The Writer's Guide to

Character Traits

*Includes profiles of
human behaviors and
personality types*

Linda N. Edelstein, Ph.D.

W

WRITER'S DIGEST BOOKS
CINCINNATI, OHIO
www.writersdigest.com

DEDICATION
To Nancy and Eve, because every once in a while life simply
offers a gift, and my friendship with each of you, like this project,
has been a pleasure from the beginning. (See Friendship Traits
in Adulthood, page 192.)

Acknowledgments

Thanks go to Barbara Monier, Patty Shafer, and my wonderful Sunday writing group,
Margit Kir-Stimon, Kathleen Slomski, and Nancy Newton, for listening and editing; to
Daniel Epstein, Eve Epstein, and Mark Epstein for advice and ideas; to Peg White for
library magic; to former students Diane Powers and Tally Izaak, who shared their research with me; and to Jack Heffron from Writer's Digest Books, who supported the
idea. Very special thanks to four young women who good-naturedly worked as research
assistants during various phases of this project—Martha Christensen, Jennifer Dubowsky, Keira Dubowsky, and Stephanie Hamilton. And an extra thanks to Keira and Jenny
for unfailing encouragement during a year when they launched their own adventures.

Visit our Web site at www.writersdigest.com for information on more resources for writers.

To receive a free weekly E-mail newsletter delivering tips and updates about writing and about
Writer's Digest products, send an E-mail with the message "Subscribe Newsletter" to newslet
ter-request@writersdigest.com or register directly at our Web site at www.writersdigest
.com.

08 07 06 05 04   5 4 3 2 1

Library of Congress has Catalogued Hardcover Edition as Follows:

Edelstein, Linda N.
    The writer's guide to character traits: includes profiles of human behaviors and personality
types / by Linda N. Edelstein.
        p.   cm.
    Includes biographical references (p. 318) and index.
    ISBN 0-89879-901-5 (hardcover; alk. paper); ISBN 1-58297-246-X (pbk.; alk. paper)
    1. Fiction—Technique Handbooks, manuals, etc. 2. Characters and characteristics in litera-
ture Handbooks, manuals, etc. 3. Typology (Psychology) Handbooks, manuals, etc. 4. Human
behavior Handbooks, manuals, etc. I. Title.
PN3383.C4E34   1999
808.3'97—dc21   99-39516
                                                                     CIP

Editor: Jack Heffron
Production editor: Bob Beckstead
Interior designer: Sandy Conopeotis Kent
Cover designer: David Mill
Production coordinator: Rachel Vater

TABLE OF CONTENTS

INTRODUCTION

Writers ask me all kinds of questions: "What makes a man have an affair? Why would a woman stalk her former lover? How can I learn what motivates a person's behavior?" These are reasonable, interesting questions. I used to point writers in the direction of heavy psychological books filled with dense ideas that even I, as an experienced psychologist, wade through with dread. I know there are many writers, both new and accomplished authors, who want to create believable characters and need accurate information about personality and behavior. My goal in writing this book has been to create a friendly reference for just that purpose. I describe the inner workings and the behaviors of ordinary and not-so-ordinary people in lists, charts, and descriptive paragraphs.

In my work I don't deal with fictional characters, I work with people. Working in psychology since the late 1970s, I understand something about the interior lives of individuals, couples, and groups—what makes them feel happy and sad, what motivates them, and what events bring them to a screeching halt. Daily, I tiptoe my way through the many layers that exist in each of us and marvel at how truly impenetrable most of that remains, to ourselves and to those around us. I am continually impressed by the strange ways people behave, and each year, when I tell myself that I have heard it all, I am humbled again by the intrigues people manage to create. Dorothy Parker was right, "people are more fun than anybody." To understand people, to write about them, and to read about them, is endlessly engaging. When we unravel their psychological puzzles, we ultimately shed light on our own lives.

This book is filled with more than four hundred lists that describe personality types, traits associated with stages of normal development, types of criminals, patterns of sexual behavior, dynamics of life events, traumas, group and organizational behaviors, traits that are found in people in various careers, descriptions of abnormal behavior, and assorted informational tidbits. We all see the outside of people: We see their behavior. To construct fascinating characters, we need a glimpse of the inside, the world that I inhabit daily. Why would a dental student become suicidal after a minor chest injury while working out? (See

From the Files on page 95.) What inspired a conventional young woman to pose for nude photos after breaking up with her boyfriend? (See From the Files on page 179.) What motivated a financially comfortable woman to embezzle money from her firm? (See From the Files on page 104.) How could a beautiful computer whiz, with a loving family and boyfriend, suffocate herself with a garbage bag? (See From the Files on page 90.) Why would a man who did not want to end his marriage tell his wife that he was sleeping with her best friend? (See page 34.) Why does a devoted sixty-seven-year-old married man spend half of the marital retirement savings on lingerie for a prostitute—in three weeks? (See From the Files on page 100.)

As an additional assist to create your characters, chapter thirteen is an elaborate index to use as a tool to cross-reference behaviors (e.g., careless), symptoms (e.g., infertility) or personality traits (e.g., grandiosity) and be referred to styles, disorders, or life stages that may exhibit that quality.

One of the strange features about being a psychologist is that everybody else is also a psychologist. I'm sure that archeologists are occasionally challenged with alternative theories of Stonehenge. And certainly lawyers are confronted with free advice on the role of independent prosecutors and celebrity guilt or innocence in criminal investigations. But the difference is that people really do *know* about psychology. We have become very sophisticated about human emotions and behaviors. The ever-increasing array of talk shows, interview shows, and "news" magazines reveals the unending desire to know about people's lives. These books, shows, and magazines also demonstrate the genuine sophistication of the man or woman on the street when we come to psychological matters. One-dimensional, uninteresting characters have become unacceptable to the reading public, who like both characters and plots.

I wrote this book because I thought it would be fun for me and helpful for others to have easy, accurate lists of qualities that hang together in personality types. It is a crash course in psychology for writers.

As a psychologist, I am the ultimate reader, always moving through an unfolding story, worrying, trying to understand, making sense, cheering, unraveling mysteries, and bearing witness to the search for a happy ending. I sit in an armchair and I read people all day long.

Introduction

This book is a synthesis of my reading, real and imagined, over the years. The lists presented here contain traits that are not my own wacky creation, but are usually mainstream ideas, accepted in psychological theory and research. Some material is on the edge, especially when I describe disorders that we still know little about. Footnotes point you to more articles and books if you want to go deeper into any of the material.

Chapter one briefly discusses the creation of believable characters.

Chapter two gets into the trait material. We begin with fully formed types of adult personalities and lists of traits for each. The styles described in this chapter are fairly complete. The traits are those normally found clustered together and are demonstrated in attitudes, reactions, patterns of living, and feelings. No one person has all the traits, and individuals have the traits to differing degrees, on a continuum from mild to moderate to strong. In mild form, most of these traits are ordinary. In the extreme, marked by →, the trait is transformed into a strong, often pathological version. In creating your characters, you can pick and choose from the list. Following each list, paragraphs about childhood and adulthood provide examples of the style.

Chapter three provides the traits associated with normal child and adolescent development, year by year. Children are still works in progress. Therefore, children and adolescents do not fit easily into defined types. However, they show certain traits based on age and stage of development.

Chapter four describes psychological disorders and the traits that define significant deviations from normal development.

Chapter five looks at criminal styles and examines styles commonly found among criminals. Included, too, are behaviors such as substance abuse that lead to criminal activity.

Chapter six lists sexual styles, including common and uncommon sexual disorders. Sexual disorders that have a predominantly physical basis are described in chapter nine.

Chapter seven presents love and marriage, from the usual to the less common dynamics in adult relationships.

Chapter eight recognizes that no matter how many plans we make for our lives, events intervene. Turn of Events offers many child, adolescent, and adult situations, from the normal to the unusual, and lists the variety of ways that individuals cope with life's predicaments.

Chapter nine describes physical problems that influence appearance, personality, and behavior. Disorders that are primarily physical in nature have grave psychological consequences. This chapter includes certain neurological disorders, substance abuse, and eating disorders. I have also included some of the alternative views of healing, which may spark some new directions.

Chapter ten offers career traits. Research has found some commonalities among people in similar professions, and these are provided in lists.

Chapter eleven describes group influences, including general characteristics of group membership and specifics associated with selected groups, characteristics of specific groups and cults, and the needs that are fulfilled by them.

Chapter twelve presents some of the lesser known information on nonverbal and verbal communication.

Chapter thirteen provides the Big Index. You can look up a symptom (e.g., sleeplessness, impotence, cruelty to animals) or you can look up a trait (e.g., arrogance, withdrawal) and be directed to the different disorders or situations where you could expect to find it.

How to Use This Book

Molly, an aspiring writer at twelve years old, spent the summer writing stories in her journal. My friend Barbara, Molly's mother and source for characterization, fielded a million questions about, "What kind of job would this person have?" "What do you think she would say?" "What do you think he would do if . . .?" Well, Molly, here are some tips on how to use the material in this book.

- Leaf through the lists and let them spark your imagination about:
    major and minor character development, or
    situations created by certain types of characters
- In chapter thirteen, the Big Index, look up a trait that interests you—one that may be central to an underdeveloped character—and build the character according to the complimentary traits. For example, the trait of *blame* offers blame of others or blame of self. Let's choose *blame of self* and refer to the six pages suggested. Eliminating the page that notes self-blame in children, two adult styles offer different presentations of the trait—the Flamboyant (page 28) covers up self-blame; the Victim (page 40) advertises it. Self-blame is also present during

depressed moods (page 87) and when certain events occur, like loss of love (page 159) or being in the throes of bulimia (page 237).

- Add traits to existing characters by locating traits that the character already possesses and seeing what other traits are usually found in that type of individual.
- Double-check traits if you are uncertain they would be found in one character.
- Choose some traits at whose existence you merely hint.
- Add abnormality to a character.
- Check the lists to see how a character would behave in extreme circumstances.
- Play up opposite traits to have a character act against type.
- Use the traits to help create external attributes, like clothes, interests, or mannerisms.
- Get ideas about ways characters grow and develop from the constellation of traits.
- Refer to boxed lists for additional details or information.
- Refer to From the Files for true stories.
- Give characters accurate careers and interests.
- Show another side to a character.
- Create authentic adult flashbacks to childhood.
- Add spice to group or family life.
- Create multiple characters who can play off each other.
- Create effective minor characters who bring information or make action happen.
- Use the chapter footnotes and read further on topics that interest you.

Reminders About Psychological Traits

- Traits cluster together to describe personality, but are rarely exclusive to one personality; for example, most traits of an Adventurer differ from those of a Conventional or a Loner, but some may be alike.
- Emphasizing one trait or another creates very different characters, even in the same style.
- When you choose heavily from either the negative or positive traits, you make the character more extreme and can create degrees of abnormality.
- Personality, by definition, is stable, but put a character in extra-

ordinary circumstances and certain traits come to the fore while others recede.

- We change and behave out of character, but not as often as we would like to believe.

- Certain periods of life give rise to predictable issues; e.g., identity for teenagers or personal mortality for midlifers.

- People tend to work and rework similar issues throughout life; for example, abandonment or anger.

- Traits are specific qualities of thinking, feeling, behavior, or adjustment patterns; for example, reactions to frustration or ways of meeting problems.

- There is not a sharp line between normal and pathological behavior. We exist on a normal ➔ pathological continuum. People can be pretty normal in certain areas of psychological functioning and disturbed in others; e.g., certain phobias may never become noticeable if the individual avoids the stimulus, whether it be heights, snakes, or bridges. We can behave conventionally in many areas and still have hidden oddities or deviances; for example, most child abusers are known to the child and very able to behave appropriately when other people are around.

- Strategies that prove adaptive at one time may fail at another. For example, a child growing up in an abusive alcoholic home may cleverly learn to be invisible as protection. That ability, necessary in childhood, may prove disastrous for the married adult who has no other way to interact during stressful periods.

- People tend to show the same traits when placed in similar situations; for example, a highly competitive man will likely show ambition in the office, on the softball field, or playing Monopoly with his family.

This book, therefore, is geared toward a psychological construction of character, of comprehending the character, of understanding the myriad of traits that combine differently each time to make each of us unique, and of constructing a person with internal consistency, so that certain elements run through the whole characterization even when some traits are out of view.

CHAPTER ONE

Real People and Believable Characters

T he traits compiled in the styles, charts, and lists throughout this book work together to help you create characters who are believable and engaging. To hold our attention, successful characters possess cohesiveness and consistency. To make us care, characters engage our empathy or emotional identification. Just like real people, fictional characters have analyzable internal lives and demonstrate interpersonal behaviors that make them believeable and draw us into their stories.

Cohesiveness and Consistency

My neighbor makes a marvelous six-layer faux Mexican appetizer. She arranges colorful levels of cheese, avocado, sour cream, beans, lettuce, and tomato, all acceptable ingredients individually, but the complementary flavors working together make the dish a real hit. I have tried to assemble something similar on the pages that follow—people ingredients—components that work together naturally, coherently, and authentically. Use some of the traits or use them all. The lists can help you imagine the depth of the character's personality. Display some traits to the reader and hold others in your own mind. Using all the traits strongly might overwhelm a character (and numb a reader), but you can play with the traits to create a character who is mild or extreme, sympathetic or repellent. The people ingredients in the pages that follow invite you to construct a unique character, not a fast-food dish where the selling point is recognizability with no surprises.

Even when a writer's imagination soars to places more fascinating than reality, characters must possess an internal cohesiveness: They must make sense. We need depth of personality to sustain a reader's interest, but cohesiveness means that the diverse elements of personality and behavior hang together in a way that readers can follow and believe. The aspects of personality must stick together. For example, a client admitted to me that she had stolen money. I was surprised by her confession, but after we talked, I understood how it happened. I could see how personality traits that I already knew she possessed, such as her arrogance, her need to impress people with a high lifestyle, her belief that because she worked hard people ought to be indebted to her, and her low self-esteem, all combined with easy access to money, could result in embezzlement. Her history contributed, too. She had successful parents who overvalued money and openly preferred her high-flying older brother. Would she have gone out with a gun and robbed a liquor store? Never. She was not violent; she had certain rules that she lived by, and she considered herself above common burglary. There was a certain logic to her behavior, including the grandiose notion that she could pay it all back and no one would ever know. These diverse traits, when revealed, hang together and explain why a woman who is a pillar of the community winds up in trouble. My understanding was retrospective; I never could have predicted an embezzlement.

People are more consistent than not. My friend Carolyn can be depended on to provide a cynical response; I get impatient when I wait in line, on foot or in the car; my daughter retreats into silence when she is furious with the family; and my client Steve falls asleep when his wife says, "Let's talk." Personality traits tend to show up repeatedly, especially when people are faced with similar events. But roles that we play, situations in which we find ourselves, and people with whom we interact elicit different traits. At work as an attorney, Carolyn compassionately explains federal regulations to an aging client with no editorializing; on vacation, I am schedule free and not impatient; with her friends, my daughter expresses herself directly and very well; and in therapy, where Steve enjoys the safest hour of his week, he loves to talk and shows no signs of drowsiness. These character traits can all be true; none have to be false.

Character can be consistent and still hold surprises. Shift the supporting players or the circumstances and different traits are revealed. Character is like looking at a box I hold up in front of your eyes. You clearly see the side facing you. You can know that segment of the box, unless I have concealed portions of it. But you are naïve if you think that one side is all there is. You know that the box has other sides, and you make assumptions about the unseen sections of the box. Some of those guesses will be correct, like the size and shape of the other sides. Other assumptions will be wrong because those sides are out of view right now. People are like the box. We see them at work and learn a bit about one side. They tell us about their history and we learn a bit more. They share their feelings about an event or we watch them react and we infer their feelings. We see them embedded in this context or that and, over time, we learn about all the sides that had been previously out of view.

Roles Influence Traits; Traits Influence Roles

Roles are a blend of personality traits and the work that person does, whether that work is president of a company, hit man, or new mother. I am more reserved and listen more attentively to my clients than when I am teaching, lecturing, or teasing the students. Sometimes (not often) I don't listen at all; I only look alert. Different roles emphasize different aspects of an individual. My work as a psychologist has trained me to listen clearly to all that is said and much that is not said. The role has professionalized the trait. My love of a good story, my curiosity about people's secret lives, and even my voyeurism probably influenced my choice of career. The trait led me to the role.

Situations Influence Traits; Traits Influence Situations

Just as our roles vary, so do the situations in which we find ourselves. Kenneth, a pedantic college professor, is very successful in the university, where he creates his own world in the classroom and spends hours doing independent math research. However, when he travels, he is companionable only as long as he maps out the itinerary hour by hour, knows the weather, and retains control of the day. Beware of Kenneth's anger and contempt when he signs on to a tour led by someone else, with a dozen other people who also have ideas about how much time to spend at each souvenir stand.

Relationships Influence Traits; Traits Influence Relationships

People elicit certain traits in each other, and the dance can become habitual. One goal in doing couples therapy is to make this dynamic obvious so that people can change their behavior. Sue says, "If you didn't always pursue me for sex, maybe I would have the time to desire you." Her husband Bob answers, "If I waited for you to initiate sex, we would be celibate." In other areas of their relationship, these traits can be seen in a more positive light. Sue is easygoing and optimistic. She has always thought that Bob is the world's best salesman. Bob is uptight and worries excessively, so Sue's support has increased his confidence. He is closer to becoming the office star than he ever imagined.

The same dynamics go on at work. Amir enjoys the last word on hiring and firing. His assistant Fred works hard to please him and is always personable, at least to Amir. As a reaction to his required agreeableness to those above, Fred shows his less pleasant qualities to those below him who, whenever possible, sabotage his projects. The power imbalance in this chain of relationships influences the feelings and behaviors that are displayed. The traits, feelings, and possible behaviors already exist in the individuals involved, are drawn to the surface by events, and create the subtleties of the relationships.

The lists of traits included in this book are internal, reactions to others, and behavioral, but rarely situation specific. You can move your character from the bedroom to the supermarket, or to the shower.

Character consistency is more effective than inconsistency because we begin to recognize the person's voice. We believe that we know someone; we know what to expect, or we think we do. Playwright Edward Albee is said to have tested his characters by imagining them in situations other than those he had created. He wanted to see if the characters would stand up outside his play. Consistency of personality does not argue against change. In literature as in life, development comes from events and growth working on the character's structure. Because you know the expected behaviors, consistency also allows you to choose to have characters act against type some of the time, like the overly cautious fellow who falls hard for the wrong woman because he feels momentary freedom.

Consistency doesn't mean that we show everybody everything at once. Occasionally a client, sad and complaining, will apologize to me, "I'm not always like this. When I'm at work (school, with others, etc.) I am strong and confident." I know. Sometimes I want to answer, "I'm not always like this—kind, calm, focused, and intelligent. Sometimes, I am anxious, dopey, sarcastic, short-tempered, and bored."

Empathy

In my work, I understand people by what they tell me about themselves and their lives, but also by establishing an empathetic connection. Empathy is that elusive exchange whereby, for a fleeting moment here and there, I walk in someone else's shoes. I get a glimpse of the universal elements in another person's struggle, feelings that we all know—love, hate, despair, shame, loneliness, fear, joy. It isn't just psychology that tries to understand and communicate universals. In his lectures at Harvard University, artist Ben Shahn described his goal in painting a particular image as trying to create "the emotional tone that surrounds disaster" more than painting a picture of a literal disaster.[1] When he succeeds, people respond to the feelings of disaster in the painting. We understand people similarly when we connect to some universal quality in them that finds its counterpart in our own private world. In literature as in life, we move closer to characters when we resonate with their emotional lives.

Understanding a character's emotional world is not the only way to generate interest. We can use props, like growing orchids, to make a character stand out. We can use a physical characteristic, like four tattoos all spelling "Mother," to make a point about personality, but the personality itself is more compelling. Props are eye-catchers, but complexity of personality sustains the reader's interest.[2] If a character engages our feelings, we wonder what happens to him or her. We want to know how the conflict turns out. To know and be conscious of the character is to remain connected and involved, even if the character's experience is far from our own.

Believable Characters

Believable characters are essential in fiction and nonfiction—in books and on the screen. Characters must be durable, fallible, and able to grow and change. Writers in all disciplines strive to create realistic characters. Authors of juvenile and adult mysteries need a fully formed hero or heroine to provide the tension because he or she is pitted

---

[1] Shahn (1957).
[2] Burns (1988).

against a personal adversary, often alone. Short-story writers need to develop characters' emotions to capture the reader quickly. Minor characters, too, require attention so they can stand on their own. Unless characters are realistic, you will intrude on and inhibit their development. You will meddle with a vacant character until believability is gone. Realistic characters tell you how they will behave.

Carlton makes the point that in Jane Austen's characters, we can appreciate reasons for their conduct in a particular situation when they are set out in the book, even if we would not give them much weight if presented to us today, in our lives.[3] When we are absorbed in the material, we feel emotion. And when we are emotionally moved, we half believe. Chatman describes a psychological model that defines character as "a paradigm of traits," more than a series of actions.[4] A character acts *because*. . . . In this way, the reader becomes conscious of the character's reality, even when that reality differs from our own.

Characters work best when you create a virtual identity for them. The character can then inhabit an imaginative space in the reader's mind, a space that you have created. Readers go along with characters as long as the characters remain coherent.[5]

The reader doesn't need to be similar to a character to be interested in him or her. The reader needs to understand and be engaged by the person, whether characteristics are shared or not. I see many people in treatment who are not like me, and I don't see me reflected in them. But, as they develop and unfold, when they allow me to know their world, I feel connected and very concerned about their "story" and its outcome.

Diversity

Traits are not confined to people; cultures also have characteristics. Contrast, for example, the individualistic nature of the citizens of the United States with the appreciation for the collective in Japan. Conflict can exist between the cultural values of individuals; the competitive drive of an Anglo boy differs from the cooperative beliefs of a Native American boy. Talking to the dead is acceptable behavior in many cultures, although in the mainstream United States a person could find

---

[3] Charlton (1984).
[4] Chatman (1978).
[5] Cohan (1983).

herself confined to a hospital and medicated for the same activity. Many, many other differences exist: Some are subtle, like the different meaning of silence in Japanese conversation than in discussions in the United States. These kinds of differences provide further opportunities for character and relationship development.

Stereotypes and Clichés

Psychology students in my graduate classes hate diagnosis because they correctly object to "labeling" or "pigeonholing" individuals. They see that the people who they treat are complex, beyond a disorder, such as "depressed." They recognize that two people suffering from the same trauma or dealing with the same emotional disorder are still very different human beings. For example, a husband whose oldest son died in a senseless car crash who goes to work silently each day, showing emotion only when he punches his fist against the car's dashboard, is grieving no more or less than his wife who, over tea with close friends, cries and talks about her sadness.

Writers hate stereotypes and clichés because both are usually unfair, often insulting, and always boring. Labels, clichés, and stereotypes all have elements of fact. Each provides us with a language shortcut because they jolt our memories. Each gives us a quick, if imprecise, way of knowing. We all find comfort and certainty with the familiar, even if it doesn't provide a great read. Stereotypes differ from clichés in that the former reduce an entire class (e.g., fat people, depressed women, or post office workers), and let the reader assume the rest. In contrast, a cliché is a hackneyed phrase. A stereotype is not identical to the real thing. Stereotypes seem to work best when characters are not created to be deep, but only to be a mental picture. Most of us find that both stereotypes and clichés fail in daily life just as regularly as they fail in literature.

Good characters break out of stereotypes. They capture our attention; they move; they get into life. This book is intended to help you create identities for your characters so they can go on to hatch plots and make mischief.

Adult Styles

T he twenty adult styles in this chapter refer to an individual's enduring pattern of inner experience and behavior. Personality development begins in childhood and remains remarkably consistent throughout life. Yes, we change and behave out of character, but not as often as we would like to believe. Therefore, we can think about personality styles and the way people behave under ordinary circumstances. When we understand how individuals usually operate, we are free to imagine how they might grow, change, and behave in extraordinary circumstances and when they behave against type.

The styles described in this chapter are fairly complete and more normal than otherwise. In mild form, most of these traits are ordinary. In the extreme, marked by ➔, the trait is transformed into a strong, even pathological version. Styles that are primarily disturbed, rather than normal, can be found in chapter four.

The combinations of traits listed on the following pages are generally found clustered together. Rarely would one person have all the traits, and individuals have the traits in differing degrees on a continuum from mild to moderate to strong. In creating your characters, you can pick and choose from the traits on the list.

Each style has traits, but traits are also influenced by the context in which people find themselves. For example, a solitary person may seem effective at work as a researcher but be ineffective and odd at a holiday party. Individuals are embedded in a context, so different situations influence how many traits are seen and how disturbed people look. Environment also shapes personality. Therefore, environment and life circumstance will enrich or distort personality, and will cause an individual to behave in healthier or more pathological ways.

Each style is subdivided into sections called **Internal** and **Interpersonal**, depending on whether the emphasis of the trait is more emotion/attitude (internal) or behaviors and reactions to others (interpersonal). For example, a character who exemplifies the first adult style, Adventurer, often remains unaware of the feelings of others, primarily an internal quality. He or she may demonstrate that trait interpersonally by ignoring social conventions or exhibiting behaviors that show him or her to be oblivious to others. Following many of the lists, you will see a short section called **Normal ➔ Extreme**. Traits that can deteriorate into abnormality usually fall on a continuum that ranges from normal to extreme rather than existing or not existing. Let's look at the Adventurer again. The wonderful normal quality of self-confidence that allows the Adventurer to take risks can become extreme and lead to poor judgments and disaster. Finally, following each list, paragraphs about childhood and adulthood provide only one example of the style.

Characters demonstrate these traits in attitudes, reactions, patterns of living, and feelings. Traits come from a blend of life experiences, internal ways that we organize ourselves, and inherited temperament. Even the fullness of the styles described here cannot make a complete person, but can be the core of a character.

To get more information and further ideas about character development, choose a trait from any list in adult styles (e.g., bold in the Adventurer Style) and refer to chapter thirteen, the Big Index, where bold is listed under Traits. The index points you to other places that particular trait, bold, appears; for example, page 80, describing the childhood of an elective mute.

Adventurer Style

The themes of the Adventurer are excitement and boldness. He or she may look or sound ordinary, but underlying most activities is the need to feel like a warrior, often unknowingly at the cost of others. More men than women are Adventurers because culture and socialization inhibit this style in growing girls, but there have always been daring women like Amelia Earhart.

Internal

Feels high levels of energy; e.g., always on the go

Bold, dominant

Unaware of the feelings of others

Leader, wants his or her own way

Competitive

Fickle, changeable

Interpersonal

Lives on the edge; needs excitement to feel alive

Thrill seeker, prepared to try anything; e.g., activities with speed
and/or danger

Enjoys the spotlight; e.g., likes to perform

Not bothered by rules or social convention

Overt interest in sex; likes having a partner/spouse

Normal ➔ Extreme

Thick-skinned, can become ➔ lacking in guilt

Confident, can become ➔ poor judgment

Forceful, can become ➔ ruthless

Extrovert, can become ➔ hostile

Rebellious, can become ➔ anti-authority

Assertive, can become ➔ aggressive

Independent, can become ➔ disagreeable with everyone

Makes impulsive decisions, can become ➔ dangerous to himself or
herself

The Adventurer is drawn to careers with excitement (e.g., pilot, stocks, sales, or managerial positions), but in the extreme can become a con artist.

Childhood of an Adventurer

From the time Mike was small, his mother told stories of how he threw himself into new situations, beginning with daring climbs on the playground equipment and a quick entry into kindergarten. In many ways, Mike was an easy child, not particularly sensitive and very friendly. Later he became the neighborhood instigator and led other boys in bicycle stunts. His mother was on a first-name basis with the emergency room staff at the local hospital. Trouble erupted when his insensitivity permitted activities that were impulsive and occasionally dangerous, like taking the family car at age eleven. Not surprisingly, his coaches had higher praise for the young man than his academic teachers.

Adulthood of an Adventurer

Mike married his college sweetheart and became a pilot for a small airline that transported freight. As a couple, they developed a large circle of friends. The only people who saw the disagreeable side of Mike were his family and the people who worked closely with him. He ran roughshod over people at home, and he barked orders, ignored rules, and disregarded the feelings of others at work. Friends saw the best in him—the fun-loving, entertaining, and gregarious man. The marriage lasted while the children were small, but after they entered high school, his wife immersed herself in her own career and Mike felt left out. She found it difficult to explain that she was tired of being home while he traveled; she was sick of taking orders and unwilling to remain invisible. He was shocked when she asked for a separation, but their children were not. Friends who had enjoyed their company for years were surprised that this pleasant couple split up, and they generally sided with Mike.

Bossy Style

The Bossy person wants to be out front—at home, at work, or at play. The themes that run through the life of a Bossy are control (of self and others) and having things his or her own way.

Internal
Driven by aggressive energy; competitive
Confident
Stubborn, likes control of self
Rigid thinking, dogmatic in opinions, closed minded
Serious
Experiences little shame or guilt
Mistrusts compassion or kindness
Has a low tolerance for frustration
Desires high status

Interpersonal

Not deterred by punishment or pain

Thick-skinned and insensitive to social approval, but sensitive to comments or attacks

Gets the job done; good at coercion

Tunes in to the weaknesses of others, and then uses that knowledge

Willing to humiliate others; sarcastic

Justifies aggression; e.g., "You've got to take care of yourself" or "All's fair"

Boastful, brusque, belligerent

Wants to be the leader in any group

Does not concede or acknowledge another point of view

Wants to get his or her own way

Avoids warmth or intimacy

Does not recognize the impact of his or her acts

Sees others as puppets to be manipulated; is domineering

Normal ➜ Extreme

Aggressive, may become ➜ reckless

Quarrelsome, can become ➜ combative

Likes control of others, can become ➜ sadistic

Headstrong, forceful, can lead to ➜ abuse

Quick responses, can be ➜ aggressive if threatened

Likes to force ideas on others, can become ➜ cruel

Communication ranges from direct to ➜ chronically rude

Poor as a follower, can become ➜ a heckler

The Bossy gravitates to careers like hotel or restaurant management, a campaign manager, an advertising executive, or a school superintendent, jobs that allow dominance but can become abusive. Mild traits are useful in sales, medical, and psychological or psychiatric fields. Often the Bossy is able to cloak negative traits in socially responsible work; e.g., business takeovers or the military.

Childhood of a Bossy

Betsy was the first born in a large family and took care of her younger sisters and many household chores. Another child might have objected to these jobs, but not Betsy. She enjoyed giving orders and believed that her instructions were in the best interests of others, even when the others disagreed. In a good mood, she was charming and persuasive, but at other times she lived up to her nickname "The General" because she was insistent and relentless, demanding that she be heard and obeyed.

Adulthood of a Bossy

Betsy became the headmistress of a boarding school, and although she performed her job to exacting standards, teachers resigned or kept their distance from her. She barely noticed their reactions because her goal was a smooth-running school. Betsy never interfered in the teachers' classrooms and she defended them to members of the board of directors, but she made endless demands and they felt trapped by her excessive, controlling manner.

Conventional Style

A Conventional lives by the rules and prefers the established ways of life.

Internal

Conservative in social matters, religion, and morals
Respects established ideas; prefers the familiar to the unfamiliar
Nostalgic
Does not understand the need to try new things or do things
 differently
Personal motto is "If it's not broken, why fix it" taken to the extreme
Loyal, has long-lasting friendships
Does not like change; e.g., resists new food, new technology, or new
 vacation spots
Avoids styles, fashion, and trends
Dependent, with strong ties to family and work

Interpersonal

Lacks trust in innovation; whatever is is best
Avoids situations that are strange, too easy, or too difficult
Confused by developmental transitions; e.g., alterations in family
 dynamics

Normal → Extreme

Personal identity depends on sameness, but can lead to → strange, secret life

Fears change, but → can be mesmerized by people totally different from self

The Conventional finds traditional careers with security, such as the clergy, appealing and satisfying.

Childhood of a Conventional

Lydia was born at home and traveled like a vagabond with her rootless parents. In fact, her name was Lake and she changed it at her first opportunity. She loved school and the reliability of learning, but the family's incessant moves meant that she and her brother changed schools yearly. Her parents believed they were exposing her to a world of new customs and excitement, but Lydia found the experiences humiliating. Her strange clothes, her parents' weird friends, and their inability to ever be like anyone else's parents were a source of distress.

Adulthood of a Conventional

Lydia worked her way through school and rarely went to visit her parents after graduation. She took great solace in knowing where she would be, when she would be there, and what she would eat, wear, and do. Her clothes and attitudes were noticeable because they were so predictable. Lydia loyally kept her friends, married the first man she dated seriously, and sent holiday cards to hundreds of people each year. Her difficulties came when her children reached adolescence and challenged her ideas in ways that she could not understand or support.

Conformist Style

The Conformist style is similar to the Conventional except that a Conformist's life centers around compliance and going along. A Conformist is responsible, sticks to the rules, and is uncreative. With others, the Conformist is a follower, goes along with others, and likes laws more than freedom. In the extreme, discipline becomes rigidity, his or her thinking becomes closed minded, and morals calcify into rigidly moralistic preaching and behavior.

Creator Style

The Creator's life gets meaning from the ability to produce new ideas or products.

Internal

Artistic, intuitive, sensitive

Observant, sees the big picture

Persistent

Does not like conformity; unconventional

Generates ideas and becomes easily absorbed by ideas

Introverted, internal focus

Internal world is a pleasant place, a respite from the outside

Tolerates ambiguity, allows disorder

Fanciful and enthusiastic

Imaginative and captured by the innovative

Likes his or her own company

Interpersonal

Can work alone for long periods

Forgetful, undependable in areas outside of focus

Not good for corporate life because he or she can be impractical

Good-natured with others, but not always sensitive to them

Reacts to stimuli emotionally and subjectively

Sees the world in unique ways

Not swayed by the group; indifferent to "What the neighbors are doing"

Normal → Extreme

Impractical, can become → accident prone

The Creator gravitates to artistic, internal work such as a poet or writer, or independent work such as a researcher, composer, tree doctor, or a geologist.

Childhood of a Creator

From the time Michael was small, he amused his father, a graphic designer, with the unique way he viewed the world. He outgrew his pads of colored paper quickly and, when his parents left for the movies, painted murals on his bedroom walls. His older brother Eric had a similarly quirky approach, but he liked mathematics and spent hours doing puzzles in his head.

Adulthood of a Creator

Michael and Eric couldn't wait to get out of high school, where they felt constrained by the rules. While in college, they began a small software company, *!Gotta be ME,* that produced stunning visual games and practically went broke several times before they hired a business manager.

Dependent Style

The Dependent's world revolves around having his or her needs met. These traits go beyond what is normally expected for a particular time of life, even in youth or during periods of trauma or illness.

Internal

Shy, humble, lacks self-confidence
Trouble with own anger or aggressiveness
Trouble initiating projects
Easily becomes anxious and fearful
Reliance on others prohibits development of independence
Wants to be liked, therefore she or he will take on unpleasant tasks
Doubts about self; sees self as inefficient and powerless
Fears abandonment

Interpersonal

Wants to be taken care of, but fears disappointment
Tries to elicit care from others; feels unable to manage well without
    help
Needs guidance; e.g., "Tell me what you think I should do"
Needs reassurance and support
Parent, spouse, boss, or friends make major life decisions
Waits for others to take action; yields to others
Fears losing approval; fears evaluation

Normal ➜ Extreme

Yields to others, can become ➜ painfully submissive
Mild, can become ➜ clinging

Needs others, can become ➔ quickly and indiscriminately attached to people

Difficulty in expressing disagreement can become ➔ silence

Considerate, can become ➔ excessively deferential and self-sacrificing

Difficulty making decisions can become ➔ allowing others to govern life

May have had an authoritarian parent ➔ learns to give in to maintain relationships

May have had an overprotective parent ➔ believes that she or he is unable to function without guidance

The Dependent seeks situations and people who will provide reassurance, approval, and instruction. The Dependent gravitates to work as a bank teller, a clerk, or a court stenographer where initiative is not required.

Childhood of a Dependent

Laura was adored by her parents for the first year, until her father became seriously ill and her mother had to care for him and work. The family suffered for years. Laura never outgrew clinging to her mother whenever possible and being afraid to upset her father. She had friends in school but was always the follower, never the leader. Teachers liked her because she was so willing to listen and obey, but she was never the favorite student because she was without any sparkle or creativity.

Adulthood of a Dependent

Laura drifted into marriage because she was grateful that Bob fell in love with her. She just took for granted that she loved him. They traveled because Bob was in the Navy, but Laura's world stayed confined to the naval bases. She followed a set routine that Bob created and raised their children to follow the rules, and it was years before she understood why they became rebellious. Laura made friends easily. She was agreeable and always the one who could be asked to sell candy for charity fund-raisers. As she got older, she wondered why people didn't seem to take her seriously, and her feelings were often hurt. No matter how hard she tried to please others, satisfaction eluded her.[1]

---

[1] Bornstein and Bower (1996).

Eccentric Style

The Eccentric marches to the beat of a different drummer.

Internal

Self-absorbed, forgetful, impractical
Better with abstract ideas than real situations and people
Attitude of being burdened
Carries on an internal dialogue
Works well alone; frustrates others
Usually has some talent that is absorbing

Interpersonal

Socially inept; distorts and misreads the behavior of others
Picks up and drops conversations at odd points
Out of touch with trends and conventions
Uninterested in others in any practical way—and it shows
No intent to harm others, but oblivious to social cues
Strange and/or eccentric behaviors

Normal ➔ Extreme

Out of touch can become ➔ isolated

The Eccentric gravitates to careers that are solitary, such as research, or work that is abstract, such as math or computers.

Childhood of an Eccentric

Jesse was always a bit of an oddball, but managed happily by having a couple of like-minded friends and being content to stay away from some of the more group-oriented activities, such as sports. Jesse did well in school, and was considered a nerd less for brilliance than for an oddball appearance, which included ever-changing hair color.

Adulthood of an Eccentric

Once Jesse figured out how to manage the practical aspects of life, like balancing the checkbook and where to put the eggs, life progressed smoothly. Work took up most waking hours, and the research lab was the most comfortable place in the world. On weekends, Jesse enjoyed searching for tin toys made in the 1800s to add to a growing collection.

Extrovert Style

If Extroverts are not the most fascinating of characters, they are among the most normal and least pathological.

Internal
Not introspective; outgoing
Not easily intimidated
Talkative
World view is optimistic; sees the hopeful side
Expressive, enthusiastic, and gregarious
Undercontrolled emotionally

Interpersonal
Belongs to groups and participates in activities
Enjoys being with others and avoids being alone
Friendly, seeks social situations
May not understand other people's depression or anxiety

Normal → Extreme
Friendly, can become → flighty, lacks intimacy, superficial

The Extrovert does well as a youth camp director, counselor, high school teacher, or missionary, all work where there is a good deal of contact with people, but it does not have to be intimate.

Childhood of an Extrovert

Jimmy got along with everyone from the time he could toddle. If he didn't have deep, special friendships, he certainly had two dozen boys and girls who liked him and included him in parties and sports. He played several sports, none well, but always with enthusiasm and was a good sport, win or lose. At home, his parents appreciated his easy manner and paid more attention to his older brother, who required additional supervision.

Adulthood of an Extrovert

One of Jim's best friends introduced him to an older man who hired and mentored Jim in business and directed him toward fund-raising for heart disease. Jim's natural friendliness gave him a competitive edge in bringing in donations for a worthwhile cause. At home, Jim coaches his daughters' soccer teams. The only real complaint comes from his wife, who is frustrated when she tries to talk with her husband about matters that require more depth of feeling or thought. He smiles, hugs her, and tells her not to worry so much.

Fall Guy Style

The Fall Guy or Girl is notable for being in the wrong place at the wrong time with the wrong people.

Internal
Gullible; does not exercise good judgment about people
Underachiever; ambition is undirected
Rarely hostile; pleasant
Narrow interests
Conventional
Not analytical

Interpersonal
Gets taken advantage of by others
Socially at ease
Overly trusting of others
Unaware of motives of others
Follower rather than leader

Normal ➔ Extreme
Follows others, can lead to ➔ danger from lack of judgment

Childhood of a Fall Guy
Greg was always the last one to get the joke. Even as a kid, he sat waiting for the explanation long after the punch line had been delivered. As far back as the third grade, his mother worried about her sweet, innocent son. In junior high, Greg had come home and told his mom how he had bought a new bike from some older kid at school. When she questioned him about it, she learned that he had been going without lunch for weeks to pay for a bike that never materialized. Greg made excuses for the other boy and talked to him, but never got the money or the bike.

Adulthood of a Fall Guy

Greg remained trusting into adulthood, and his friends loved him for it. He was warmhearted and listened to every one of their problems or ideas. Unfortunately, he also listened to others who were not benign and lost all of his savings in an investment scheme to raise albino buffalo.

Fearful Style

Life for the Fearful is driven by inhibition and fears of rejection.

Internal
Withdrawn
Easily feels criticism
Self-deprecating
Problems being assertive
Unhappy
Avoids stress

Interpersonal
Socially inhibited; uncomfortable in social situations
Feels inadequate and anxious in the presence of others, but longs
    for closeness
Ultrasensitive to others; restrained in intimate relationships
Concerns about physical appearance
Image of self is socially inept and unattractive
Fears involvement with others unless certain of being liked
Belongs to few groups

Normal ➜ Extreme
Fears embarrassment, leads to ➜ avoiding activities if they may
    cause discomfort

Childhood of a Fearful

Rob's parents were divorced when he was four, and his father moved out of state. His mother threw herself into a series of remarriages; none of the new husbands had much use for a small, shy boy. Rob longed to belong but was always in the way until he got an after-school job at the drugstore. They kidded him about being an old man because he was so responsible and serious, but Rob kept that job for many years.

Adulthood of a Fearful

Rob married Deb almost by accident. She had come in to the drugstore so often that they fell into being a couple. She still pursues him to talk or have sex, and he still has trouble responding. Then she gets angry and stops speaking to him for days. He is hurt each time it happens, but has no idea what to do differently.

Flamboyant Style

Life for the Flamboyant contains themes of love, sex, competition, and disloyalty, always with a lack of authenticity, as if the person shows more or expresses more than is really felt.

Internal

Dramatic, easily upset, and emotionally unstable

Seems "flaky," flighty, and insubstantial

Always a sexual undercurrent; interprets much behavior as sexual

Underlying poor self-esteem and self-blame

Indirect and devious

Naïve and simplistic, immature, excessively emotional, and childish

Feels like the evil seductress or seducer

Gets depressed because he or she feels like a bad person

Hard to think clearly; feels like an insubstantial person

Not aware of own seductive or aggressive behaviors

Not very clear on picture of self; does not see self as responsible for actions

Attention seeking, demanding, wants nurturance and support

Provides an ongoing melodrama for others; appears dramatic or phony

Physical symptoms (headaches, weakness, chest pains) develop under stress

Emotionally overdone; positive and negative feelings are both expressed flamboyantly

Interpersonal

May see self as sex object; may see others as sex objects

Creates triangle relationships (as the "other" man or woman)

Competitive with individuals of the same gender

Exhibitionistic; dramatic in social situations

May have been emotionally or sexually exploited by adults

Vain, promiscuous, and jealous

Relationships are superficial, but important because of the need for attention

Manipulative; plays games to try to get whatever he or she wants

Women lack good relationships with other women and are hostile to weak men

Normal → Extreme

Attention seeking, may lead to → suicidal gestures, without intention to do harm

When feelings are intense becomes → disorganized, overwhelmed, not functional

The Flamboyant gravitates toward careers where emotional experience can be directly shared, (e.g., art, design, media, show business), or work where intuition is rewarded.

Childhood of a Flamboyant

Nicole grew up as the only daughter in a family where her father was overly seductive. Even when she was a child, he confided in her too much and talked explicitly about sex. She and her mother became locked in a competition for his affection. This cold distance between mother and daughter always remained. Nicole's normal needs for nurturing were not met. There was little opportunity to get attention from others because the family kept to itself and was not at ease socially.

Adult of a Flamboyant

Nicole needs attention, whether at work or play, and she pouts when it is not forthcoming. She has become very flirtatious and uses her body effectively to call attention to herself, but she is shocked when men take her seriously because she is not sexually promiscuous. Nicole has few close women friends: She is competitive and accuses them of disloyalty. In return, they find her to be insubstantial, and friendship with her is too much work to maintain.

Hyper Style

The Hyper's life is active, but not always with direction.

Internal

Overactive in thought and behavior

Grandiose
Careless
Changeable
Self-centered
Easily excitable; unstable moods
Elated; high
Thrill seeking

Interpersonal
Outgoing
Active
Energetic
Poor company

Normal → Extreme
Excited, may lead to → outbursts of euphoria
Moody, may lead to → explosive anger

Childhood of the Hyper

Randy got into trouble before he even got to school. He was running and jumping, knocking kids over, and breaking knicknacks from the time he could move around on his own. Family life became unpleasant because all his parents' energies went to control him and his sisters felt very left out. Randy didn't just make noise; he developed an explosive temper that seemed to erupt for no reason, frightening his family. His sisters pulled away and began staying at friends' houses whenever possible.

Adulthood of the Hyper

It is easy to pick Randy out of a room where a meeting is being held. He is the fidgety, jumpy one, twitching and wiggling. Randy is happiest when he has someplace to go, a game to play, or anything that has motion. His wife complains that he cannot listen to her. His friends love his readiness to entertain but never dream of going to him with an intellectual or emotional concern.

Loner Style

The Loner's life seems to be directionless; loners drift, with little strong attachment to anyone.

Internal

Comfort is found in being solitary

Rarely expresses anger

Appears unambitious because he or she reacts passively to tragedy

Has difficulty responding to significant life events

Does not reveal him- or herself easily

Is harsh toward self

Chooses hobbies and interests that allow him or her to be alone; e.g.,
computers, math

Appears bland and cold, with little emotional reactivity

Interpersonal

Indifferent to the approval of others; cares little about what others
think of him or her

Does not engage in the usual social smiles and nods

Oblivious to social cues; unable to bond with others

Detached; does not want social relationships and lacks skill to deal
with others

Avoids emotional entanglements; very restricted emotionally

Not interested in sex; often does not marry and does not change if
he or she marries

Appears superficial or self-absorbed due to lack of interest in others

Few, if any, close friends; may be close to a sister or brother

Does not get satisfaction from being a member of a family

Finds social closeness difficult, maybe even terrifying

Other people are a source of pain, not comfort

Normal → Extreme

Solitary, can lead to → gravitation toward harsh environments

Detached, can lead to → retreating to insure safety

The Loner's style is not to be confused with temporary states of withdrawal (emotional numbness or freezing) when individuals are in strange circumstances (immigrants) or reactive to tragedy (intense grief).

Childhood of a Loner

Bob was born to parents who thought they wanted a child, but in reality were unready to meet the needs of an infant. The subtle but cold, even hateful, environment helped create a young boy filled with the feeling, "I shouldn't exist." He made little eye contact with people. He tried to tune out unpleasant experiences. He was alone, emotionally as well as physically. Bob learned to avoid love early. The world of people became a frightening place.

Adulthood of a Loner

Bob's life is geared to avoid rejection and failure. Any situations that are reminiscent of earlier difficulties cause the old behaviors to repeat. Bob fears strong emotion, so he stays distant, with intermittent bouts of getting close to people. Generally Bob does not feel deeply anymore. He shows little in the way of facial expression or emotion. His eyes show deadness and he seems stiff; his body is constricted. He appears even-tempered, whining, and never very happy. He had a few euphoric bursts when he met Carol, but he needed to manage their closeness and distance, so she felt too controlled. Even with the control he exercised, the relationship ended with Bob feeling "trapped like a rat in a cage," and he told his cousin that he had been willing to "chew off my leg to get out."

Man's Man Style

The Man's Man appears one-dimensional because only certain qualities are allowed to emerge.

Internal

Exaggerated masculine qualities
Coarse
Fears weakness
Hides powerlessness or impotence
Adventurous and aggressive
Worldly and sexually experienced
Demanding and hard
Ambitious; needs to win
Compulsively masculine, with no desire to change

Interpersonal

Lacks individuality
Lacks originality
Emphasizes male interests; likes traditional male pursuits

Inflexible about masculinity

Response to trouble is to beat it

Likely to have rocky relationships with women; may look for Ultra-
Femme woman

Normal → Extreme
Masculinity can become → one-dimensional

Childhood of a Man's Man
Richard was aptly nicknamed "Brick" early on. He loved sports, guns,
and physical activity of all sorts. He always performed well because
he was driven more than many of the other boys, not because he had
specific talents. He wanted to go to a military academy.

Adulthood of a Man's Man
Brick married and told everyone that his family meant the world to
him, but somehow he was never home for birthdays or other occasions.
He was always off on an exciting project that impressed his friends
and got his name in the local paper. He was injured in a mountain
climbing accident, and the confinement that followed precipitated a
long depression.

Passive-Aggressive Style
For the Passive-Aggressive, days are lived under a negative cloud.

Internal

Sulky, resentful, and sour (may be
hidden)

Reserved, pessimistic, and ill-tempered

Jealous

Hostility gets suppressed, so passivity
is left to see

Cannot remain passive, so a bad mood erupts

Always looks for the worst

Self-image is being misunderstood by others

Tension arises from swings between passivity and aggression

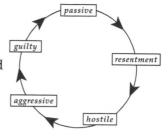

Interpersonal
Nagging
Not physically abusive but has short-lived bursts of temper
Intense relationships
Hates anyone having power over him or her
Infuriates other people
Behaves in indirect ways
Tries to comply but cannot last for long

Normal → Extreme
Passivity can lead to → actions against those people who are close

Childhood of the Passive-Aggressive

Chuck was an agreeable child until he had to make a choice or until his parents told him to do his chores: "You can't make me!" He wallowed in indecision but hated following orders. When he had to study for a test, he fell asleep over the book; when he had to pick up bread from the store, he was strangely detained at school. He made intense rebellious stands at odd times that angered everyone around him, and then he felt ashamed.

Adulthood of the Passive-Aggressive

Chuck married a tough, controlling woman, which satisfied his passivity, but there is no room for healthy aggression. His methods are more subtle than they were in childhood. He began an affair with his wife's best friend, a mild woman with few demands that cannot easily be met. For a while it was enough to keep a secret from her, but in a major argument he "slipped" and told her. His wife was devastated. That affair ended, but several years later another one began. Friends can't see this side of him; they enjoy the mild guy with a good (if somewhat stinging) sense of humor.

Personable Style

A Personable makes for one of the best friends or colleagues around.

Internal
Unruffled, calm, mature, and cooperative
Flexible, warm, easygoing, casual, and trusting/believing

Not creative
Goodhearted; accommodating
Hardworking
Not a risk taker
Laughs
Works better with people than with ideas

Interpersonal
Participatory
Insightful about people and alert to environmental cues
Likes working in group projects rather than alone
Gets along with everyone; well liked
Joins groups and clubs to make friends, not for causes

Normal → Extreme
Fears loneliness, can lead to → hasty marriage
Enthusiastic, can lead to → hasty, poor decisions
Sees the good in people, can lead to → being gullible or being manipulated
Interested in being with people can lead to → hypochondria to get attention
Wants others to like him or her, can lead to → compromising one's own beliefs
Socializes too much, can lead to → doesn't get own work done

Childhood of a Personable

Joan had more good friends than anyone else. She was never afraid of new people and found them all to be interesting. She found the kid sitting next to her in school more enjoyable than the subject matter, with predictable results. She was a natural leader and understood how to get consensus. These abilities carried her through much of her school years.

Adulthood of a Personable

Joan met her husband through her large network of friends and embarked on the next stage. Married life was more difficult because she had multiple responsibilities and, for the first time, found herself envious of others and keeping track of her girlfriends' successes. When she didn't have time to attend to her extended family, she felt guilty; when they showed up unexpectedly at her house, she was flattered but overwhelmed. Before long, she was on a assortment of boards and committees. It took Joan a long time to set priorities in her life and to make decisions putting herself and her family first.

Problem Solver Style

The Problem Solver can stumble by being too capable for others and not capable enough for himself or herself.

Internal

Resourceful
Faces reality but may lack imagination
Can exercise restraint; disciplined
Reliable and mature
Stable; not easily influenced by emotions of others
Emotionally steady, with no wide swings or dips in feelings
Self-starter; achieves goals; high achiever
Healthy
Pleased with himself or herself; little self-blame

Interpersonal

Sticks to projects; perseveres
Not easily disturbed
Savvy in relationships; knows how to get his or her point across
Not easily panicked; good under fire
When life gives him or her a lemon, she or he makes lemonade
Recognizes problem ➜ generates options ➜ makes choices ➜ follows
   through

Normal ➜ Extreme

Coping skills can lead to ➜ being overly self-sufficient

Childhood of a Problem Solver

"Evan was born efficient," his mother always crowed. And that was a good thing because Evan's mom was always in emotional high gear and got little done. Evan figured out how to work the kitchen appliances, how to read, and how to make friends who invited him places that allowed him to escape his home.

Adulthood of a Problem Solver

Evan went to college on a scholarship and moved far away. He rose quickly in his company, and everyone values him. He will never take over the top job because he has no creative vision, but he will always be able to beautifully implement the plan. Friends depend on him, and now his mother is calling to suggest that Evan set her up in a nearby apartment. Some days Evan feels weary and can't figure out why.

Resilient Style

Life is no different for a Resilient than for others, but they have the remarkable ability to recover from the losses and disappointments.

Internal

Generally happy

Productive

Copes with adversity with a minimum of stress

Motivated; effective problem solver

Takes responsibility for his or her own life

Good sense of humor

High ethical standards

Faces problems and takes personal control

Interpersonal

Has personal goals; e.g., fame, power, money, career growth, community, children

Interested in others as well as interested in self

Ability to concentrate

Uses physical activity to combat stress

Maintains strong support network[2]

Normal ➜ Extreme

Independence can become ➜ inability to depend on others

Childhood of a Resilient

Sara's first experience with loss was the death of her grandmother. Luckily, Sara's family took the time to listen to her feelings and to

---

[2] Flannery (1997).

explain the circumstances. When she had nightmares about it, her parents calmed her down and treated her fears with compassion. Over the years there were other disappointments; Sara lost her footing temporarily but was able to feel confident that she could survive and have some degree of mastery over her life.

Adulthood of a Resilient

Unfortunately Sara's adult life was also marked by losses. She was widowed in a freak accident while she was still in her twenties. She deeply grieved the death of her husband but faced the difficulties and concentrated on her baby and herself. She moved ahead slowly at first, but felt that it was up to her to make a life for the two of them. Although her friends and family were helpful, Sara's attitude was that failure was not an option.

Show-Off Style

Internal

Active and alert

Doesn't tolerate frustration well

Immature

Not helpful

Expressive

Emotions shift

Undercontrolled and aggressive

Ostentatious

Interpersonal

Showing off interferes with relationships

Effective with people and tasks

Socially outgoing

Can be oblivious to others

Wants to be admired

Sarcastic

Hard for him or her to share

Normal ➜ Extreme

Expressive can become ➜ aggressive

Childhood of a Show-Off

Doug was a favorite on the playground. He made up great games with uninhibited zeal and led the crowd in early drinking and smoking attempts. In school, however, the teacher said he had a fresh mouth and had no inkling of how to behave around the other kids.

Adulthood of a Show-Off

Doug has channeled his show-off qualities very well. He is a lawyer who runs his own firm and appears often in the courtroom. Most of the time he is enjoyable because of his quick wit and outgoing nature, but everything has to be under his direction and has to be done his way. When he went on a vacation with a bunch of old friends and dominated every decision and conversation, they swore to each other that they would never travel with him again.

Ultra-Femme Style

The Ultra-Femme is to women what the Man's Man is to men. Not surprisingly, they often wind up together.

Internal
Stereotypic feminine behaviors
Exaggerated qualities of naïveté and innocence
Nurturing, passive, and soft
Takes on traditional feminine roles
Constricted emotionally; self-pitying
Helpless and dependent
Indirect, modest, and coy
Idealistic

Interpersonal
Reluctant to express anger or conflict
Accepting of male behaviors
Flirtatious; boosts men's egos
Submissive and yielding; seductive
May doubt own adequacy as a woman

Normal → Extreme
Flirtatious can lead to → loss of herself

Childhood of the Ultra-Femme

From the time Kimmie was a little girl, she was rewarded for her adorable behaviors. Her father doted on her, especially after raising her older brothers. She turned to her father for advice, but had more trouble finding a way to be with her mother. Kimmie had lots of friends and was sought after by girls because she was cute but not threatening; boys enjoyed her without taking her too seriously as a girl.

Adulthood of the Ultra-Femme

Kimmie kept her friends and added more, but whenever they were in a crisis they turned to others, never to her. Guys flirted with her, and her unending innocence seemed to evoke either care or manipulation in them. Kimmie steered clear of personal crisis until her fiancé changed his mind and she experienced feelings with which she had no prior experience—pain and rage.

Victim Style

Life for the Victim is filled with the themes of lack of self-determination and control.

Internal

Long-standing impotent rage that is not strongly felt

Unaware of his or her own hostile behaviors

Feels weak; wants to feel safe

Pessimistic and negative about life

Feels and acts burdened

Feels little pleasure; pleasure results in anxiety so it must be avoided

Turns self-denial into social concerns; e.g., "I cannot buy new shoes because others have none"

Inhibited, serious, responsible, and unassuming; e.g., "I must keep going"

No deep emotions of love or hate

Vaguely depressed and helpless when left alone

Interpersonal

Feels mistreated; distrustful of others

Tries to please others, but self-sacrifice leads to bitterness and more suffering

Self-image is one of suffering; pride comes from being able to "take it"

Goal is to avoid abandonment

Self-blame allows him or her to continue loving others who may treat him or her badly

Demanding; inordinate need for affection

Sexual dysfunction in relationships; unable to receive pleasure

Dependent on others, but relationships often repeat humiliation and defeat

Complains but does not change; displays defeat to the world; says, "no one can help"

Frustrates those who want to help, makes them ineffectual, and arouses their anger

Indirect; appears compliant but may be secretly manipulative

May have learned to enjoy defeat as a way of surviving with pride

Tries to be good; will "go along" to avoid being alone

Behaviors seen in work and interpersonally

Wants to arouse guilt in others, and hopes that guilt will become love

Normal → Extreme

Lack of self-care can lead to → trouble, e.g., marries an alcoholic or sticks with an abusive boss

Unassertive can lead to → endlessly stuck, e.g., stays with a career in which she has no talent

Proud of sacrifice, being able to "take it," can become → depression and suffering

Continued efforts that result in debacle can lead to → feeling hopelessly trapped

Fear of being alone can lead to → denial of danger from others

Confuses mistreatment with affection, which leads to → poor judgment of abusive behaviors

To avoid abandonment → endures verbal, physical, or sexual abuse

Childhood of the Victim

When Sally was born, her mother had exhausted herself raising three other girls and had no patience for another. Each time Sally tried to assert herself normally, whether at two years old, "no potatoes," or three years old, "I want to wear the purple pants," or ten years old,

"I like the piano better than the violin," she was crushingly defeated. The conflicts, and *defeats*, at the hands of her parents were consistent, if not brutal. She was often accused of being "willful," and punishments were attempts to bring her into line. The times that Sally remembers most fondly are the periods of childhood sickness when she enjoyed her parents' solicitation and encouragement.

As she grew up, Sally's small attempts at independence were met with criticism. Her complaints were sympathetically received. Sally's anger went underground, and what remained in view was a compliant young lady who never achieved much.

Adulthood of the Victim

Sally dropped out of school and began working in a lawyer's office. The work was steady but she resisted all efforts at learning new and challenging tasks. The boss liked her reliability and seriousness. Sally wed the first man who insisted on marriage. He was an alcoholic and Sally's friends tried to help her change the situation or leave, but Sally took a strange pride in sticking with him. She made excuses for his behavior; she covered up for his absence at family functions. Her friends and older sisters eventually tired of attempts that were always listened to but never acted on. Sally felt their distance, and this proved to her that there was no one she could trust and no help available. She became even more afraid that her husband would leave and she would have no one.

CHAPTER THREE

Child and Adolescent Types

C hildren are not miniature adults: Personalities are not yet fully formed; they are still works in progress. Therefore, children and adolescents do not fit into defined styles like the adults in the previous chapter. However, children and adolescents can be expected to show certain traits based on age and stage of development. This chapter provides the traits associated with normal development and some of the milder ways that young people run into trouble. Other chapters provide more information about children and adolescents. Chapter four describes psychological disorders, which lists more severe disturbances; chapter eight contains some child and adolescent traumas, and chapter nine has disturbances associated with adolescents, such as substance abuse, addictions, and eating disorders.

Forty-eight percent of all Americans between the ages of fifteen and fifty-four experience a psychological disorder during their lifetime. Many begin in childhood.[1] It is estimated that 7.5 million, or 12 percent, of American children and adolescents suffer from mental disorders.[2] Life is stressful, and even when growth and development are normal, kids have a complex world to negotiate.

The most normal children are not usually the most interesting. One large-scale research study followed almost two thousand boys for twelve years and found all but fifty to be free of psychopathology, *but*

---

[1] "Psychological Sources: Essential to America." American Psychological Association practice directorate. February 1995.

[2] Report Card on the National Plan for Research on Child and Adolescent Mental Disorders: The Midway Point. Institute of Medicine (IOM) Committee for the Study of Research on Child and Adolescent Mental Disorders. February 1995. rptcard.htm@wwwaacap.org

these "normal" boys were also described as "lacking in imagination and creativity, and were highly limited in their interests and activities," so, the interesting fictional character may need a couple of quirks.

Child Development

Some form of a "self" (a single, distinct, integrated body that experiences feelings and has intentions) probably exists before birth. Other aspects of the self, such as the ability to plan, reflect, put experience into language, and share knowledge, require maturation.[3]

Babies are born with individual temperaments that can be seen most clearly during times of stress. The different dimensions of temperament are listed in the left column of the chart below. On the right, the range of temperament gives you a continuum of possibilities from which to choose.

Dimensions of Newborn Temperament

Dimension	Range of Temperament	
Motor Activity	listless/quiet	restlessness/energetic
Mood	placid/easy to soothe	easy to cry/irritable
Approach/ Withdraw	passive/avoids new things	active/seeks stimulation
Distractible	easy to distract	stays focused
Attention	short attention span	persists
Response	little intensity	high-energy reactions
Adaptability	low sensitivity to change. . .	strong reactions
Sensibility	low threshold of response . .	tolerates change
Regularity	regular functions.	unpredictable
Impulsivity	restrained	impetuous

During infancy, the world is a physical place. A newborn infant's pleasure comes from sucking, feeding, and being held, all physical activities. During the next months, the physical world remains central but expands as baby learns to grasp objects, turn over, and explore his

---

[3] Stern (1985).

or her limited surroundings. Therefore, the traits of infancy are more often physical than internal.

We rarely see a young child as the central character in a story, but the following traits provide accuracy for any minor characters and give you a basis for interaction among characters, such as between parent and child.

We follow Pat through the first ten years.

The First Year
0 months–2 months old

The newborn is far more of a person than many people believe, and the days are filled with periods of alert inactivity, when Pat is wakeful but not busy or eating.

Physical

Knows his mother; turns to the smell or voice of mother

Prefers seeing faces to looking at patterns

Likes the human voice better than other sounds

Actively moves his arms and legs, his eyes examine the world, and he seeks stimulation

Mimics what he sees; e.g., Dad sticks his tongue out, Pat will slowly try to do the same

Pat was born with preferences about what pleases him to look at, and sunshine is one of his favorites. The stimulation of light coming through the window and the sounds of people moving in the house excite his entire nervous system and capture his attention. After some time lying and watching the patterns of light, Pat's hunger grows and sweeps painfully through him. The peace ends and he cries out in deep, gasping breaths.[4]

2 months–8 months old

The infant already seems to be a more complete person. Pat begins to know herself; e.g., she intentionally moves her arm.

---

[4] Stern (1990).

Physical
Begins to explore the environment and sits up with the aid of her own hands
Play is not only regulated by adults, Pat also tries to engage them

Interpersonal
Increased recognition of her separateness as a person from her mother
Curious
Seems to know the difference between toys (inanimate) and people (living)

Pat has become more social. She smiles, coos, and makes eye contact for long periods. Pat especially likes human faces but was frightened by the grimaces made by her older brother. Later, she snuggled in her carriage while the family strolled through the local art fair. Startled by breezes, high and low noises, and changing sights, Pat remained calm as long as she sensed her family close by.[5]

8 months–12 months old
Noticeable changes occur. Pat gains subjectivity, the knowledge that he has a mind and so do others. This milestone allows him to communicate differently, and life becomes increasing interpersonal. Pat also loves to show off his physical accomplishments.

Physical
Can sit up; crawls
Hands grasp objects, hair, and toys
Manipulates objects with hands; learns through touching
Drawn to pictures that reflect his mood; e.g., chooses drawing similar to his own sad face
Sleep problems begin from accumulated stimulation due to activity

Internal
Fearful; stranger anxiety is shown as distress in the presence of unfamiliar people

[5] ibid.

Recognizes other people as separate from himself, with distinct bodies and different thoughts

Interpersonal
Sharing is seen when Pat points to an object and checks back with his mother
Teasing is possible; e.g., plays peek-a-boo, hides toys, or holds a toy out and pulls it away
Changes into a more sociable person and loves an audience

Pat's favorite game now is peek-a-boo. He also remembers where toys are hidden and excitedly enlists his mother's help to find objects.

Pat is firmly attached to his family and babysitter, and not just to feed him; he wants their company for emotional reasons—soothing, comfort, or help regulating his ups and downs.[6] The most disturbing occurrence for Pat these days is the array of strange people that he sees. His acceptance of them is low.

Neglect   **From the Files**

Regurgitation without a medical condition may be sign of neglect or poor parenting. The child vomits and rechews food without disgust. This condition is usually seen in young children three to twelve months old. Another trait of neglected infants is poor attachments, either the failure to respond to others or the reverse, indiscriminate attachment to others.

Toddlerhood

Toddlerhood begins with the ability to walk. Lurching steps usually start in the second year, between ten months and sixteen months. In toddlerhood, we begin to understand more of the developing internal world of the child.

1 year–2 years
Physical
Rounded body and a head-thrust-forward walk describe "toddling"

---

[6] ibid.

Thinks with her feet; walking allows her her first taste of
   independence
Explores, bumps into people, and knocks into objects
Loves to run and be caught, climb stairs, close doors, and close
   books
Likes to grab things, throw and pull at objects
Hand movements are improved but she has no fine finger abilities yet

Internal

Uninhibited, she touches and tries things that make this age
   dangerous
Thrilled with herself and feels omnipotent
Walking around in this enlarged world also increases tension, and
   she craves reassurance
Comfort is sought in hair twirling, thumb sucking, a blanket (security
   object), rocking, or head banging

Interpersonal

The world becomes a bigger place with the ability to walk, but she
   still likes to be carried
Walking greatly helps separation from caretakers
She physically explores, but checks back to be sure Mom is still in
   sight[7]

Pat lurches across the room, first tripping over a cord and bringing
down the lamp, and then moving on to the new porcelain figure that
Grandma bought. Her thrill turns to fear when she hears the crash and
then her mom yells. She bursts into tears and crawls back to her blanket.

2 years–3 years

The development of language is a major milestone for the young child.
Language emerges during the second year, and at twenty-four months
Pat has a vocabulary of more than fifty words; during the next six
months, he will be able to create small sentences. His favorite phrases
are "Me do it" and "No." The struggle between independence and
dependence occupies him during this period.

---

[7] Ames, Ilg, and Haber (1982).

Physical

Body control is not complete; turning sharp corners requires preparation

Going-to-bed problems continue from accumulated stimulation of activity

Loves throwing things

Deals with toilet training; begins self-control with body

Internal

Is often overtired and overexcited

Fears noises from vacuum cleaner, animals, toilet flushes, or draining tub water

Lives in the present; not much sense about past or future

Interpersonal

Beginning of sibling rivalry because he has to share attention and love

Temper tantrums include screaming, throwing himself on the floor, hitting, kicking, and biting, often because he is frustrated by his limited ability to communicate

As Pat gets closer to three years old, he is making the transition from toddler to child. Physical activity gets smoother. He retains an image of his parents in their absence and understands that they will return.

Childhood
3 years old
Physical

Body is at her command; she runs smoothly, walks securely, and loves outdoor play

Begins to learn gender differences

Boys play rough and more physically than girls

Internal

Wants to do things correctly "Dis way?" and conforms to routines

Doll play is more imaginative for both boys and girls

Books and music are of interest

Childhood Explanations   From the Files

Greg came into therapy as an adult and insisted that his father beat him because he was a bad boy and talked back or dropped his cereal. Greg insisted, "If I could have been good, he would not have beat me." Greg took the blame for two reasons: (1) His version gave him some control over what had been random and terrifying, and (2) he had been too young to realize that his father beat him when the man was drunk, no matter what the little boy was doing.

Likes humor; e.g., enjoys being asked, "Is your coat green?" when it is red

Interpersonal
Friendlier; e.g., "We go for a walk?"
Capable of sympathy and is pleased when she pleases others
Listens, wants to learn, and likes to tell stories of her adventures
Language is fun and can be used to ask "How?" "What?" "Why?" and "When?"[8]

Pat has become a psychological being. She has reached another landmark—she thinks about and makes up explanations for the things she sees around her. She can now create a story from the diverse details in her life, and she chatters a lot.

4 years old
Physical
Can do some things by himself; e.g., play outdoors
Boys grab genitals as tension reliever
Excessive, energetic, high drive, can move well, is speedy, and has good balance
Fingers are under control to do fine tasks like buttons or catching a ball with his hands
Can feed, wash, and dress himself

---

[8] Ames and Ilg (1976a).

Internal

Exuberant, expansive, and highly sure of himself

Emotions are extreme: loves a lot; hates a lot; laughs loud, and cries, kicks, and spits hard

Lively mind, enjoys newness, and loves exaggeration; uses his fluid imagination

Vastly increased vocabulary and likes language

Grasps concept of time and seasons and activities associated with each; e.g., swimming

Interpersonal

Has realized that adults are not all powerful and he can get away with mischief

Hates changes made by parents; e.g., a new haircut

Intrigued by elimination, "poo," so he tries out "dirty" words and makes "poo-poo" jokes

Likes to hear true stories

Likes everyone's humor; changes familiar songs and stories into new silly versions

Friendships are strong, and he is learning how to get along with others

Resistant to adult commands, he knows his own mind and rejects the suggestions of others

Bedtime gets easier because he likes to play with books and stuffed animals in bed[9]

Pat feels a certain amount of power these days. He is expansive and funny, sometimes going overboard and tempting the other members of his family to squash him. He "loves" or "hates" everything, often without any reason that is apparent to anyone else, but the family is being tolerant.

5 years old

Internal

Calmer and quieter than a four year old; enjoys life (e.g., "Today is my lucky day")

---

[9] Ames and Ilg (1976).

Imaginary Friendships

Imaginary friends appear when a child is between three and ten years old.

The Child

Dramatic but normal aspect of childhood

Not indicative of psychotic or prepsychotic disturbance

Occurs equally with girls and boys

Children temporarily stop playing with imaginary friend when playmate arrives

May share imaginary friend, but often will not

Not just a phenomenon of only children, lonely children, or quiet children

Imaginary friend may be a playmate, her conscience, or a way to govern behavior

Imaginary friend is often blamed for misdeeds; e.g., "Freddy did it!"

The best qualities in the child are brought out by the friend; e.g., love, care, and kindness

Child has a chance to practice behaviors and work on understanding

Major function is companionship

The imaginary friend disappears, often with no explanation

The Friend

May do exotic activities that a good child cannot allow herself

Is distinct and has set features

May require a seat at dinner and a plate

May never appear in public

May be an animal; may be the same sex as the child or the opposite sex

May have an ordinary or a fantastic name[10]

Secure; loves mother; not adventurous or daring

Serious and thoughtful; self-controlled; likes to practice (e.g., print her name)

Matter-of-fact; likes to be certain and accurate; is factual and concrete

---

[10] Fraiberg (1959); Sommers and Yawkey (1984).

Capable of self-criticism

Believes that if she does good, good happens; if she does bad, bad happens[11]

Interpersonal

Usually begins kindergarten, so she meets other children and learns new behaviors

Conscious of rules and feels rage when punished unjustly

Pat sits on the floor in the living room, watching her mother bounce her new baby brother and chat happily with a friend. Pat stares silently, and the visitor offhandedly comments, "What a thoughtful girl," interrupting the child's elaborate fantasy of stuffing cake up the baby's nose until he stops breathing. This is Pat's first extended experience with intense anger that she cannot express.

Separation Problems at 5 and 6 years old

Terrible anxiety about separation from home and/or parents

Fears about being alone

Anxiety seen in physical complaints; e.g., "I have a stomachache"

Avoids school; e.g., "I'm sick"

Happens more often in closely knit families than in more distant families

Problems often precipitated by stress

Middle Childhood

Middle childhood occupies the period from six years old to ten years old and is generally marked by the ever-widening circles in which children move. The world quickly expands from family to school, peers, and playgrounds. The physical world is replaced in importance by the world of activity and relationships.

6 years old

Internal

Tension is seen in wiggling, kicking table legs, and swinging arms

---

[11] Ames and Ilg (1979a).

Cannot choose, especially with small matters; e.g., "I want the blue
   shirt" and as soon as Mom takes the clothes from the drawer, "*No,
   I want the red shirt*"
Insecure, so he loves praise and flattery

Interpersonal
Begins building practical relationships
Beginning of need for increased independence from parents
Competitive and stubborn; e.g., "Make me"
Does what is asked and then does the opposite; e.g., picks up the
   shoe and drops it again
School and playmates increase separation from parents[12]

Six-year-old Pat was in the hospital overnight for the first time. His
mother discovered that everywhere Pat had been, he stole an item: a
magazine, a toy, or some food. This was unusual behavior for Pat, who
had always shared with his brother and sister. Pat could not explain.
He simply looked frightened and mute. The explanation? It is likely
that Pat was afraid that his possessions at home were being taken by
others; that the hospital was experienced as a place that was taking
something from him, and in a six-year-old way, he was desperately
attempting to replenish his meager resources.

7 years old
Physical
Awareness of her body; may avoid public bathrooms; dreads
   exposure

Internal
Introverted, absorbed; a time of withdrawal, pulling in, and calming
   down
Worries, inner tensions, and fears; e.g., late for school, the dark, or
   ghosts
Aware of herself; Pat wants her own room
Tension seen in muttering, mumbling, and wiggling loose teeth
Plays with pencils; draws and erases

---

[12] Ames and Ilg (1979).

Can tell time, and wants a watch; increased understanding of time and knows days and months

Bad and good are slowly becoming abstract concepts rather than orders from parents

Interpersonal

Can take other people's needs into account

Wants mother to listen to complaints, often about dislike for the opposite sex

Potty jokes end

Interested in babies and pregnancy more than sex[13]

At seven, Pat is not easily known: There is much life under the surface that is not readily apparent. She watches, her mind rushes, and her hands fidget.

Characteristics of the Unpopular Child in Middle Childhood

Has fewer skills of making friends

Not adept at managing conflict; e.g., answers "Punch him"

Aggressive, silly, babyish, and a show-off

Anxious; uncertain about own worth

Less resourceful; doesn't know how to manage people well

---

8 years old

He suddenly is less a child and less afraid. He is expansive; he takes everything he learned at seven and uses it in the world.

Physical

His world is expanding; likes to go to the zoo, museums, and places of interest

Wants to explore so he walks or bikes, and even is willing to try new food

Physically better coordinated so sports are more rewarding

---

[13] Ames and Haber (1985).

Internal

Likes his own objects and money and hoards possessions

Aware of his personal qualities, appearance, and others' responses to him

Evaluates his own failures and mistakes and can think logically

Intellectually more curious; enjoys reading

Interested in life processes; beginning to understand death as an event in all lives

Enthusiastically friendly; less self-centered; recognizes the views of others

Can picture a series of actions so he can run an errand

Interpersonal

Interested in human relationships, even nosy about others

Jealous of siblings with mother, but has a smoother relationship with father

Loves to talk and with emphasis; e.g., "It was *awful*"

Often has a best friend, and there is less play with the opposite gender

Secrets with friends are not shared with parents

Likes specific clothes, special brands, board games, dice games, and cards and wants to win

Hard to understand group compromise: "But I want to play a different game"[14]

Pat has a great love of animals and shows tenderness to them. Of course, he still feels free in telling his family that "the shirt you bought me sucks."

9 years old

Internal

Deepening of emotions creates a lack of self-confidence

Difficult to make choices and decisions

Wrapped up in herself and is overly sensitive

Anxious about her health; complains about her physical well-being

Can understand changed rules, but likes standardized rules

---

[14] Ames and Haber (1989).

Common Childhood Fears (Ages 6–12)

Unlikely worries such as being attacked by snakes, tigers, or lions

Realistic worries such as being late for school

Other worries:

> Being adopted
>
> Someone in the family becoming ill or dying
>
> The house burning down
>
> Someone close having an accident
>
> Being followed by a stranger
>
> Being kidnapped

Interpersonal

Resists adult supervision and is critical of others

Pat is into what her father calls "the sulks." He has learned not to tease her because that always results in a slammed door, but he has no idea how to communicate with her and has decided to wait it out. That seems fine with Pat, who prefers reading and talking with friends.

10 years old

Physical

Tension is still seen in nail biting or hair twirling

Clothing choice is more important than baths and washing

Girls and boys are still the same size

Girls show approaching puberty, softening, and a waist; girls worry about breasts

Girls are more aware of sex than boys; boys question little about sex

Girls bike, run, play table games, collect things, draw, write, and perform plays

Boys play in large groups: ball games, biking, table games, collecting things, drawing, and constructing things

Internal

Gaining poise

Fewer fears and nightmares[15]

---

[15] Ames, Ilg, and Baker (1989).

Peer Groups of Middle Childhood

Groups become important around age ten

Peer groups are preferred company to parents

Gives children information about their own roles and status

Helps form attitudes and values

Shapes concepts of adult world

Leadership develops

Norms develop that govern the group

Adolescent Development

Adolescents authoritatively discuss sex, love, self, friendship, religion, society, justice, and the meaning of life. Conversations are endless, and phones, notes, and e-mail are a way of life. Beginning at this time, abstract thinking allows adolescents to form concepts, so they can think about how one thing relates to another and about social institutions, and they can question possibilities. The young people are trying desperately to define themselves and gain an identity. For parents, adolescence can be a trying stage because their sons and daughters become egocentric and self-absorbed while they figure out who they are—all very annoying, but normal. For many parents, their children's adolescence occurs while they are struggling with midlife issues, an unfortunate combination of events. More dangerously, adolescence brings a sense of invincibility and unlimited power, so young people are more likely to take chances. Accidental deaths are highest for young men between the ages of fourteen and twenty-four years old than any other age group.

Early Adolescence
11 years old
This marks the beginning of adolescence.

Physical
Seems to be in constant motion

Girls are showing more physical development than boys

Some boys have begun a growth spurt; some boys have erections

Doesn't like to sleep and doesn't like to wake up

Aware of and has definite ideas about clothes

Experiences body pains of undetermined origin

Internal

Egocentric

At best—alert, imaginative, and energetic

At worst—lying, self-centered, quarrelsome; has a conscience but may lie or steal

Money may take on importance, and plans to spend can be thought out

Emotions run high; anger and tears occur often

Getting a sense of humor; silly

Interpersonal

Quick to criticize

Has high standards of behavior for others, lower for himself or herself

Not helpful to family around the house

Trying to become free of parents to gain independence; resistant and rebellious

More critical of mother than father; e.g., *"She says I can't go"*

Behaves better to others outside of home than in the home

Is interested in all that goes on; gossips

Difficulties with siblings; competitive

Less casual and more discriminating about friends

People are more important than play

More critical of school, even with kids who like it

Has close, mutually shared relationships; good relationships outside the family

11 years old–13 years old

Puberty has begun. There are significant differences in puberty for boys and girls.

Boys

Physical

Boys are less comfortable with body changes than girls

Masturbation is a means to control excitement or to soothe himself

Boys get slimmer hips, muscles, facial hair, and sweat glands—they
grow and gain weight later

Boys no longer look solid; they look like they will break objects with
their awkwardness

Boys dream about buildings with equipment and bombs, tubes, and
periscopes that go up and down

Hormonal levels change as puberty begins

Internal

Gruff exterior covers gentleness that is best seen with pets

Lazy and conflicted between being active vs. passive and dependent
vs. independent

> Wake him up and he is angry
> Don't wake him up and you are uncaring
> Tell him to sleep and you are interfering

Interpersonal

Provokes fights

Competes with height, competence, spitting, and telling tales

Girls

Physical

Invested in her own body; some begin to diet

Better prepared for menstruation than boys are for ejaculation

Untidy rooms

Girls gain weight, hips widen, grow (to age fifteen), and develop
sweat glands

Internal

Girls dream about idealized love and pop stars

Girls underreact with indifference or overreact with sarcasm, tirades,
and tears

Interpersonal

Still likes cuddling by family

Less need to be independent; tolerates connectedness

Independence seen as she borrows Mother's clothes and then criticizes them

12 years old—boys and girls

Physical

Maturity rates are now noticeably different; girls are more physically developed

Both still experience body pains of undetermined origin

Many have tried drugs, cigarettes, and alcohol

By the end of the year, the average twelve-year-old girl has achieved 95 percent of her adult height

Twelve is the average age of menarche

Boys show greater variations in physical and emotional development

Boys have erections spontaneously and from sexual stimulation, anger, horseplay, and fear, all of which is puzzling to them

Masturbation is common, especially in boys

Genuinely hungry often

Girls begin to worry about weight

Sleep is more restless, but arguments about bedtime diminish

Bathing is more under control than subtleties like hand washing

The "right" clothes are very important

Internal

Evens out temperamentally, but emotions are shapeless

Enthusiastic reactions of all kinds (positive and negative)

Greater moral development

Increased sense of humor

Tries to hide feelings but emotions, especially anger, are not under control

Humor takes on sarcastic tones, and they love double meanings

Knows own positive and negative qualities

Distinct abilities become apparent; e.g., athletics, math, or music

Conscience speaks clearly

Interpersonal

More distant as a person, so they are less critical of parents

Friends are a source of support and pleasure; e.g., "All my friends have a later curfew"

Boys and girls notice each other

Girls attend parties hoping for romance; boys attend parties to horse
around and eat

Enterprising twelve year olds are figuring out ways to earn money

Compares oneself to others; looks for similarities and differences

Each sex likes the other; girls show more interest

Individuals are heavily ruled by the group

Loneliness becomes frequent company for many kids during these years. Heather has been neatly cut out of her clique. She doesn't quite know what she did wrong, but no one is calling or talking to her. She will eat lunch in the school library today rather than sit alone in the cafeteria.

Davey suffers from the awkwardness of a growing adolescent. He overheard the basketball coach rebuke the team captain, who suggested that Davey be left on the bench. Davey dreams of being a success at the sport and getting the attention he craves.

13 years old
Physical
Girls continue steady physical changes

Change seems abrupt in boys—genitals grow, voice deepens and
cracks, nose sticks out of face, and growth still occurs in spurts;
50 percent have experienced ejaculation

Eating continues, but manners and table behaviors improve

Very particular about clothing; notice their own grooming but not
their rooms

Majority have tried cigarettes, drugs, or alcohol

Internal
Physical and emotional withdrawal; wants to get rid of dependency
on parents

Seems to be pulling thoughts together

Sour, cloudy, and uncertain disputations

If not happy, very ethical and concerned with right and wrong

Internally they are very busy even when the exterior seems stagnant

Enjoy their own rooms

Money never lasts; always broke

Worry about a lot of things

Humor is crisp and sardonic, and sarcasm increases

Good mimics of teachers, siblings, and parents

Scrutinize outer selves first, and then inner selves

Think globally about world issues; e.g., hunger, peace, or animal
rights

Interpersonal

Needs privacy; doors are closed and locked (e.g., "Leave me alone!")

Parents nag and adolescents reply with one-word answers: "OK"
or "Nothing"

Embarrassed by parents

Different relationships develop with mother and father; may still
talk to mother, but father is easier for homework instruction

Dates and attend parties; girls like parties better than boys do

Still argues more with mother than father

Boys are still comfortable in groups to do things (although may have
a best friend)

Girls' friendships are closely knit; maybe three of them, with two
often ganging up on one

Beginning to dislike authority

Increasingly sophisticated about ethics, right and wrong, white lies,
and accepting blame

Maria has begun to fail in school. Until her parents' divorce last
year, she had been a top student. Her mother figures that Maria cannot
concentrate because she is upset about all the changes in her life. That
analysis is true but not complete. Maria is also angry and guilty. She
is angry that her foolish parents have separated, but she is guilty
because she isn't sure that she is free from some responsibility for the
mess. Her solution is to punish them all, especially herself. Failure is
an effective self-punishment for real or imagined crimes.

14 years old

Reorganized post-puberty provides boundless energy.

Physical

Overwhelming majority use drugs, alcohol, or cigarettes

Girls look like young women; their physical development is well
under way

More variety in development for boys; greatest growth spurt, looks
masculine, and has a deeper voice

Boys go from unself-conscious to modest

Most boys masturbate regularly and understand ejaculation

Girls are cleaner than boys, but both continue to be particular about
clothes

Involved in activities, sports, and groups

Internal

Emotions are more shared; less turning inward

Wants more freedom; willing, sometimes eager, to argue

More drive toward the opposite sex

Knows right and wrong, even when doing wrong

Interpersonal

Highly critical of parents; family is the problem more than school
or friends

Father now joins mother as an object of criticism; parents don't
understand

Teens listen to father better than mother

Parents say kids demand everything, appreciate little, and get insulted easily

Disturbance appears in the father/daughter relationship as she matures and dates

Same-sex and opposite-sex friendships may be dissolving and
reforming

More pleasant with people outside the family

Understands money better but cannot hold on to it; many expenses

Some find work

Boy-girl relationships shift rapidly

Shame is the experience of being inadequate and visible for all to
see. Talia had the wrong clothes for her new school, and several girls
made a point of telling her. Eddie got put down by a young girl in a
voice so loud that he was sure that the entire school heard her laughing
rejection of him. Mary Lou silently begs to die every day in sex educa-

tion class because the discussions remind her of the long-standing sexual fondling that she has endured at the hands of her stepfather.

General Traits of Middle Adolescence
Most physical changes have taken place
Want to know reason for society's rules
More secure about emerging identity; frees them from parents
Identifies with an adult
Imitates others; tries mannerisms
Small percentage make vocational choice

Middle Adolescence
15 years old
Physical
Minimal response; restricted energy
Sexually active to varying degrees

Internal
Deepening capacity to reason
Limited emotional and intellectual expression
Thoughtful and reflective rather than expansive and expressive
Pulls together thoughts and organizes perceptions
Tries to evaluate and hold on to a perspective
Unadaptable; unhappy

Interpersonal
Individualistic and often unpredictable responses
Conflict with authority; rebellious; negative toward family
Friends becomes very significant; looks for things to do with friends
Experimenting goes on with friends; likes getting away with things
Bounces against family limits; can evoke anger in parents

Molly was picked up by the police because she was hanging out in the playground after curfew. Max was picked up later in the week for spray-painting some garbage cans. Both are good kids trying some new limits. Molly and Max both know where to buy drugs but haven't experimented with them—yet.

The sixteen to twenty-one year old moves in the direction of continuing to become a more clearly defined individual. The conflict becomes "I want to be independent, but I don't want the pain of separation."

16 years old
Physical
Body growth smoothes out

Internal
Becoming future oriented
More self-sufficient
Introspective; daydreamers
More straightforward
Develops deeper interests; is more creative and imaginative

Interpersonal
Warm toward and interested in others
Sensitive to and aware of others
Concerned about relations to others
Driver's license is milestone

Heather is in her first "serious" romance, meaning they are experimenting with sex. Heather's parents have figured out some of it, but are arguing over whether the safe sex talk will encourage her even further—or is it information that teenagers *need* these days. What they haven't caught on to yet is that when Heather says she is sleeping at Megan's house, Megan has just told her parents that she is at Heather's.

Early Adult Transition
17 years old–21 years old
Terminating adolescent structure—initiating preliminary steps in the adult world
Separation from parents creates a vacuum; the rules of one's parents are disappearing and there are no replacements
More autonomy
Consolidation of identity in sexual choice

Vocational choice becomes a concern

Vacuum makes individual receptive to new people and ideas

The Twenty Most Common Dreams of College Students

1. Falling
2. Being attacked or pursued
3. Trying repeatedly to do something
4. School, teachers, and studying
5. Sexual experiences
6. Arriving too late
7. Eating
8. Being frozen with fright
9. A loved person is dead
10. Being locked up
11. Finding money
12. Swimming
13. Snakes
14. Being inappropriately dressed
15. Being smothered
16. Being nude in public
17. Fire
18. Failing an examination
19. Seeing one's self as dead
20. Killing someone[16]

---

[16] Griffith, Miyagi, and Tago (1958).

Psychological Disorders

Mental illness is less about brain malfunction and more about personality disorders. Disorders, by definition, mean that people deviate in substantial ways from the norm. Disorders also exclude behaviors that are a result of cultural differences or that are acceptable actions elsewhere. For example, in certain Native American tribes, talking to the dead is commonplace; mention those conversations in mainstream North America, and heavy medications might be ordered.

Problems in Child Development

When development is not routine, children and adolescents can be described, in part, by the traits that define their disorder. This chapter provides traits of many disorders, from mild to severe. Even when an individual cannot remember early events, those experiences influence adult behaviors. If a newborn boy lies neglected in a dark room, his cries unanswered and his needs unmet, it is unlikely that he will have any memory of those months. However, the influence of mistreatment will be seen years later in issues of trust and care. Even further back in time, a girl conceived and born after an older sister died has no knowledge of the tragedy. Yet her parents' reactions to her will be partly formed by events that occurred before her birth. Problems unsolved by one generation are passed down to the next.

Some problems that we see in childhood and adolescence can happen at any time of life. Children, like adults, can be depressed or psychotic, or can have a substance disorder or an eating disorder. In this chapter, disorders are described alphabetically under general headings of Child, Adolescent, and Adult. The disorders listed as childhood problems are those that begin early and are seen primarily in young people. The problems listed here under disorders of adolescence are those that most commonly begin during that period. Some disorders end; others continue throughout life.

Early Influences Shape Personality

Each child is born with a basic temperament that is shaped by life events. When a child fits nicely with her parents and her environment, she flourishes. When circumstances are adverse, the child suffers. Some circumstances are innocent; for example, I treated a young woman who was an artist. Unfortunately for her, she was born into a family of accountants—nice people, but they had no idea what to do with her, and she suffered from feeling different and unvalued. In a more serious instance, a young man had been born with heart defects that required repeated surgeries until he was fifteen. His mother had already nursed her own parents through fatal illnesses and hated taking care of him. Whatever normal shyness he started with became distorted, and he was a withdrawn, ashamed, and angry young adult by the time I met him. In these ways and innumerable others, childhood personality and past experiences shape the present.

Several of the disorders below may appropriately have been included in chapter nine, but because they are so closely tied to youth, they have been listed below. These include common difficulties of childhood, such as tics, stuttering, and bed-wetting or enuresis. Less ordinary problems that have a strong physical-emotional link are also here. These are skill disorders, autism, and encopresis.

Mild Disorders of Childhood
Anxiety

The anxious child doesn't behave badly. In fact, she or he is too withdrawn and fearful to get into any trouble. Many children outgrow their anxiety completely, and others get it pretty much under control and remain mildly anxious adults, but some go further into themselves and have no peer relationships, are cold and unresponsive, secretive, like to be alone, and refuse to communicate very much. This last group may become the adult Loner personality.

The Anxious Child
Shy, timid, and tense
Depressed and sad
Hypersensitive and easily hurt
Feels worthless
Self-conscious; e.g., easily embarrassed
Lacks confidence
Cries frequently
Aloof and worried[1]

Heather was always shy, but since she began school she has cried every morning and is frequently sent home with stomachaches and nausea. Heather's mother hates to admit it, but she loves being so essential to her daughter. School isn't the only problem. Heather's mother arranged playtime with a sweet girl across the street, but just when Heather was getting comfortable at Amy's house, Amy's father came home angry and upset. Even though he didn't speak to either of the girls, Heather heard him yelling in the other room and has refused to go back to play.

Bed-Wetting (Enuresis)
Enuresis is of little concern until after the age of four. At that time, it begins to interfere with a child's ordinary life. He cannot engage in activities without fear that he will wet his clothing. Normal childhood pleasures, such as sleeping at a friend's house, become impossible. The child becomes ashamed and fearful.

Bed Wetter
Usually wets at night; wetting is less common during the day
Behavior is not voluntary
Child does not mind being wet
Self-esteem suffers a negative impact

---

[1] Achenbach (1982).

Regarded badly by peers

Subject to teasing

More common in children who are aggressive

More common in children who have difficulty adapting to new
situations

Parents and teachers get angry and punish him, with little effect[2]

Billy was toilet trained at three but has always had a problem with
wetting the bed at night while he is sound asleep. Occasionally, when
he is engrossed in an activity, he wets his pants during the day. His
parents were not worried because his father had similar trouble as a
child and outgrew the problem by age four. But Billy passed his fifth
birthday and nothing improved. The other kids are now aware of the
problem, and a couple of the boys tease him. The teachers try to intervene at school, but he is quickly becoming the kid that is left out of
sports and group activities. These rejections fuel his shame and self-
hatred, and recently he frightened his mother by screaming that he
wished he was dead.

Billy differs from Greg, a four-year-old boy in his preschool who
intentionally urinated on his mother when she lay down for a nap.
Greg also has a problem, but his behavior was intentional, probably
arising from confusion and anger about his parents' separation.

Involuntary bowel movements, or encopresis

Less common than bed-wetting

Occurs at inappropriate times

The child may have been trained at one time and stopped, or never
trained

More common during the day than during the night

Children are usually under stress

Defiance

This child has difficulty being properly assertive so she overdoes the
rebelliousness. An extreme version is the Conduct Disordered child,
described in the next section, Moderate and Severe Childhood Disor-

---

[2] Achenbach (1982).

ders. Conduct disorder is more worrisome because violence is present and the future possibilities are more negative.

Defiant Traits
Negative; hostile
Loses her temper
Argumentative; refuses to listen to parents and teachers
Touchy and easily annoyed
Parents become annoyed and perplexed
Blames others; does not want to accept responsibility
Low self-esteem
Difficult to appropriately separate from her parents
Behaviors are attempts to gain emotional control in relationships
Behaviors regulate distance between the child and her parents
Finds it difficult to be properly assertive
Swings from withdrawn to bullying[3]

Samantha is a twelve year old whose soft features cloak deep negativity. She has been running away from home for the last year and is on the verge of failing school. Sammi has had a rough time. Her parents divorced three years ago, and her mother has been chronically ill for a long time. Sammi alternates between trying to be helpful to her mother and intentionally disregarding everything that she is told. Life is further complicated by Sammi's older sister, a star student and athlete. Sammi can't find a place for herself and falls into angry rebelliousness very easily. She does not have a strong peer group, so there is little support available. Running away often seems to be the best solution, sparing everyone the arguments and hurt.

Obsessiveness
Children go through normal phases of worry, but the obsessive child is chronically fearful without a justifiable cause. This can become more severe as time goes on.
Anxious, tense, filled with worry, and fearful
Conforming
Needs reassurance; very sensitive

---

[3] Mones (1998).

Seems mature
Learns to control feelings, especially joy
Guilt keeps her anger under control
Models herself on parents' authority

Megan is a serious little girl, and adults who talk with her forget that she is only seven years old: She seems much older. Her father wishes that she would be a bit sillier, more like her little sister, but Megan is not a lighthearted child. She is very conscientious and does beautifully at school and playing at friends' houses. Other mothers always compliment Megan on her good behavior and adherence to rules. However, Megan's parents have begun to worry. At first they felt very lucky to have a daughter that followed rules, kept toys clean, and did not get into trouble. Recently, her mother confided to a friend that she would be thrilled to see Megan laughing and filthy in the back yard. They see an anger inside Megan that erupts periodically, and they are concerned that their daughter is overly controlled and restricted in her emotional development.

Overattachment

Themes of fear about separation run through every day
Anxious about any separations from parents
Worries that bad things will happen to parent; e.g., "Don't have a
   car crash!"
Worries excessively about being taken her from parents; e.g.,
   kidnapping
Avoids school because bad situations could happen while she is
   away
Has trouble going to friends' houses; cannot sleep at a friend's house
   or at camp
Threat of separation from parents means a tantrum, terror, or begging
Physical symptoms occur at an imminent separation; e.g., nausea,
   vomiting, or headaches
Fantasies and nightmares are about separation
Calls and/or writes excessively when she has to be away; e.g., at camp

Karen would like to be with her mother all day long. She doesn't even want to go out with her father or older brother. She is filled with dread when she goes to school each day and often vomits before leaving the house. She insists that friends come to her house and avoids any activities that will take her away from home. When her parents suggested camp, she got hysterical and locked herself in the bathroom. Karen had always been close to her mother, but after her mother was in a car accident, separation had become much more difficult. No encouragement or reassurance lessens Karen's unspeakable fear.

Tics are sudden, recurrent, repetitive motor twitches
Cannot be controlled for any period of time
Various motor tics are
> eye blink
> smelling things
> childhood tics generally disappear unless they mark the onset of a disease

Various vocal tics are
> barking
> echokinesis—imitation of someone else's sounds
> coprolalia—repeating "bad" words
> Tourette's—one vocal (i.e., echokinesis) and several motor tics (e.g., jumping and grimacing)

Moderate and Severe Childhood Difficulties
Like most problems, the following disorders range from mild to severe. The following traits are descriptive of the severe forms of each disorder. To create milder forms of these problems, use few traits or mild forms of the traits, or demonstrate that the behavior can be easily controlled.

Attention-Deficit Hyperactivity
Lately this disorder has become popular and is being used to explain normal behaviors that are unattractive and to ignore other problems, such as pervasive anxiety or anxious depression, that could show similar symptoms.
Fidgets or squirms in a seat at school or at home
Trouble remaining seated when asked
Trouble concentrating; easily distracted and has a short attention span
Fails to finish things that he starts
Acts before thinking; e.g., impulsive

Needs a lot of supervision

Cannot wait for his turn in games or in groups of other children

Talks out of order; calls out in class

Trouble following instructions, even when he intends to do so

Shifts from one activity to another

Interrupts other people; intrudes into conversations or activities

Trouble playing quietly; runs and jumps on furniture

Too much talking and not enough listening

Loses things; e.g., books, assignments, toys, or equipment

Sluggish, lazy, and drowsy

Often first pointed out by a teacher and always begins in childhood (before age seven)

The school's standard of behavior highlights already existing problems[4]

Kevin's parents took him to see a psychologist because they were at the end of their patience. He had always been active, always jumping around and always noisy, but after the birth of his sister when he was three, life went downhill. Going out with Kevin, even to the local fast-food restaurant, was particularly unpleasant because he chattered and wiggled constantly. In kindergarten, the teachers alerted Kevin's mother that he was difficult to manage in class and, over the years, the bad reports never stopped rolling in. The other kids in his class said that Kevin couldn't be a "true friend," and he remained one of the less popular children.

Kevin's older brother and younger sister had none of these behaviors; in fact, they were hardworking and responsible, so the contrast was sharp. The three of them did not get along, so family vacations just about stopped. The constant fighting, Kevin's need for more than his share of attention, and his aggressive behavior threatened to wreck the family.

Two of the worst disorders of childhood are autism and childhood schizophrenia. Schizophrenia is rare in children, and only about 5 percent of cases of this disease begin before puberty, but it does occur and has all the same characteristics found in adults, as described in a later section of this chapter, Problems in Adult Development. Schizophrenia

---

[4] Garber, Garber, and Spizman (1990).

can disappear, recur intermittently over the lifetime, or progressively get worse. Autism always appears first in childhood and almost never gets better.

Autism

Autism is a severe and pervasive impairment in communication, with delay of or lack of language and poor social interaction (e.g., no relationships and no reciprocity)

Always apparent first in childhood

Unaware of others; e.g., treats people like objects

No idea of another person's distress; no ability for empathy

No ability to play and no reciprocity

Prefers solitary activities and is passive

No interest in or ability to make friends, no sharing, and no taking turns

Absence of attachment

Does not come to caretaker for comfort when hurt or tired

No ideas about privacy

No communication; little or no speech

Makes repetitive sounds; monotonous, screeching, or melodic

No nonverbal communication (e.g., no smiles), has a steady stare, and 50 percent never speak

Strange stereotypic, restricted, repetitive body movements; e.g., head banging on walls, flapping, or hand-twisting

Insists on sameness; reacts badly to any change (e.g., mother cannot move a chair)

Follows same dull routine day after day; unchangeable rituals

May attach to one object; e.g., carry a paper bag around

The doctors knew something was wrong by the time Alli was one year old, and her mother knew they had a problem even earlier when her daughter stiffened and never seemed ready to be held. Alli didn't babble the way most infants did, but no one knew how bad the problem would be until several years later. Alli was diagnosed as moderately autistic and spent hours each day in solitary activity, often banging on the piano. Other days, she sat in her room rocking or thumping a doll against the floor. Alli hated to be touched or disturbed. When her mother tried to distract her, Alli made horrible grunting sounds and fought her. Alli's mother cried endlessly during the first years, when her daughter treated her like a piece of furniture, but she got used to the endlessly bizarre behavior; others never did. Alli was institutionalized at age fourteen.

Conduct Problems
In a child can become Bossy in an adult
Dislikes social rules; i.e., disobedient and defiant
Can be violent and aggressive
Fights, behaves cruelly to people and pets, destructive, and bullies and threatens people
Loud, attention seeking, and a show-off
Destructive; e.g., vandalizes property
Obtrusive
Temper tantrums; e.g., blows up easily
Aggressive; e.g., fights, hits, and is assaultive
Hates to take directions; impertinent, smart, and impudent
Has school problems and lacks self-control; i.e., boisterous and noisy
Not deterred by fear
Lacks desire to please others; e.g., uncooperative and inconsiderate
Mistrustful and untrustworthy; lies

Behavior → Extreme
Believes that others are bad and harmful → allows violent behavior
Hates to lose → so cheats

Tom went from being difficult at age five to impossible at age twelve. He had been suspended from school repeatedly for hitting other kids and being disrespectful to teachers. The school social worker tried to get him involved in football, figuring that a sport would provide some outlet for his aggression, but Tom could never follow the coach's rules and was thrown out. It was not unusual for Tom to walk down the street with a key in his hand and happily run a scratch along the newer cars at the curb. Tom's brothers and sister stayed away from him until he broke the leg of his sister's kitten when he threw it into the air, and then they beat him. It made no difference.

When child conduct problems also include bad companions, gangs, being truant from school, running away from home, stealing, lying, and cheating, the odds go up for future trouble and run-ins with the law.[5]

Depression

We do not like to believe that children can be depressed. Childhood depression is also one of the most difficult disorders for adults to identify because it is hard to observe the expectable symptoms of guilt, self-blame, feelings of rejection, low self-esteem, and negative self-image. In children, depression is often marked by physical complaints, refusal to go to school, emotional outbursts, fears, underachievement, insomnia, anger, or isolation.

Children get more notice when they behave badly than when they are lethargic and uncommunicative. Even when adolescents report severe depression, parents and teachers are often dangerously unaware of the situation. Depression can be mild, but I have included it in the moderate and severe listings because the consequences of child and adolescent suicides are grave.

For a list of traits, see Depression, Adult Styles, in this chapter.

Gender Identity Disorder

Upset about being their own gender, either boy or girl

Does not want to wear clothing of gender; e.g., girls wear boy's underwear

Hates one's own body, particularly any evidence of gender; e.g., breast or penis

May insist that the other body parts will grow; e.g., girls says penis will grow

May pretend to have other organs; e.g., boy hides penis to look like vagina

Girls may urinate standing up; boys may urinate sitting down

Cross dresses

Enjoys activities associated with other gender

Behavior → Extreme

Vocal about wanting to be the other gender → insists that she or he is the other gender

---

[5] Quay and Werry (1979).

Childhood of a Transgendered Individual

When Johnny was three and announced that he was a girl, everyone grinned and corrected him. At four, when he dressed in his older sister's clothes and insisted on urinating sitting down, his mother tried to be understanding. At five, he announced, for the first time, that he hated his penis and wanted to cut it off. One evening, Johnny's father walked toward the house and said hello to a cute young girl playing on the lawn before he recognized his son. He lost his temper. Johnny tried to conform. He was a fine athlete, played tennis all through school, and had friends that were boys and girls, but never lost the sense that biology had played a terrible trick on him. When he went to sleep at night, he prayed to wake up as a girl.

A person who continues to feel this way as an adult is usually considered transsexual. A man may choose to live as a woman and vice versa. In some instances, the individual will take hormones and have his or her body surgically altered to become the other gender, a process called *sexual reassignment*.

Mental Retardation

Abilities all depend on the level of retardation—mild, moderate, or severe

Can be a result of a genetic abnormality, a birth defect, or trauma at or after birth

Wide range of retardation, from mild to severe, with different levels of ability

Significantly below average intelligence

Significant trouble in adaptation; e.g., social skills, communication, and daily living

Trouble reaching adult levels of independence and responsibility

Cannot progress in some areas; e.g., speech skills

Adaptation also depends on personality, motivation, education, and opportunities

Down syndrome is a common cause of retardation and has specific physical features

Causes of retardation:

        30—40 percent unknown

        hereditary factors—Tay-Sachs, Down syndrome

prenatal problems—trisomy 21, alcohol consumption, or
  infection
birth and perinatal problems—prematurity, malnutrition,
  trauma, or lack of oxygen
physical disorders—lead poisoning, trauma, or infection
environmental problems—complication of severe mental
  disorder; deprivation

Mutism
There are rare children who are able to talk but refuse to do so.
  Refuses to speak in several important settings; e.g., school or friend's
    home
  Able to speak and able to understand language
  Usually willing to talk at home
  Begins early, before school years
  May not be noticed until school or settings outside the home make
    it evident
  Can last for weeks to years
  May have an overprotective mother
  May have had an early trauma; e.g., hospitalization

Childhood of a Mute
Heather was a beautiful little six year old who seemed normal except
for one very strange behavior—she spoke only to her mother and to
her best friend. Watching Heather, it became clear that shyness was
not at work; in fact, Heather seemed bold and very much in control
when she wasn't talking. Other little girls wanted her to talk to them
and felt left out when Heather turned to whisper to her best friend.
Heather's adoring mother, an older nutritionist, never could understand where this behavior came from, but was thrilled when, two years
later, it gradually disappeared.

Skill Disorders
There are children who have a marked inability to do a certain activity,
but have normal abilities in other areas. These disorders are not indicative of mental retardation, and children perform adequately in other
areas. The following list provides some of the idiosyncratic disorders.

Arithmetic Disorder—Cannot develop arithmetic skills: math operations, copying numbers, counting objects, or reading math signs.

Writing Disorder—Cannot adequately spell, use written grammar, punctuate, or organize paragraphs.

Reading Disorder—Cannot adequately recognize written words or comprehend written words.

Speaking Disorder—Cannot adequately express himself or herself in words: uses limited vocabulary, has trouble acquiring new words, or uses short sentences and simple grammar.

Problems in Adolescent Development

The disorders described previously may continue into adolescence; the disorders described next generally begin in adolescence. Other problems that begin in adolescence, eating disorders and substance abuse, are fully described in chapter nine under Physical Disorders.

Self-Cutter

Self-cutting is repetitive, nonlethal cutting of the body, usually beginning in adolescence. Cutting indicates problems, usually trauma or a personality disorder, but does not involve major mutilation, which is psychotic.

Usually females (males get into more accidents that do bodily harm)

Usually begins by adolescence; rarely starts in adulthood

Often occurs concurrently with an eating disorder

Often ends spontaneously

Is done in isolation

Transforms emotional pain into physical pain

Feels removed from her own body during the cutting; e.g., "I watched myself cut" or "It was like I wasn't there"

Does not want to die: This is not a suicide attempt; in fact, she fears inadvertant death

Self-hatred

Anger at herself for having needs and feelings, and for lack of control in life

Must cut until blood flows

Feels calmer and relaxed afterward

Feels shame; e.g., "I'm a freak"

Trying to be independent

Reaffirms identity and boundaries of skin; e.g., "I exist if I bleed"
    Competing explanations for cause of self-cutting

Manipulative or attention seeking; e.g., "I wanted someone to ask
    what was wrong"

Result of rape or childhood sexual abuse; e.g., "I'll show you how
    bad you made me feel"

Self-punishment

Discharge of anger; e.g., "See what I can do"

Self-purification; e.g., "I had to get rid of the badness"

Pleasure or tension release; e.g., "The feelings were building. Then
    afterwards, I was calm"[6]

Childhood of a Self-Cutter

Leslie was sexually abused during childhood and into early adolescence. She never told anyone and tries not to think about it. As the stresses of adolescence piled up, she began to cut herself. The first time she had been drinking and dropped a glass. As she picked up a sharp piece, she used it to cut her arm. She watched the blood flow and felt relief. After that, she bought blades, saved them especially for cutting, and cut her arms and breasts whenever the tension was unbearable.

Adolescents who mutilate themselves do not want to die: Cutting is not about death as much as it is about rage and pain.

Other adolescents want to die.

Warning traits of adolescent suicide

Talks about committing suicide

Abrupt changes in personality

Gives away prized possessions

Previous attempt at suicide

Harms self in less obvious ways

Increases use of alcohol and/or drugs

Inability to tolerate frustration

Sexual promiscuity

---

[6] Himber (1994); Suyemoto (1995).

Withdrawal and rebelliousness
Inability or unwillingness to communicate
Truancy; runs away from home
Family disruptions
Neglects academic work and has difficulty concentrating
Hostile behavior (e.g., unruly at school and fights with friends)
Theft and/or vandalism
Depression
Neglect of personal appearance
Unusually long grief reaction to loss, sadness, or discouragement
Inactivity and boredom; extended apathy
Carelessness and/or accidents
Occasional evidence of bizarre thinking; e.g., delusions
Eating disturbances and weight change
Sleep disturbances; e.g., nightmares or insomnia

Childhood of a Potential Suicide

Juan's personality began to change in his junior year of high school. His grades dropped and he began drinking and smoking pot regularly. When he borrowed the family car, he ran into a pole and suffered a concussion. His parents tried to talk with him but he refused and withdrew further. His parents drove him to the emergency room after they were told that he had given away his prized compact disc collection.

Problems in Adult Development

The following styles can range from mild to severe, depending on the number of traits and the severity.

Disordered Styles

Anxious/Nervous Style

Anxiety is very common in normal proportions and as a disorder.

Internal

Constant worry that life cannot be controlled
Worries may shift from one thing to another; e.g., from child's welfare
    to own incompetence
Feels restless, tense, or irritable

Feels like danger is always around the corner

May have sleep problems

Interpersonal

Likely to come from a fearful family: Anxious parents create anxious children

Easily reactive and sensitive to others' approval or disapproval

Worry affects other areas of life; e.g., relationships, work, or play

Childhood of an Anxious

Janet was a clinging child, afraid to venture away from her parents or older sisters. She was well behaved and obedient, but in second and third grade she vomited each day before going to school. She was afraid to take the normal risks of childhood.

Adulthood of an Anxious

Janet made friends, married her high school sweetheart, and lived in the same town in which she grew up. She settled for low pay and low independence because she believed that challenging work would be unattainable. Janet was also hired for those jobs because she appeared nervous and employers figured she would be compliant. After her children were born, she gradually cut down on her activities, and her husband came home early to drive the kids to their appointments. Janet liked to stay in; she talked to friends on the phone and she ordered groceries by phone.

Within the Anxious style, three distinct subtypes exist.

1. Agoraphobia—Marked by fear of places or situations where one could be trapped and help would not be available

    Avoids situations that might bring on fear

    Behavior is increasingly limited as more places/situations are threatening

    Increased reliance on others

    Fears to do activities alone

    No escape; e.g., crowds or travel in vehicles

    Changes behaviors to avoid fears

2. Panic—Marked by expectations and occurrences of panic attacks (sudden onset and short duration) that make a person feel like she or he is dying and wants to flee

Pounding heart; sweating

Shortness of breath; fear of dying

Fear of losing control; e.g., incontinence, fainting, or going
insane

Dizzy

Can happen when life is disrupted by moves or losses

Becomes ashamed and embarrassed about fear

Often changes behavior to avoid fear

3. Phobic

All types elicit

Sweating

Desire to escape

Irrational response

Excessive response

Clear and limited fear

Immediate and persistent fear

Fear that begins before awareness; feeling more
uncontrollable

Specific phobias, fears of special things such as snakes, speaking in public, or heights, are common in children but are usually outgrown. Common phobias are heights, flying, close spaces, being alone, storms, animals, blood, and water. People with phobias rarely have just one during their lifetime. Fear of heights is the number one phobia of men and fear of animals is number two. With women, the reverse is true.[7]

When the specific fears persist into adulthood, they fall into four types.

Type	Age at Onset	Trait
Animal—spider, snake	age seven	high excitement
Natural environment type (heights)	childhood	
Blood—injection—injury type (dentists)	age nine	low excitement (fainting)
Situational (claustrophobia, tunnels, flying)	twenties[8]	anxiety (fear of going crazy)

[7] Curtis et al. (1998).
[8] Merckelbach et al. (1996).

Black-and-White Style

Black-and-White style is marked by instability in life. Adolescents often appear to have these traits, but a major distinction between youth and adulthood is that in adolescence much of the instability is due to hormonal changes and identity development, which is temporary. In adults these traits are not temporary and are very difficult to change.

Internal

Swings between fears of abandonment and engulfment

Shifting image of self and others

Impulsive, can be seen in acts of harm to self by cutting, self-mutilating acts, reckless driving, sex, or substance abuse

Self-destructive acts usually caused by threats of abandonment or others leaving

Moods are intense but shift easily; e.g., despair can pass into calm within hours

Holds grudges about perceived hurts

Ruins their chances when success is near; e.g., destroying a relationship that is healthy

May attempt suicide in the swings of feeling, especially to ward off loss or abandonment

Poor at tolerating stress

Interpersonal

Wants to be one with someone else to avoid feeling alone and empty

Relationships are unstable and, at the extreme, are chronically dysfunctional

Even their constant crises get repetitive, and so they become boring to others

Swings from love to hate of others over small events

Vacillates about plans, career, and decisions

Switches sexual choices easily, including sexual relationships with both men and women

Thinks others are wonderful and admires them, and then sees them as worthless

Histories are often replete with parental loss, neglect, abuse, or serious conflict

Adulthood of a Black-and-White

After high school, when Susan got her first job, she began a series of intense, unsatisfying relationships. She yearned for closeness from friends and lovers but, at the first misstep, was so wounded by their behavior that she became hurt and enraged and pulled away. They had gone, in Susan's eyes, from wonderful to trash. Susan even tried a few homosexual relationships, more looking for closeness than because of sexual desire.

Depressed Style

Moods refers to a frame of mind, including emotions, and can be fleeting, such as anger when a driver grabs your parking space. But when mood is pervasive and defines a way of life (for example, a person suffering with depression), we can think of mood as defining a personality style such as Depression.

Most people feel sad from time to time. Where does depression begin and normal dejection end? How do we know when we have depression rather than appropriate grief in response to some loss?

Grief traits only:

Feelings are justified by a genuine loss, such as unemployment, the
death of a loved one, illness, disaster, or rejection
Feelings are temporary
Feelings are induced by events
Feelings, although intense, move through a process and joy returns
Symptoms such as poor sleeping, over- or undereating, or crying abate

Traits that commonly exist in Depression, Grief, and ordinary Sadness:

Internal

Pessimistic; sees a dark future
Poor morale; dissatisfied
Apathetic; lack of energy for coping
Irritable

Lack of joy
Distracted by fears, worries, and/or self-analysis
Overestimates difficulties, feels insufficient, and underestimates self
Excessively sensitive and easily wounded
Exhausted
Feels helpless, trapped, or blocked
Sees death as a way out; wants to die
Speech may be somber, slow, or flat; tone may be discouraged

Interpersonal

Aloneness may lead to drug or alcohol addictions
In the throes of a new love or interest, he is overly optimistic
Despairs and longs for relief and love
Seems resentful about having to be a responsible adult
Weakened sexually; e.g., wants contact and snuggling but no passion
Seems normal for periods but inevitably crashes
Difficulty sustaining an adult adjustment to people and work
Passively withdraws from others or makes excessive demands on others
Wants nurturance from others; wants to be assured of their devotion
Openly discuss their worthlessness and demonstrate helplessness;
    evoke guilt in others
Anger and resentment exist but are displayed subtly to avoid rejection
Persistent in demands, needs, bitterness, and worthless protests
Preoccupied with self
Obsessively worries about troubles
Life is a well of hopelessness
Image of self is worthless
Suicide becomes an increasing possibility as an escape from pain or
    humiliation

Physical appearance associated with Depression is

Shoulders pulled forward and rounded
Chest seems shrunken and collapsed
Shallow breathing
Chronic tension in body
Head forward; tense muscles around the neck and jaw
Eyes look needy
Looks physically weak

Depressed people particularly fear abandonment and therefore may rush into relationships even while they silently rage at all the past abandonments.

Physical symptoms of Depression are
Sleep difficulties and early morning wakening
Fatigue; prone to illnesses
Lowered drives for food, sex, and pleasure
Physical complaints, bodily aches and pains, or headaches

Suicide
Ninth leading cause of death in the United States
20—65 percent of people who commit suicide have made at least one previous attempt
80 percent of individuals who succeed gave definite warning of their intention
Suicides are most predicted by
> presence of a specific plan
> access to a specific weapon
> preparation; e.g., a will or giving personal items away
> history of suicide in close relatives
> feelings of hopelessness
> disorders of depression, alcoholism, or schizophrenia

Not all people are certain, common to have mixed feelings and still go ahead

Traits of People Who Commit Suicide
Common to have fantasies about suicide
More men than women complete suicide because they use more lethal weapons; e.g., guns
More women than men attempt suicide; e.g., pills
Older people commit suicide more often than younger people
Older white males have the highest success rate
Married people have the lowest rate
Young people fifteen to nineteen years old are the fastest growing group of suicides
Adolescents may be copycat from friend or exposure to media

People do not believe their suicidal thoughts are irrational, so they do not look for help

May be an impulsive act; e.g., an adolescent reaction to spurned love or severe rebuke

May be calculated; e.g., an elderly man who saves his medicine to get a lethal dose

May be a desire to get revenge; e.g., a man whose wife leaves him for his brother

May be a desire to get attention; e.g., a wife whose husband and children have lost interest

May be a desire to get sympathy; e.g., a person who is suffering without recognition

Cannot reconcile past image of self with present situation; e.g., a failed marriage or business

Suffering from psychosis or suffering from severe depression or manic depressive illness

Represents an escape from responsibilities of (continued) life

Hopelessness[9]

From the Files

Years ago, I treated a high school computer whiz. She seemed to have it all—brains, beauty, and a cute boyfriend, but she came to see me after her father accidentally found her drunk, trying her best to suffocate herself in a plastic garbage bag. She almost succeeded. She wanted to escape a pressured life that she had not chosen but was trapped into living. This delightful young woman was so filled with self-hatred that she saw nothing wrong in wanting to destroy the object of her hate—herself.

Grief

Grief is the normal range of emotions that accompanies loss; for example, shock, numbness, sadness, temporary depression, helplessness, confusion, inability to concentrate, anger, and even the fear of going

---

[9] Clinard (1963).

insane from the intense emotions. Grief becomes a disorder under two conditions—chronic grief and absent grief.

Chronic grief is a disorder where the survivor never lets go, never moves forward in the emotions or in life. The loss is always as fresh as it was in the beginning, and the adaptation is to freeze life at that day. Miss Havisham in *Great Expectations* may be the classic character of chronic grief. More subtle instances can be seen when rooms are left forever untouched or deceased people remain forever spoken of in the present tense. One client continued to write and mail letters to her son who had died in Paris: She pretended that he had extended his stay. Chronic grief may result in suicide for the survivor, who sees death as the only path to reunion.

Absent grief is also a disorder where the survivor never lets go but, on the surface, the disorder looks very different from chronic grief because no emotion is displayed. No outward signs of normal grief reactions can be seen. This does not refer to the earliest days of grief when the survivor may be in shock or may need to put personal feelings aside to help others (natural disasters) or get tasks done (funeral). Absent grief does not refer to privacy issues and personal beliefs about decorum. Absent grief goes beyond the stiff upper lip and means that the emotional nature of the loss is not acknowledged; for example, the father whose twenty-year-old daughter was killed and he forbade her name to be mentioned, took her violin and locked it away, and expressed no feelings to anyone either in public or private.[10]

Hypochondriac Style

The Hypochondriac is so consumed with physical complaints that other aspects of personality disappear in this disturbance.

Internal

Pessimistic, dull, and complaining

Selfish, self-centered, preoccupied

Ineffectual

Complains about aches and pains that cannot be explained by a medical condition.

Misinterprets bodily symptoms; e.g., fainting is imagined to be cancer

---

[10] Edelstein (1984).

Vague complaints; weakness and low energy

Usually not factual or good reporters of symptoms

Little information comes back from lab tests

Holds on stubbornly to illness; when challenged, says "But there are always diseases that doctors don't know about"

Uninterested in psychological explanations; little insight

Gathers information to support existing ideas

Interpersonal

Uses several doctors at the same time, confusing the issues

History of complaints that persist for years

Vehemently argues in favor of illness

Controls people and environment with complaints

Different symptoms across cultures

Childhood of a Hypochondriac

Ethel had a very difficult childhood: immigration to the United States with her family, the death of her father, and abandonment by her mother. She remembers many years of never having enough food, clothes, or care.

Adulthood of a Hypochondriac

Ethel married a very gentle man and only had one son because she wasn't strong enough for more children. Her physical problems worsened when her husband had to go into the army. The problems never stopped. Her pains begin in her toes and go up to her scalp. Going out to eat is even a problem, but friends try to be patient with her food restrictions and seating requirements. Her complaints have never been restricted to one part of her body. Her history of pain includes different body sites, sexual problems, and gastrointestinal disorders, all experienced at one time or another with no medical condition found.

Conversion disorder is an unusual form of hypochondriasis in which the symptoms are dramatic (e.g., blindness or paralysis) and still no medical condition can be found. The name "conversion" came from the old belief that an individual "converted" unresolved psychological problems into physical problems, so the body, rather than the mind, suffered. The person is not faking and suffers greatly.

> ### From the Files
>
> A talented attorney suddenly began having fainting spells. Comprehensive and repeated medical exams found nothing, but she insisted that it was purely physical and discounted the fact that these spells began after she watched her daughter run from her arms into the street and get severely injured by a passing car.
>
> A forty-year-old bond trader who hated his work and was failing financially experienced a heart attack on the job. Later it was found that he had no physical problems, although the symptoms had mimicked a coronary exactly.

Narcissistic Style

The hallmark of narcissism is that these individuals are less than meets the eye.

Internal
Grandiose
Shows off
Low self-esteem
Lacks empathy for others
Needs admiration

Interpersonal
Accuses others of what is inside one's self but uncomfortable to experience; e.g., "You are envious of me" when the envy is really inside

Under pressure resorts to extreme views of others, self, or life; e.g., partner is seen as *all bad* and self as *all good*

Extreme views can shift back and forth; it is difficult to integrate a mixed view

The Narcissist gravitates to careers where attention and admiration are available. Politics is a good choice because it allows competition and manipulation. Religious careers are good because there is a built-in audience.

Childhood of a Narcissist

The parents have used the twins to fulfill their ambitions. Johnny is given piano lessons from age four because his father was too poor to continue lessons as a child. Johnny's mother sits in the room when he practices, brags to her friends about his skill, and threatens him, "It will break your father's heart if you quit." She also ignores his genuine interests and skills: "What is that stupid ball game you play?" His father forgets to pick him up from soccer practice. His twin Jenny is entered in beauty pageants, her hair is lightened, and she is taught makeup and flirting. The family spends a great deal of money on modeling, clothes, and lessons, but there is no time for sleepover parties and homework. "A good-looking girl like you doesn't need an education," her father says. Her mother whispers, "You will marry a very rich man and take care of your old mom and dad, right?" Jenny's talent for math is overlooked, and she never learns how to relate to other girls: She learns only how to compete with girls and flirt with boys and men.

Adulthood of a Narcissist

Because they have been treated like objects, they treat themselves and others like objects. "I can play any piece on the piano," John boasts. He treats lesser players with contempt *unless* they are willing to adore him. Jenny, too, is happy when she is adored, when that rich husband tells her that she is the most beautiful woman in the room. If her husband fails, if he needs her, if he is distracted or ill, she is alone and frightened. She may need an admirer or a lover to bolster her self-esteem. Over the years, both need more and more to feed their frail sense of self.

Friends say, "I never feel like I'm saying the right thing around Jenny" or "I always feel inadequate around John." Friends find them lively to be around, shining stars, but over time others see the selfishness, the self-absorption, and the intense need to be at the center of activity.

Obsessive Style

Life for the Obsessive is a series of preoccupations with order, schedules, cleanliness, and perfectionism.

Internal

Long-term anxiety

From the Files

A muscular twenty-seven-year-old dental student, dressed in skimpy shorts and a tank top, came into my downtown office and confessed that he wanted to die. He was so serious about suicide he had to be hospitalized for protection. Why? He had injured a small muscle in his chest. He could still work out. He could continue to build his body. He did not miss any schoolwork and could continue to become a dentist. *But* he could not have the perfect chest that he *had* to have. The injury was psychological more than physical.

Intellectualized ways of thinking and relating protect against anxiety
Needs to be in control to feel safe
Insecure; difficult to relax; reserved
Sentimental
Realistic, logical, and level-headed
Skeptical; critical of self; harsh voices guide actions
Looks for rules to guide decisions because of uncertainty; plagued
   by self-doubt
Inflexible and rigid; tense; high-strung
Overly attentive to rules, details, and lists
Precise; stubborn
Collects things and is reluctant to throw objects out
Self-image is industrious and hardworking

Interpersonal

Overly strict about ethics and morality
Misses the big picture; focuses on the details
Feels that love has heavy obligations
Not good with pleasure; turns fun and leisure into work
Tends to be logical and intellectual; hides aggressive feelings
Fears loss of control or going crazy, but that rarely happens
Looks for sanctioned ways of being judgmental and controlling;
   critical of others
Poor time management, so others are delayed and inconvenienced
Often values work and productivity to the exclusion of everything else

Wants others to do tasks his way; gives detailed instructions to
others

Expects subordinates to be deferential; wants to please superiors

Believes that there is only one way to do things

May be stingy with money, compliments, and ideas; hard to acknowledge others' viewpoints

Contemptuous of frivolous people

Gets angry when control is taken away

Expresses affection in a controlled manner

Appears stilted or dull; speaks in a formal manner; dresses with
restrained style

Does poorly in novel situations

Extreme ➜ Very Extreme

Excessive fear of harm to self, others or property leads to ➜ compulsions (ritual behaviors) such as of washing, checking, hoarding,
excessive arranging, or cataloging

Striving for perfection or symmetry leads to ➜ compulsions such
as having shoes tied perfectly or walking through the center of
a doorway

Perfectionism leads to ➜ eating disorders

Lack of emotional expressiveness leads to ➜ addictions or
hypochondriasis

In order to avoid feeling anything too long, can become ➜ impulsive
on rare occasions

The Obsessive gravitates toward careers where systematic or technical skills are rewarded, "driven" qualities are appreciated, and emotional response is limited. They are very successful in careers if their
traits remain mild. They are excellent at rational, detailed, disciplined
work (e.g., accounting, technology, research) and superb at rules to be
enforced (e.g., judge, dean, or soldier).

Childhood of the Obsessive

Timmy's parents were very exacting, each in their own way. Mother
liked the house to be very tidy, and Father had a multitude of moralistic
rules that had to be followed. Expressions of spontaneity were quickly
discouraged. Timmy thought that his parents loved him but understood

that their own comfort came first. It wasn't a fun household. Timmy's sister had an easier time because she was naturally passive, but Timmy was active and aggressive, so he felt awful about himself rather frequently. Timmy found it difficult to get angry and rebel against his parents, so his aggression and passion were muted and he became like his parents.

Adulthood of the Obsessive

As an adult, Tim is a hard worker, is controlled, and is a decent family man. He is considered stubborn rather than aggressive, but inside he worries all the time and feels physically ill frequently. At work people think he is fair but not creative. He pays a lot of attention to the details of each project and is effective, although he never feels finished. Tim doesn't want to do anything wrong, but his wife chides him that lovemaking is routine, he pinches pennies, worries unnecessarily, and their life together has grown increasingly boring. She says that he keeps her at arm's length. She often asks him if he is angry, and he usually says (and believes) he is not, but he *seems* angry to her and to his children. Because he holds in the anger, he also holds in the love. When relations are poor between them, she feels that he controls her and cannot see her point of view. He suffers over these accusations but intellectualizes them away and can do little to change.

> Obsessiveness may be partly inherited.[11]

When Obsessiveness gets extreme, the obsessions often focus on body, food, safety, or cleanliness.

Bowel Obsession

Fear of losing bowel control in public

Irrational concern

Anxiety

Other obsessions usually co-exist

Family history of fears

Often begins with an accident of losing bowel control

---

[11] Clifford, Murray, and Fulker (1984).

Distress at being away from a bathroom

Afraid to travel and afraid to be on public transportation[12]

When Obsessiveness gets extreme, we often see strange compulsions as an integral aspect of the style.

Compulsions

Compulsions simplify the environment to make the world more
   manageable

Repeated thoughts about contamination

Need to have things in a particular order

Repetition of aggressive thoughts

Repetition of sexual imagery

Common rituals are

> cleaning; e.g., hand washing, housecleaning
>
> ordering; e.g., straightening objects
>
> checking; e.g., the stove, the garage door, keys
>
> demanding reassurance; e.g., asking questions repeatedly

Mental acts of repetition; e.g., prayer, counting, repeating words

Magical acts of protective behavior, e.g., saying particular numbers,
   wearing certain clothes, touching a talisman

Avoids particular objects

Differences between normal and abnormal rituals are not about the ritual itself, but about the severity of performance and the extent to which the compulsions cause distress and interfere with functioning.

Severe Disorders of Adulthood

The styles that follow are some of the most extreme in psychology. Although the styles in chapter three offer traits that can create a severe or pathological character, the range is broad. These styles do not have a normal counterpart. These are disturbances, even though some people can lead normal lives by using medications and learning how to cope with the problems and suffering.

Severe Abnormality is Diagnosed By

Degree of disturbance

---

[12] Muris, Merckelbach, and Claven (1997).

Duration of disturbance
Severity of feelings and symptoms
Loss of awareness of reality
Behavior is very different from norms of society

Manic Depressive Style (Bipolar Disorder)

Manic depression, or bipolar disorder, is a disability that can exist in any personality style. At least two million (1—2 percent) Americans suffer from bipolar disorder which, when out of control, takes over a person's life. Medications (usually lithium carbonate) are almost always needed to stabilize the mood swings; when the medications are effective, a person leads a very normal life and the problems are invisible. It may take years to correctly diagnose this illness. Men usually start with a manic episode and women start with a depressive episode, and years can pass between episodes. Of all the mental or emotional disorders, bipolar disorder has the greatest genetic component, meaning that in the families of individuals who suffer from manic depression, there is a likelihood that some relative also has manic depression or depression without highs. Stressful life events often precipitate the first and second episodes, but after that little correlation exists between events and episodes. Both the manic and depressive cycles can last for days, months, or even years.

Depression may exist and cycle with manic highs
Depression can range from mild "blues" and increased need for
    sleep to hallucinations, delusions, or suicide
Depression may never exist and highs cycle irregularly
Mania is a "high" with euphoria, little sleep, vast amounts of energy,
    wild thoughts, and reckless behaviors
Highs recur; can go from mild to ➜ extreme mania

Delusional Style

No particular oddities, except for delusions that can be bizarre (not likely in this world) or reasonable (can happen). Either way, the event is not true.

Five Types of Delusion

Danger Delusion   Believes that one is in danger; e.g., being followed,
                   poisoned, or abducted by aliens

Love Delusion   Believes that same person is in love with him or her

Years ago, a lovely sixty-four-year-old woman came in and described her sixty-seven-year-old husband as out of control. He talked so fast that she could not understand him; he had wild ideas about where they should move and what they should do; he was interested in sex in ways that she had not seen in years; and he seemed to go without sleep. After questioning her, it appeared that he had a similar episode fifteen years before. Suspecting bipolar disorder, I encouraged her to bring him in to a psychiatrist to be evaluated for medication. Before she could act, the news worsened. He crashed into a depression. The depression was compounded by shame when he confessed that he had spent more than $80,000 of their retirement money on clothes and jewelry for a prostitute.

Jealous Delusion	Believes that one's partner is unfaithful
Body Delusion	Believes that one has a disease or a defect
Grand Delusion	Believes that one is a famous person or has inflated worth or power

Multiple Personality Style

This is a complex, chronic, uncommon, dissociative disorder.
   Disturbance of identity
   Disturbance of memory
   Post-traumatic condition
   Dissociative states develop as protection against negative stimuli
   Continues in abusive or neglectful relationships
   Difficulty with stable relationships

   Classic multiple personality has distinct personalities or fragments of personality.
   Each personality takes full control in his or her state
   Primary personality may not be aware of others
   Primary personality may be terrified at emergence of others
   Amnesia—inability to recall important personal information (not ordinary forgetfulness)
   One in five cases resist detection

50 percent can have symptoms be quiet for a year or more; small
  percentage brag about disorder
Hard to figure out and may take months to recognize; feels confused
World seems unsympathetic, overwhelming, and frightening
Other personalities emerge spontaneously during crisis
Individuals have been told "You seem like a different person"
Chaotic family history
Medical history of headaches, unexplained pain, and complaints of
  a sexual nature
May have suicide attempts, self-mutilation, hallucinations, or symp-
  toms of post-traumatic stress disorder
Behaviors that identify other personalities include:

> spontaneous amnesia
> use of word "we"
> conflict can occur among "alters" or nonmajor personalities
> spontaneous voice or accent changes
> involuntary movements
> changes in handedness
> changes in facial muscles
> catatonia
> handwriting changes
> mood shifts
> pseudohallucinations, where voices argue among them-
> selves or make comments

Extensive psychiatric history with treatment failures
Other people can have strange reactions to these individuals; for
  example, losing track of time, forgetting, or other mild dissociative
  phenomena

Suspicious Style
Internal
Evasive
Stubborn and dogmatic
Dwells on own frustrations
Anxious
Preoccupied by doubts
Sees self as different from others
Guarded; always alert, so may appear quiet or cold

Self-righteous
Cannot tolerate criticism; very sensitive to others

Interpersonal

Suspicious with no basis in fact; suspiciousness impairs relations
   with others
Argumentative
Feels persecuted; always distrustful, so needs to be self-sufficient
Looking for the "truth"; sees nothing as benign, sees malevolence
   in all actions
Suspect plots; scrutinizes actions of others
Assumes that others will cause intentional harm; feels harmed and
   retaliates angrily
Suspicious of interference of others
Blames others; distrusts motives of others; hard to believe in loyalty
   of others
Does not confide in others because of fear that others will share
   information
Interprets honest mistakes as intentional harm
Misinterprets jokes and distrusts compliments
Holds grudges; is unforgiving
Can be pathologically jealous
Collects "evidence" to support beliefs
Very controlling in relationships; poor at collaboration
May be outgoing and argumentative because of suspiciousness
Often involved in legal disputes
Very aware of power and rank
Likes simplistic formulations

Normal → Extreme

Stress → can become temporarily psychotic; may have delusions

Suspicious people may be successful in large organizations where
intrigues are always in motion, or in careers like law where adversarial
relationships are part of the fabric of the work. They can also succeed
as cost estimators or investigators, where the ability to quarrel is an
asset.

   The Suspicious style is not to be confused with the cautious behavior of immigrants, refugees, or minorities who must navigate an unfamiliar and/or unfriendly society.

The Suspicious style may be apparent in childhood or adolescence as odd or solitary behavior with few close relationships; this kind of young person attracts teasing.

Psychopathic Style

This style is described again in chapter five because it is frequently the basis for criminal activity.

Internal

Easily bored

No conscience; amoral; deceitful; lies

Motivated by money

Aggressive and reckless

No guilt about poor treatment of others

No strong feelings

Impulsive and irresponsible

Ignores conventions

Feels no sense of belonging to family or community

Nonconformist

Rationalizes own behavior

Interpersonal

Others cannot appeal to a sense of right or wrong

Can be violent if thwarted

Criminals are usually nonviolent because of lack of investment

Fails to conform to social norms or laws

History of irresponsible performance in school, jobs, and financial obligations

Socially maladjusted

Alienated from others

Dislikes and resents authority

Usually delinquent when young

Usually involved with the law

Easily charming with others

Makes a good initial impression; others are dismayed when traits are revealed[13]

Behavior → Extreme

Disregards the rights of others, can become A4 violates rights of others

---

From the Files

A stunning, feminine woman came to my office for treatment because she had been caught stealing money from her firm. Zell had no regrets and had trouble understanding why her mother was so upset. Zell charmingly explained that the money was available, she wanted it, and she took it. The cash supplemented her income. Without a word to anyone, Zell drove off in a large Mercedes a few months later with her only girlfriend's husband.

Schizophrenic Style

Of all the adult styles, schizophrenic is the most abnormal. Contrary to popular belief, individuals who suffer from schizophrenia are rarely violent or homicidal. They may appear very bizarre, even frightening, but are usually harmless to others. The first schizophrenic "break" usually occurs when an individual is in his or her late teens to early thirties.

Delusions (false beliefs, often persecutory, firmly held in spite of contrary evidence)

Bizarre delusions are also common; e.g., alien thoughts are inserted in the mind

Disorganized speech is a key trait; e.g., rambling, makes no sense, wanders from topic to topic, incoherent, and/or provides answers that do not respond to questions

Bizarre thinking is seen in weird speech, unusual associations, and/or illogical connections

Disturbed moods; e.g., may go from very stubborn to peaceable

Peculiar disorganized behaviors; e.g., disheveled, inappropriate sexual behavior, agitation, talking to self, and/or rarely initiates goal-directed behavior

---

[13] Abrahamsen (1983).

Strange gestures, jumps around, or performs sexual acts in public

Confused; responds to internal stimuli, not to clues in the outside world

Hallucinates, meaning that any sense can be affected; the most common is auditory

Auditory hallucinations include hearing voices that comment, threaten, or instruct

Apprehensive and plagued by self-doubt

Socially alienated and feels misunderstood

Anxious and avoids new situations

Hard to concentrate

Can be out of control and impulsive

Withdrawn, secretive, and inaccessible

Experience themselves as strange

Usually flat in speech, expressionless, with little body language

Inappropriate affect; e.g., laughs or cries without reason or shows no emotion

Feels estranged from self; feels not real

Types of Schizophrenia
Paranoid

Does not seem as strange as other types of schizophrenic, can seem normal at first

Preoccupied with delusions and/or hallucinations about persecution or grandiosity; e.g., "the FBI has planted bugs in the showerhead" or "I am Napoleon"

Catatonic

Immobile or mute

Excessive motor movements lead to bizarre postures or movements

Traits of individuals who have later become schizophrenic

This disorder is rarely seen in children, and there are few definitive hallmarks in childhood that can predict a later schizophrenic problem. Several possibilities are

Difficult, inhibited, withdrawn, and unresponsive (as infants)

Flat, irritable, and easily distracted (as children)

Low reactivity; poor motor functions such as coordination and balance (as children and adolescents)

Low joy at all ages; shy and introverted (girls)

Disruptive; displays inappropriate behavior (boys)

Flat—little facial expression, poor eye contact, nonresponsive, and lack of voice inflection (as adolescent)

Low social competence (as adolescent)

Signs of relapse in individuals who suffer from schizophrenia but are in remission

Anxiety and irritability

Depression and withdrawal

Strange, uninhibited behaviors

Changes in thought and speech

Beginning to sound suspicious or have delusions

Drugs Used to Control Psychotic Symptoms

Since the introduction of antipsychotic drugs in the 1950s, the lives of schizophrenic individuals have improved greatly. Symptoms are often controlled, and hospitalizations can often be minimized. Unfortunately, there are severe side effects from the drugs, especially tardive dyskinesia.

Unusual disorders related to schizophrenia

Brief Psychosis, which is characterized by delusions, hallucinations, catatonic symptoms, and strange speech (all described previously), but the symptoms last for a very short period (one day to one month) and the individual returns to full, normal functioning. Often, this disorder occurs after an overwhelmingly stressful event.

Shared Psychosis is a disorder that is shared by another individual (e.g., spouse or parent) which develops as a result of close living with a person who has schizophrenia or suffers from delusions. The new, shared disorder is similar to the delusional person's original problem.

Drug-Induced Psychosis is diagnosed when hallucinations or delusions are caused by the physiological effects of drugs such as alcohol, amphetamines, cannabis, cocaine, inhalants, and the effects of withdrawal from drugs and/or alcohol.

There are many kinds of delusions, but the popular ones are about persecution, religion, and fame. One interesting delusion is having been captured by aliens and taken to a space ship. This one holds particular interest because a good number of the people who make these claims are *not* delusional.

Contactees usually fall into one of two categories: those with mental problems and the others, who are more difficult to figure out because they are nonpsychotic, respected members of the community.

Alien abduction experiences have been reported by thousands of people. All report being taken by nonhuman entities and subjected to experiments or procedures. Many cannot be classified as psychotic.

Normal

Respected member of the community; e.g., teacher, minister
Frightened and panicked by the experience
Reports contact to police or air force seeking a reasonable explanation
Wants anonymity
No hallucinations or psychosis in the past
No history of hoaxes[14]

Abnormal

History of mental problems and aberrant behavior
Delusional
Claims of receiving signals from aliens
Leads a strange life in general
Has had other occult experiences
Seeks publicity
No fears of ridicule
Does not report experience to legitimate agency
Organizes clubs and uses group to promote sighting
Has great detail about planets, aliens, and flights
Has been given a mission by aliens[15]

---

[14] Jacobs (1975).
[15] ibid.

CHAPTER FIVE

Criminal Styles

In This Chapter

♦ Styles of People Who Commit Nondeadly, Nonsexual Criminal Acts
♦ Styles of Rapists and Others Who Commit Sexual Crimes
♦ Styles of Murderers

T his chapter examines Criminal styles and lists the traits associated with specific types of criminal activity. To enrich a character whose criminal behavior is designed from this chapter, you can refer back to chapters on childhood, adolescence, or adulthood—not simply chapter four, which describes disorders, but also the more normal Adult styles found in chapter two will help fill out the personality. It is easy to see how some Adult styles lend themselves to criminal behavior. For example, a character exemplifying the Dependent style (page 22) might make a fine accomplice because she was afraid to speak up. The Fall Guy (page 26) is ripe for becoming a victim in a confidence scheme. More seriously criminal, a character who exhibits the Narcissist style (page 93) could be caught up in his grandiosity, embezzle money from his real estate investors, and tell himself, "They owe it to me. Look at all that I have done for them." He is convinced that his behavior is not wrong because "I'll pay it back. I can always make money." When he is caught, he tells his wife, "Other people do much worse" or "I'm entitled to a bigger share of the profits," and he tells himself, "I'm a successful man who needs to maintain a certain lifestyle so others have confidence in me." He also blames others: "They interfere with my ability to do my job."

In this chapter, first we have the styles of people who commit nondeadly, nonsexual criminal acts, listed in alphabetical order. Second, we examine styles of rapists and others who commit sexual crimes. Third, we examine styles of murderers.

Information in the boxes scattered throughout the chapter may be helpful to character development in a general way.

Motives of Perpetrators From the Mildly Awful to the Genuinely Evil

A goal is envisioned; people may be in the way

Passion, resentment, dislike, and hatred are not prime factors

Convinced that the outcome merits the deed

May be setting things right from past injustices

Evil deeds are seen in a greater picture of good

Seems less wrong to the perpetrators than to the victims; e.g., "It wasn't so bad"

Perpetrators see outside influences as having great power: "It wasn't in my control"

Perpetrators don't feel fully responsible; e.g., temporary insanity: "I couldn't help it"

Perpetrators have no desire to remember: "Let bygones be bygones"

Events vanish quickly into the irrelevant past

May see one's self as under threat or attack; e.g., "I had to beat my wife, she was going to leave"

Perpetrators remember events very differently than victims; both memories are distorted[1]

Hit man Martin Blank's mantra in the movie *Grosse Point Blank* was "They did something that brought me to their door."

Criminal, Arsonist Style

(also see *Criminal, Pyromaniac Style*)

Usually a juvenile male

Poor school record; often still lives with parents

Often the fire is a group activity

May be a spontaneous act

Sets fires out of maliciousness

Wants to destroy a specific place; e.g., a church

Place is near home

If situationally motivated, he does not return to the scene of the crime

Chad and Tommy played Nintendo and commiserated about how unfairly Mr. Mettanick, their high school teacher, was treating them.

---

[1] Baumeister (1997).

Both knew that their parents were going to see awful English marks on their report cards. Later they walked over to the school, sat in the playground, and pretended to tell Mettanick off. Chad and Tommy topped each other with plans for revenge. The next week, they broke a window and set fire to the auditorium curtains.

Individuals Have Other Motives to Set Fires

Desire to gain attention
Get revenge on someone; fire is simply one method
Concealment of another crime; e.g., murder
To collect insurance
To dissolve a business
To ruin a competitor

Criminal, Career Style, Ordinary

Conventional crimes; e.g., burglary, forgery, embezzlement, and/or theft
Repeats; crime is a way of life
Commits large numbers of crimes
Goal is to gain something; e.g., money, property
Specialization in nonviolent crime; prefers no injury
Hangs out; most comfortable with others like himself or herself
Minimal planning and forethought
Begins crime at an early age
Early signs of predatory behavior
Daily life has a constant tension and high level of awareness
When imprisoned, spends time trying to gain status
Criminality in family of origin
Often drug or alcohol abuser
High unemployment
Justifies behavior; e.g., "Everyone is more or less dishonest"
Irresponsible
Self-indulgent, proud of success[2]

---

[2] Walters (1990); Korn and McCorkle (1963).

By age twenty-five, John had been picked up by the Chicago police dozens of times, had been prosecuted four times, and been in jail once. Breaking into homes and cars was the way John made his living. His territory was the North Shore. He expected to get caught occasionally. He was encouraged by his crowd and by his family, who worried about him and looked the other way when a new television or disc player came into the house.

Criminal, Career Style, Professional

These traits are compared to those of the Ordinary Criminal.

More intelligent and polished

Uses more efficient and intricate techniques

Crime has higher stakes

Considers himself skilled

May have had a regular job; not criminal by origin

Begun later in life; has some social skills

Plans carefully

Prefers crimes such as stealing from jewelry stores by substitution, confidence games, passing illegal checks or money orders, shakedown or extortion, or "grifting"[3]

Criminal, Confidence Specialist Style

Specialist

May work "short con" or "long con"; e.g., requires more or less time and money for scam

Victims of scam do not always go to the police because they may have skirted the law in the deal

Presentable, personable, and well dressed

Ability to gain confidence of others; intuitive

Patient, congenial, and a good talker

Determined; good ability to withstand anxiety

Little in common with the petty criminal

Derek and a woman begin casual conversation in a coffee shop. Weeks later, after showing much interest in her troubles, Derek reluctantly confides that he has important friends in a certain African nation

---

[3] Korn and McCorkle (1963).

who need to bring money to a U.S. bank for safekeeping. His friends fear governmental chaos and, because they are highly placed, may be in danger. They have never been to the United States and are frightened of being taken advantage of by sharp Americans. They need to locate trustworthy individuals who will sponsor them at banks. They are more than willing to pay for this service.

Criminal, Counterfeiter or Forger Style
General Traits
Almost a creative artist

Draws inspiration from others' work

Intends to deceive the buyer/receiver

May be an entirely new conception; e.g., an "early work of . . ."

Always based on someone else's technique

Good technical ability

Justification is "If I can paint a picture that people buy as a Monet,
 I must be as good as the original"

Buyers, dealers, and experts do not like to believe they can be duped

Rarely women

Often, the motivation is a battle of wits against the expert

Success bolsters self-esteem

Financial gain may be secondary to creating a sensational object

May be a one-time event or a career

Amateurs are motivated by envy, jealousy, inferiority, and desire for
 attention

May be desire to "prove" a theory

Specialties
Forger, Archaeological
Items may include skulls, weapons, pottery, or engravings

May have a real piece but tries to pass it off as being of earlier origin

A cottage industry in certain areas is selling "Indian arrowheads." The actual flint in the area is from the correct age. The techniques to make the arrowheads are the same as those used thousands of years ago. The difference is that today's teenagers are the arrow makers.

Forger, Artistic

Items include paintings, drawings, furniture, sculpture, ceramics, gems, ivories, or lace

May run a reputable business in restoration

Respected

Ages pieces; e.g., knocks a nose off a statue so it looks older

Adds worm holes or creates patina and sells a piece as older

Forger, Literary

Items include manuscripts, autographs, first editions, or "new" works

The work may have been created with innocent intent many years ago

May have political motives; e.g., forged documents to incriminate a person

Forger, Criminal

Items include coins and paper money, false and altered checks, wills, deeds, copyrights, letters, postage stamps, or false identity papers

Very popular during wartime

Hope is to get rich quick

Major goal is financial gain

May be a gambler

Money may be forged to flood market and cause political chaos

Identity may be forged to gain position, title, or money; e.g., a son who is believed drowned reappears and is accepted years later by a grieving, wishful mother[4]

Forger, Checks

Check forging is no longer the elaborate business that it once was, so the long-term artistry is not needed

Spontaneous; not carefully planned

Situations are exploited as they arise

Impulsive, rapid worker

Manipulative; may impersonate others if required

Tends to be migratory but stays within a region

Loner; avoids personal relationships and other criminals

Tense; blunders when tension gets high

---

[4] Cole (1956).

Expects to get caught somewhat regularly

Spends money fast when he has it; e.g., gambling

Suspicious and distrustful

May be well educated and come from a professional family[5]

Criminal, Delinquent Style (Female)

Delinquent is a term that usually refers to a young person who is breaking laws.

Hard; comfortable on the street

Unforgiving

Violent toward other girls; competitive with other girls

Sees prestige in sex, boys, and older men, and brags about sexual prowess

Gains a sense of power from sex

Feels betrayed by mother but hopes for reunion with her

Angry at mother, but fiercely attached to her

Usually has absent father

Mother of a Teenage Criminal

Addicted to drugs or alcohol

Offers daughter no protection

Chooses men over her daughter[6]

Liz is in a state-run home until she is eighteen. She was expelled from the public high school for cutting another girl with a broken bottle and is not getting along much better in the institution. Her drawings and stories are heartbreaking accounts of assault, abandonment, and betrayal, but dealing with her aggression and hostility day to day leaves people tired and hopeless. Liz has not had one visitor in eight months.

Criminal, Delinquent Style (Male)

Assertive and aggressive

Unafraid; impulsive

Unconventional

Extroverted; poorly socialized

Defiant, hostile, and suspicious

---

[5] Lemert (1958).

[6] Berger (1989); Calhoun, Jergens, and Chen (1993).

Sadistic

Mental problems

Destructive[7]

Criminal, Gambler

High comes from seeking novelty; excited by new things

Does not see the risk that stops other people from gambling

Aggressive

Believes that personal skill will win, and denies the nature of randomness

As children, less anxious, more delinquency, theft, and early gambling

Impulsive, fearless, and carefree[8]

Criminal, Habitual Petty Style

Very common; easily caught

Often arrested; has long criminal record

Rarely commits felonies; always sticks to petty crime

Began at an early age

Has extensive connections in the underworld and thinks of him- or herself as a criminal

Not sophisticated, lazy, and irresponsible

Is a failure in social situations

Eventually, he or she finds it impossible to get legitimate work[9]

Criminal, Kleptomaniac Style

Cannot resist impulse to take things; repetitive

Does not need the items

Is not stealing for financial gain

Not planned beforehand; mostly situational, taking place in a store

Often gives away items as gifts

Sometimes hides items or throws them away

Need to steal builds beforehand and is reduced by the theft

Not dangerous; does not lead to more severe stealing

---

[7] Wilson and Herrnstein (1985).
[8] Vitaro, Ladouceur, and Bujold (1996).
[9] Clinard (1963).

Joanne steals when she feels bad about herself. She was fired from her job for talking on the phone too much, knew her boss was right, got depressed, and began shoplifting, a crime she had not done in three years. She felt smug and powerful. For months, stealing was the only activity that made her feel good about herself. She stopped— temporarily, at least—when she got another job.

Criminal, Late-Blooming Style

No history of criminal behavior

Not young

Needs structure; strong external controls have weakened over time

Domineering mother or religion kept him or her in check

Growing older frees the existing, but suppressed, criminal attitude

Foundation was laid early but remained dormant until controls broke

Intrusive to others; likes to control others

Irresponsibility is now unchecked; self-indulgence is now loose[10]

Everyone always felt sorry for Marta and wanted to like her, but never did. She stayed home to care for her aging mother after her brothers and sisters had married and moved far away. Marta had a way of snooping into other people's business and gossiping about them in a holier-than-thou fashion. After her mother died, people rallied around her for a while. Vandalism began that fall, but the police wasted years before they were able to pinpoint fifty-six-year-old Marta as the culprit who had been defacing and destroying property.

Criminal, Looter Style

Frustration leads to aggression

Strikes out indiscriminately

Opportunistic

Usually an employed person; not the poorest individual

Often works with a partner or with a family

Stays in own neighborhood and rarely loots elsewhere

Rare during natural disasters; more common during civil problems

All races, men and women, adults and young people

Looting is public, in full view of others[11]

---

[10] Walters (1990).
[11] Quarantelli and Dynes (1970).

Ellen and Jorge were drinking beer and watching the NBA championship game when the hometown team won. Excited, drunk, and already angry from a week of hard work, they roamed the streets singing songs with made-up lyrics. They watched some guys set fire to a car and got excited. Ellen grabbed a rock and shattered a stereo store window, and without even thinking, they snatched whatever they could and ran away laughing.

Criminal, Occasional Offender

Does not make a living from crime

Crime is fortuitous, a chance opportunity

Likes the thrill

Acts when he or she needs money (check forgery is common with occasional offenders)

Does not think of himself or herself as a criminal

Unsophisticated in criminal techniques

No knowledge of "fences" or organized underground

Makes no effort to progress to crimes of greater skill[12]

Laurie worked in the business office of a tool and die company. Her father was a well-respected foreman in the plant. Laurie had been hanging out with a couple of wealthy young women, and when Christmas rolled around the girls had a wonderful time shopping. To keep up with her friends, Laurie opened the petty cash drawer and helped herself. She did not touch it again until May, when everyone wanted to go to Las Vegas for a big weekend.

Criminal, Pyromaniac (Fire Setter)

(also see *Criminal, Arsonist Style*)

Usually young adult men, often unemployed

Usually begins in childhood; repeats

Socially inadequate, particularly in heterosexual relationships

Deliberately sets fires

Setting the fire is exciting

Often sticks around to watch the fire

Feels thrilled and satisfied seeing the results

---

[12] Clinard (1963).

Not set for any particular reason, not revenge or gain

Likes everything about fires; e.g., creation and destruction

Indifferent to results

May look for work near fires; e.g., forest ranger, volunteer fireman

Two cases show how arson can be very different crimes.

The Japanese author Mishima wrote *The Temple of the Golden Pavilion*, based on a real-life incident where a monk burns a Zen temple in order to completely possess its beauty. Contrast that obsession to the story of a twenty-year-old California man who had started setting fires when he was five. He loved the flames and, as he matured, found the fires sexually arousing. He was angry when the fires were put out. When he was caught for another crime, he told the police that he "couldn't help himself." This case has a clear sexual overtone, even though the arsonist was unaware of his motivation.

Criminal, Skyjacker Style

Usually a man

Not a very accomplished person; wants to distinguish himself or
   herself

Often fired or unemployed at the time of the crime

Shy and introverted; women dominate him

May come from a family where father is violent

Father has probably died prior to the crime, freeing son's aggression

Often has religious mother

Mother has made son her confidant

Timid and sexually passive[13]

Criminal, Stalker

Stalking is an abnormal or long-term pattern of threat or harassment (unwanted pursuit) against an individual. Five percent of U.S. women are or will be victims. It is estimated that 200,000 people in the United States are stalking someone.

There are five distinct styles of stalking.

Obsessional

This is the largest category and includes most batterers.

---

[13] Hubbard (1971).

Male; knows the victim who is usually an ex-spouse, ex-lover, or
  former employee
Conducts a campaign of harassment
Wants to get the person back; cannot, so stays close with tormenting
  punishment

Love Obsessional
Stranger to the victim
Obsessed; wants to make the victim aware
Does not really love the victim, but has a deep pathological
  attachment
Not psychotic in the usual sense

John Hinckley's attachment to actress Jodie Foster and his desire to
impress her by shooting the president falls into this category.

Erotomania
Usually female, occasionally male
Delusion that the victim, usually someone famous, is in love with
  him or her
May not have other delusions
May have begun with an innocent glance from the other person
Loner or withdrawn, usually

False Victimization
Conscious or unconscious desire to be seen as the victim
Falsifies physical abuse
Blame love object for stalking and hurting them

Psychopathic
This is the most dangerous stalker and often a killer.
Male
Dangerous; may be serial killer
Predator; no love or delusion involved
Detached

One of the newer ideas about stalking behavior is that stalkers, as
children, had a history of insecure attachments. Later in life, stalking

becomes a way of repeatedly trying to get a person to remain close to them—a reunion. Instead of letting go, the stalker first seeks proximity. Later, when rejected, the stalker wants to retaliate by hurting, controlling, damaging, or destroying the object of his love.[14]

Symptoms of Victims of Stalkers
Make lifestyle changes 94%
Change work 37%
Relocate 39%
Have prior knowledge of stalker 74%
Anxiety 83%
Sleep disorder 74%
Fatigue 53%
Appetite problems 45%
Has suicidal thoughts 24%
Headaches, nausea, or indigestion % varies[15]

Criminal, Successful Style
Commits crimes within structure of society; e.g., business
Engages in unethical or illegal acts with a high payoff
Crimes have low rate of detection
Crimes have smaller penalties
Trapped by overconfidence and a sense of invulnerability[16]

Criminal, Thief (Professional)
Has nothing in common with the amateur
Has array of technical skills and manual dexterity
Migratory
Rarely uses violence, so needs verbal skills and some charm
Isolated from general society, feels like an outcast
Always suspicious of people[17]

Criminal, Violent Style
May have minimal or no provocation to act

---

14 Powers (1997).
15 *Journal Watch for Psychiatry* (1997).
16 Walters (1990).
17 Sutherland (1937).

Aggression is not inhibited
Fear of consequences is insufficient to stop crimes
Punishment did not deter him or her
Belongs to a culture of violence
Value is placed on power
May have been subject to violence as a child
May have witnessed violence or subjugation
Coached into violence by peers or mentor[18]

Criminal, White-Collar Style

(see *Narcissistic* for personality traits)
High-status occupations
Crimes are generally committed in conjunction with work; e.g., business, law, labor, labor union official, politician
Is in a position of trust
Has power and influence
Separates business and personal ethics; e.g., "Business is business"
Business morals may be low, while personal morals may be normal
May play other roles; e.g., respected citizen
Does not see himself or herself as a criminal; may be a lawbreaker
Justifies actions; rationalizes behavior
Associates with others like himself or herself, therefore less objective scrutiny
Has reciprocal relationships with similar others
Contempt for law; feels above the law
Arrogant
Often conceals criminal acts through elaborate organization
Learns potential illegalities through business knowledge; e.g., insider trading
Sees himself or herself as above other people
Importance of status, outsmarting others, and possessing symbols of power

Computer-Related White Collar Crime

New; usually ex-computer programmer, engineer, or data entry clerk
Knows techniques of erasing information

---

[18] Athens (1992).

General Traits of White-Collar Crime

Intent to commit a wrongful act

Disguise the purpose

Relies on the ignorance or carelessness of the victim

Victim voluntarily takes action to assist the offender

The violation is concealed[19]

Wants to gain by stealing money or selling information

Uses skills to steal money; moves it to an accessible location

Criminal, Wife-Batterer Styles

There are three distinct styles of Batterer: Violent Psychopath (also see Psychopath, page 127), Family Violent, and Emotionally Volatile.[20]

Batterer, Violent Psychopath

(Also see *Psychopath* in chapter five)

Violent to everyone

Violent in many situations

Belligerent

Contemptuous

More use of alcohol

Psychopathic traits

Batterer, Family Violent

Majority of spouse abusers

Less severe and less aggressive

Suppresses angry emotions

Feels remorse

Batterer, Emotionally Volatile

(Also see *Loner* [page 30] and *Black-and-White* [page 86])

Violent only within family

Socially isolated; few friends

Socially incompetent; doesn't know how to behave with others

---

[19] Geis and Stotland (1980).
[20] Holtzworth-Munroe and Stuart (1994).

Values and Attitude Traits of Violent People

Looks for catharsis, the need to express overwhelming feelings at anyone available

Craves excitement; i.e., planning, implementing, and getting away feels thrilling

Desires escape or needs to flee from pressured situations

Wants justice or retribution from perceived wrongs

Has religious/political beliefs; e.g., terrorist activity is justified

Selfish, personally entitled, wants material gain, and has disregard for others

Poor self-esteem; e.g., any threat of inferiority, blame, or humiliation evokes violent response

Self-indulgent; e.g., abusive to make other people cater to assailant's needs

Avenue of self-expression; e.g., anger that the wished for outcome was denied

History of severe abuse teaches violence as punishment

Has always believed that he or she is a bad, defective person

Wants social acceptance, and violent behavior satisfies a group or gang[21]

Depressed

Feels inadequate

Emotionally volatile

Sexual Criminals

Exhibitionist

Sexually aroused by urges and fantasies of exposing genitals to women

Usually male and feels manly while exhibiting himself

Sometimes masturbates while exhibiting himself

Not usually physically dangerous

May hope to arouse observer or may believe the observer will be aroused

Likes being noticed, even if it is negative attention

---

[21] Flannery (1997).

Extreme ➜ Repeatedly acts on urges and exposes genitals to stranger

The statistics on exhibitionism are skewed by society's norms—women who expose themselves in public are rarely arrested as exhibitionists, and women showing themselves is considered more acceptable.

Sexual abuse is considered to be any behavior that is inappropriate. Children, adolescents, or adults can be sexually coerced or abused. The abuse may be violent, such as rape, or it may be manipulative, such as an older brother toward a younger sibling. Victims don't always know whether or not they have cooperated, especially if the abuse is at the hands of someone they care deeply about (e.g., a parent or sibling). Victims are even more confused about how they should have responded (e.g., scream, tell someone, tell someone later, or refuse). Children often do not have words to explain the interactions until they are older, especially if the abuse was limited to nonviolent fondling combined with displays of affection. Sexual abuse can also occur within a marriage: It is not confined to underage children. The age of the individual, his or her relationship with the abuser, the circumstances of the abuse, and the length of time that the abuse has gone on are all variables in the reaction of the abused.

Perpetrator of Sexual Abuse
Usually male
Uses coercion, trickery, or force
Offers privileges, attention, and/or rewards
Threatens retaliation and reprisal
Urges secrecy
When the abuse is between an adult and child, 80 percent know the child, and 50 percent have the child in their care at the time
Cautious in public
Has poor boundaries; i.e., unknowing of appropriate personal limits

Two Types of Perpetrators
Tyrannical Type
"King of the mountain"; his behavior expresses his lack of respect for others

Inhibited Type

"Mr. Mom"; his behavior replaces an affair; he denies inadequacy
or rage

Excuses

Denial: "It was an expression of love"
Justification or distortion: "It's not really sex"
Blame the victim: "The child didn't stop me"
Blame others: "Her mother shouldn't have left her"

An incestuous relationship began with a mother and her only child,
a boy, when he was seven. He had nightmares and crawled into bed
with her. First she fondled him, but they had intercourse from the time
he was twelve until he turned sixteen and became interested in a girl
at school. He refused his mother; they had a violent argument and the
boy killed her.

Nymphophile

Sexual desire for female children, usually prepubescent
Aroused by lack of pubic hair and other signs of immaturity
Heterosexual; may also desire women and may marry
Justifies behavior: "I was teaching her about love" or "Better than
with an awkward boy"
Usually knows the girls
Shows interest and gains her trust
Fondling may be more frequent than intercourse
Feels guilt
Convinces himself that the desire is mutual
Convinces himself that child is able to give consent
Insists that he feels affection
Avoids violence; takes pains not to frighten the child
Knows how to behave appropriately in public[22]

Pedophile

Sexually aroused by urges and fantasies to have sex with a preteen
child

---

[22] Masters (1966).

> ### *Adult Traits Associated With Childhood Sexual Abuse*
> Damages or destroys healthy, normal attitudes toward sexuality
> Damages comfort with one's own body
> Difficulty in sexual situations
> > disease
> > impotence
> > premature ejaculation
> > sexual pain
> Depression
> Phobic disorders; anxiety
> Memories often do not return until adulthood
> Prone to violence (one-third)

Repeatedly acts on urges and has sex with a preteen child
Often attracted to a particular age of child (may be as specific as
    age eight to ten)
May have been abused in childhood
Pays a great deal of attention to the child
Show generosity and affection to the child
May court a woman who has an appealing child
May, in extreme situations, abduct a child or swap children
May threaten the child to ensure silence
Child can be a boy, a girl, or both, depending on the perpetrator
May limit himself to exposing genitals or masturbating in front of
    the child without touching the child
May engage in more complete acts of sex
Excuses himself by saying that the child was to blame: "It was no
    big deal" or "No harm done"

Pedophilia takes many forms.

Eric, forty-two, had been released from prison on bond. He had no
place to go, so his sister took him into her home. Before the first weekend ended, Eric had fondled his niece.

Pornographer
Often isolated, and their activities are reading or watching sexual

material without ever abusing a child; others may engage in sexual activity

Assaults their own child or neighbor children

In denial about seriousness of acts

Convinces himself/herself that

> the child encouraged the behavior
>
> he or she was kind to the child
>
> activities were mutual
>
> no harm was done because sex was done with patience or love

Psychopath

A psychopath is not necessarily a criminal, but the traits make it easy to become one.

Internal

Easily bored; no strong feelings

No conscience; amoral

Deceitful; lies

Motivated by money

Aggressive and reckless

No guilt for behavior or poor treatment of others

Impulsive and irresponsible

Nonconformist; ignores conventions

Doesn't feel a sense of belonging to family or community

Rationalizes own behavior

Interpersonal

Others cannot appeal to sense of right or wrong

Can be violent if thwarted

Criminals are usually nonviolent because of lack of investment

Fails to conform to social norms or laws

History of irresponsible performance in school, jobs, and financial obligations

Socially maladjusted and alienated from others

Dislikes and resents authority

Usually delinquent when young; usually involved with the law

Easily charming and makes a good initial impression

Others are dismayed when negative traits are revealed

Disregards rights of others, can become ➔ violates rights of others[23]

Rapist

Sexual criminals who have strong needs for repetition or ritual cannot change, so they follow a pattern; e.g., physical characteristics of the victim, engaging in the sexual act in certain ways, or use of words or phrases. Because the ritual is a need, he cannot easily vary his behavior.

Rape results from different, often overlapping, motivations, seen in the traits described below.[24] In addition to the following types of rapist, some men commit rape during the commission of another crime, but the rape is secondary to the criminal.

General Traits of a Rapist

These traits are found in many of the following specific styles.

Lacks self-confidence at an early age; does not want to feel helpless

Often hypermasculine or macho

May have been abused as a child; used to be a victim, now is a victimizer

Witnessed violence in his family

Began assaults in childhood and adolescence

Hostile toward women; discharge of anger is satisfying, not the sex

Believes that aggression and dominance are aspects of male sexuality

Relies on peers to support rape

Justifies behavior; e.g., "She didn't behave the way she was supposed to"

May have trouble with erection and/or ejaculation during the assault (30 percent)[25]

Rapist, Acquaintance Style

Social relationship exists, often of short duration and the assault usually occurs on a date

Usually begins with consensual interaction

Little expressed aggression

No severe injuries to the victim

Victim feels that she knows the man well enough to be alone with him

---

[23] Abrahamsen (1983).
[24] Douglas et al. (1992).
[25] Moglia and Knowles (1993).

Usually situational

Rapist usually has good social skills and no involvement in criminal activity

May use alcohol or drugs to facilitate the assault

Convinces himself that victim was consenting, even if she is unconscious[26]

Rapist, Angry Style

Act is an expression of anger and rage

May choose a victim he knows or a stranger

Impulsive; often coupled with alcohol or drugs

Sex replaces anger and the victim replaces some hated person

History of perceived slights, insults, and rejections by many people over the years

Hates women generally; may direct anger toward girls or elderly women instead of adults

Insults, humiliation, and punishment are as important as the rape itself

Can range from verbal aggression to murder

Rapist, Exploitation Style

Act is impulsive and predatory

Little sexual fantasy; mostly situational and having contact

Prowls for a woman to exploit sexually

Wants woman to submit

Rape, Group Style

Friends, or a gang with allegiance to each other, commit sexual assault

Can be planned or impulsive

Individuals are usually attempting to be part of a group and give in to peer pressure

Leader of the group is commonly the instigator

Followers go along out of fear of, or respect for, the leader[27]

---

[26] Abel and Osborn (1992).
[27] Revich and Schlesinger (1978).

Rapist, Power-Reassurance Style

Acts as expression of rape fantasy

History of sexual preoccupation

History of living out sexual perversions; e.g., strange masturbatory practices, voyeurism, exhibitionism, obscene calls, or fetishism

High sexual arousal and loss of control results in distorted perception; e.g., wants to date the victim afterward

Core of the fantasy is that victim will fall in love with him

Feels deeply inadequate as a man; e.g., believes no one in her right mind would have voluntary sex with him

Rapist, Sadist Style

Planned, not impulsive

Violence exceeds what is needed to make the victim comply with his wishes

Sexual arousal is a result of the pain or fear inflicted; e.g., whipping, bondage, burning, or cutting.

Victim is usually injured moderately to severely

Victim is usually unknown and unsuspecting

Rapist has history of behavior problems

Predatory

Enjoys taking by force, sometimes objects as well as sex

Goal is control and power, not sex

Rapist, Sexual Style

Act is an expression of sexual-sadistic fantasies

Cannot separate sex from aggressive feelings; e.g., aggression heightens sexual feelings or sexual arousal increases rage

May begin as a seduction

Fixates on body parts that have sexual significance; e.g., breasts, buttocks, anus, genitals, or mouth

In addition to rape, there are other types of sexual assaults that arise from psychological problems. Some men do not have physical contact with their victim, but the motivation is still sexual gratification. At one extreme we have the man who gets an isolated wrong number when dialing the telephone and impulsively blurts out obscenities. At the other extreme there are men who engage in long-standing, patterned compulsive behaviors, such as creating routes for peeping in windows or carrying a video camera to film people or behaviors that interest them sexually.

Some acts of sexual assault are predominantly coercive because the offender uses power or position to get the other person to comply. Force is not needed and no severe physical injuries occur; dominance or authority is enough (e.g., employer, police officer, therapist, teacher, coach, or physician).

Another form of sexual assault to be considered is domestic sexual abuse; that is, between people who have a relationship with each other (e.g., partner/partner or husband/wife). Adults may be legally married or in a common-law relationship. They may be a same-sex couple. Domestic sexual abuse often has a conflict already established (e.g., money or work problems), and often has alcohol or drugs as the precipitant. The other difference between sexual assault on a stranger vs. that on a partner is that the latter escalates from a quarrel that intensifies into hitting, biting, and throwing things before the assault.

If the victim is a stranger, the rape suggests that a compulsion is driving the attack, which may indicate that the perpetrator is a serial rapist. For profiling purposes, serial rapes that increase in the degree of physical force used can signal serial murder potential.[28]

Murderers

Murderers (Not Justifiable or Accidental)

People do not like to kill. In World War II for instance, only 15—25 percent of combat infantry were willing to fire their guns. By the time soldiers went to Korea, 50 percent of combat infantry were willing to shoot. In Vietnam, the figure was up to 90 percent. People have become more willing to kill because of desensitization, conditioning, and denial. Desensitization encourages contempt, thereby allowing men to convince themselves that the enemy is different—not human. Conditioning develops the quick behavioral reflexes of shooting. Repetitive training allows soldiers to shoot and forget that they are hitting real people. The price paid for the ability to kill can be seen in the increase in post-traumatic stress reactions (see chapter four). These processes have found their way into the general culture.[29]

---

[28] Holmes and DeBerger (1985).
[29] Grossman (1995).

Murderers are people who have committed a murder. Therefore, no one style exists that includes all individuals. Most murders are *not* career criminals. Many have never been previously arrested. The following are styles where the crime was not accidental, such as a driving accident, or justified, such as self-defense. Each style has distinct traits associated with a particular kind of murder.

Murderer, Argument Style
Blue-collar, young adult male with little education
Uses violence to solve problems
No sexual assault
May be using drugs or alcohol
Had verbal or physical dispute with victim
History of violence; e.g., fights, but not murder
Knows victim
Sloppy murder; not planned; may have involved drugs or alcohol
Victim may have insulted murderer publicly or have a history of
    assaultive behavior

A young Marine with a history of violence picked up a provocative woman; they got drunk and attempted to have sex. She taunted him about his lovemaking and teased him about his body. He strangled her in a rage.

Murderer, Domestic Style
Can be parent/child or spouse/spouse
Plans murder to look like an accident, suicide, or death by natural
    causes
Cannot control internal impulses
Usually behaves better toward the victim just before the murder
Demonstrates care and concern toward the victim

Murderer, Erotomaniac Style
Murderer has fixated on someone
Victim can be known, especially a person of higher status or a
    celebrity
Preoccupied and consumed by the victim
Almost always stalks the victim

Has probably sent gifts or letters
Does not expect any gain, money, or sex
Looking for spiritual union with the victim
Wants to own the victim
May be motivated by real or imagined rebuff
Relationship may be entirely imagined
Believes that victim has sent secret messages
Plans the murder carefully

Murderer, Extremist Style

Not a professional hit man but does belong to a group. Murder is
committed in the name of a body of ideas. The ideas can be politi-
cal (e.g., murder of Robert Kennedy), religious (e.g., Hizballah
extremists), or racist (e.g., KKK)
The victim represents opposite beliefs
Others may be killed because of association with the intended victim
Looks for public place
Stalks or watches the victim; usually ambushes the victim
Plans escape
Has a history of hating a particular group
Follows the media accounts
Often had a difficult childhood
Looks for a purpose in life— the group satisfies that search
Uses a weapon of distance; e.g., a rifle

Murderer, Female

Murderers are still mostly men. For authenticity, here are distinct traits
that women murders possess.
Age range twelve to sixty-five years, average age is thirty-one years
60 percent are, or have been, married; 40 percent are unmarried
Often unemployed
One-third have a past history of violent crimes
One-half have an arrest record
Crime is usually result of a quarrel
Weapon is usually a gun or knife, not poison
Crime occurs in the home—in the kitchen (1950s), the bedroom
(1990s), or the den (1990s)

Occasionally, in especially aggressive murders, crime is not in the
   home, but in the street, alley, or yard
Usually murders a person known to her, and crime is spontaneous
Murder usually takes place at night, between 8 P.M. and 2 A.M.
Usually women (80 percent) kill men who were lovers or friends
Kill children more often than men do, often after a history of abuse
   and neglect
Rarely kill strangers (7 percent)
Alcohol is involved
Usually not premeditated
Murder may be the end result of a fight begun by the victim; often
   precipitated by rage, jealousy, anger, or revenge[30]
Murder may be an effort to stop physical abuse before the abuser
   kills her; believes that there is no escape

Murderer, Incidental Style
Unplanned
Murder committed during panic and confusion or on impulse
May have been startled by an alarm or a scream
May be novice or experienced criminal
Victim was threat to the success of the other crime
Kills while committing another crime; the legal term is *felony murder*
Alcohol or drugs often increase perpetrator's volatile nature

Murderer, Inheritance Style
Motivated by financial profit
Has a close relationship (i.e., business or personal) with the victim
Victim is chosen because of the money involved more than bad
   feelings
May plan carefully or be spontaneous, depending on personality
May try to stage murder to look like an accident or natural death
Suffocation or poison is often the chosen method because these
   methods may escape notice
A trigger (e.g., money problems, fight), makes murderer act
Is nervous, has tight alibi
May delay notifying authorities or being available for questioning

---

[30] Mann (1996).

Murderer, Passionate Style

Responds to a crisis; e.g., cheating spouse caught in the act

Sees murder as the solution to a problem

Knows the victim well

Feels provoked

Unplanned; reactionary

Murderer, Professional Style (Hit Man or Contract Killer)

Hit men are generally married and have families who are completely unaware of their professional activities.

Kills for material gain; e.g., money or favors

Work is kept separate from all other aspects of life

Emotionally distant; can discuss murders matter-of-factly

No emotion; murder is simply business as usual; usually no relationship with the victim

May be a member of organized crime

Kills by surprise; spends little time at crime scene

Kills fast; orderly

Uses sophisticated weapons that indicate a specialist

Comfortable with killing; does not overkill

Guns may be stolen and/or left at the scene to avoid being found on killer

Little history of stealing or sexual assault

Often has a particular style of killing, whether knife, cyanide or gun

Has history of violence

Premeditated; e.g., stalking but without attachment[31]

Murderer, Product Tampering Style

Murders by sabotaging a product; e.g., aspirin, baby food, or soft drink

Wants money through lawsuit on behalf of victim, extortion of company, or business; e.g., competitive company goes under and stock falls

Must make it look random

Often has more to gain than money; e.g., bad marriage ends or collects insurance

Others often die but are not intended victims

---

[31] Douglas and Schlesinger (1980).

> ### *Traits of a Person Who Hires a Hit Man*
> Has personal conflicts or business competition with victim
> May have recently changed behavior to show concern toward victim
> Has excellent alibi; may have been highly visible
> Has excellent recall of events surrounding murder, and is less good
>   about other details

Murderer, Psychotic Style

(See the traits of psychosis in chapter four under *Schizophrenic*)

The individual suffers from delusions and is out of touch with reality. Most delusions are harmless, and most psychotic individuals are far more likely to suffer themselves than to make anyone else suffer. Usually, the person has a history of hospitalizations. The delusions for a psychotic murderer may involve persecuting, relentless voices telling the psychotic individual to kill. Or the delusion may involve a belief that the psychotic individual is someone else (e.g., the Great Avenger), and has a job to do. Or the psychotic individual may believe that he or she is being pursued by an evil force or a member of a secret society, and murder is the only way out of danger.

> Mentally ill people are not usually violent criminals, but violent criminals are often mentally ill. Studies indicate that major mental illness and substance abuse is overrepresented in criminals.[32]

Murderer, Sexual Styles

There are two sexual styles: Planned and Opportunistic.

Planned
Usually murderer is male and victim is female
Sexual elements are part of the murder
May be rape (before or after murder) or symbolic rape
Obsessive about details
Looks for a certain victim; e.g., age, appearance, or lifestyle

---

[32] Cameron et al. (1998).

Captures victim; often moves her to another place for the murder
and the disposal of the body

May take a trophy from victim; e.g., jewelry, driver's license, or body
parts

Behaves aggressively toward victim; e.g., bites

Socially adept

May impersonate someone else; e.g., a security guard

Opportunistic

Usually murderer is male and victim is female

Sexual elements are part of the murder

Sexual mutilation may be part of the murder

Often overkill as an enactment of a fantasy

Unplanned; opportunistic

Impulsive, under stress; no plan

Lives near the scene of the crime

Feels inadequate

Sloppy; random

Socially inept and lacks interpersonal skills

Lives alone or with parents

Odd; nocturnal

Murderer, Serial Offender Style

The behavior reflects his personality. The crimes are not committed
for greed, jealousy, or profit. He is not getting revenge against a close
victim. The victim is a stranger. The murderer is almost always male
and usually white, between eighteen to thirty-five years old.

Complex motives make finding him difficult, but a profile emerges
with continued offenses

He becomes better and more ritualized with each killing; the rituals
have meaning for the killer

May be charming, articulate, and glib, but could also be an angry,
ineffectual loser

Wants domination, manipulation, and control over others

History of bed-wetting, fire-setting, cruelty to animals, solo breaking
and entering, or sadistic rape; stealing women's underwear during a burglary is a sign in this direction.

May take a trophy from the victim; e.g., ring or body part

Rarely expresses hatred toward those close to him

> ## *Psychological Experience of Imprisonment*
> Trapped; no physical escape
> Psychological route is only escape
> Forced contact with others in prison society
> Loss of self-determination; e.g., few choices available
> Loss of privacy; everything that happens is discussed by anyone
> Must follow orders; e.g., roles are assigned and maintained
> Subject to jailhouse public opinion and fast-spreading rumors
> Exposed
> Desires power, usually physical and status symbols; e.g., dress or
>   visits
> Must behave submissively
> At the whim of the informal inmate social system, whose tools are
>   blackmail, threats, social ostracism, death, and mental torture[33]

Lives in a fantasy: Fantasy is about killing, and murders are attempts
  to fulfill fantasy
History of childhood abuse (physical or emotional)
Usually chooses victims of the same race
Loner; raging; inadequate
Crimes may be precipitated by a stressor
Compulsion to kill increases after time; becomes overwhelming[34]
Killer begins to decompensate and get sloppy; some want to be
  caught at this time because they feel out of control[35]

Murderer, Simmering Style
Accumulates hostility
Has history of frustration; becomes obsessed with trivial problems
  (e.g., IRS misfiled forms, even after problem is solved)
Unable to separate trivial problems from real source of tension: self
  or relationship change
Not experienced in murder
Plans well
Has poor history of working out conflicts in school or relationships

---

[33] Korn and McCorkle (1963).
[34] Douglas and Olshaker. *Journey Into Darkness* (1997).
[35] Revich and Schlesinger (1978).

Usually has long-standing conflict with victim, but may not be close
Becomes quiet about injustice as the plan takes shape
Link to the victim may not be obvious because it may exist primarily
    in his mind
May react because of feeling rebuffed
May seek revenge for a perceived wrong
Revenge murder may mean multiple victims
Murder is a relief and is seen as restitution
Cannot deal with increasing tension; act of murder relieves tension[36]

Murderer, Visionary Style

Psychotic; has delusions
Victim is related to the delusions
History of mental illness; history of violence related to delusions
Feels murder was morally justified
Does not flee
Can be cult leader or cult member

Styles in Organized Crime and the Criminals

Traits of the Organization

Organization has hierarchy with clear relationships, obligations, and
    privileges
Leaders use force and violence for internal discipline
Maintains immunity from government or legal interference
Operation is large with vast finances
Often specializes; e.g., drugs or gambling
Strives to become a monopoly
Power rests with leaders

Traits of Members

Members use force and violence to eliminate the competition
Career is almost exclusively in a criminal syndicate or ring
Great allegiance to leaders
Code of personal loyalty
Follows code of behavior
Has long history as ordinary career criminal

---

[36] Schlesinger (1996).

Sexual Styles

P eople care about being sexually normal—preferably sexually superior—and one of the ways that individuals evaluate how well they are doing is by comparing themselves to others. In the arena of sexuality, however, comparison becomes difficult because people have no way to know what other people are *really* doing, how they are doing it, or whether they are having fun. That may be why external sexiness is so important: It becomes a substitute for genuine information.[1]

Traits of normal sexuality are presented first, followed by problems that people experience. When problems involve children, nonconsenting adults, coercion, or violence, they become criminal acts and are described in chapter five.

Traits of Normal Sexuality

Infancy

Erections occur neonatally and throughout infancy and childhood

Infants' introduction to their bodies is by being held, cuddled, and hugged

Babies' worlds are primarily physical; i.e., feeding and holding

Toddlers are increasingly aware of their bodies as they learn control of elimination

---

[1] Tiefer (1995).

Childhood and Early Adolescence

Most children enjoy touching their genitals (masturbation).
Children just enjoy the physical sensations, without fantasies (different than adults)
Obsessive masturbation can signal a problem
Boys and girls are fascinated with the changes their bodies undergo
Children compare themselves to others, overtly or covertly
Both genders are often unprepared for sexual nighttime dreams
Daughters flirt with fathers, asking, "Will others find me attractive?"
Sons flirt with mothers, asking, "Will others find me attractive?"
Children rehearse adult roles; i.e., boyfriends and girlfriends

Adolescence

Girls look like young women before boys look like men
Masturbation is common
Sexual experimentation to varying degrees; heterosexual or homosexual
Looking for role models and validation of sexuality

Types of Adult Sexual Orientation

Bisexual

Sexual attraction to members of both sexes

Heterosexual

"Straight"
Sexual attraction to members of the opposite sex

Homosexual

Lesbian or gay
Sexual attraction to members of the same sex

Asexual

Absence of sexual attraction

Love Maps

Personal preferences of who is attractive; e.g., men or women, tall or short

What is a sexual turn on or off; e.g., bald men, large breasts, or blondes
Influenced by hormones, genetic makeup, early experiences, and
    growing up

Traits of Sexual Problems

A survey of more than three thousand men and women, ages eighteen
to fifty-nine, found that 43 percent of women and 31 percent of men
regularly suffer from a lack of interest in sex, an inability to reach
orgasm, or some other sexual dysfunction.[2] The twenty-one problems
that follow are a mix of problems—some have a physical basis and
some are exclusively psychological. The problems that are violent or
abusive, such as rape or sexual abuse, are in chapter five.

Addict or Sexual Compulsive

An addict is a person unable to adequately control his or her sexual
behavior. The term refers to more than excesses in frequency or partici-
pation in certain types of sex. The addict cannot control behavior de-
spite the risk of potential adverse consequences; e.g., jobs, marriages,
health, or a high government office may be sacrificed because of reckless
behavior. Compulsive sexual behavior occurs more often in men than
in women. Not all of the following traits will be seen in the same
person. However, the compulsive aspects are always present.

Frequent sexual encounters

Compulsive masturbation

Seeks new sexual encounters out of boredom with the old ones

Desires to get excesses under control but is unsuccessful at attempts
    to stop behavior

Engages in sex without physiological arousal

Behavior is self-destructive; behavior may jeopardize marriage or
    career

Convinces self that the behaviors are OK; e.g., rationalizes that "It's
    not *real* sex"

Spends excessive time in sexual behaviors, thinking about sex, and
    sex encounters

Has desire for excitement and may ignore other responsibilities

Guilty, lonely, and/or angry

---

[2] The Journal of the American Medical Association, February 1999.

Lacks control in other areas of life

Continues in spite of adverse consequences

Believes that sex is the answer to his or her problems

Has difficulty being emotionally intimate; relies on sex instead

Sex is the main mode of expression, but the feelings do not have to be intimate

May have had a childhood marked by little control

Childhood may have had blurred boundaries or abuse

Most common compulsive sexual behaviors are masturbation and continual affairs (often both simultaneously) while married[3, 4]

Apotemnophiliac

Rare sexual compulsion satisfied only when one has an amputation of his or her body

Can stage an accident (e.g., hunting) so that professional amputation is required[5]

Aversion

Persistently avoids genital contact

May have sexual desire but is repelled by the idea of sexual contact

Can become ill; e.g., nausea, diarrhea, vomiting, or sweating

Avoidance may be a way to deal with sexual anxiety

Vulnerable to this disorder after a trauma; e.g., rape

Can be caused by sexual abuse, sexually repressive parenting, or pressure from partner

Body-image or self-esteem problems cause vulnerability to the disorder

There are married people who never have sexual contact with their partners

Bestiality

Individual performs sexual acts with an animal

May have preferences about male or female animals

Rarely an exclusive sexual interest; usually supplemental or a diversion

---

[3] Gold and Heffner (1998).

[4] Gold, Steven and Heffner, Christopher. *People* Magazine, March 23, 1998, p. 12.

[5] John Money coined this term.

Likes sex with people

Occasionally occurs because of shame about small penis size

Some individuals are too anxious to have sex with another person

Some people believe that one gains supernatural powers or cures disease

Animals that are preferred because of size and stability are dogs, sows, mares, heifers, and apes[6]

Traits of All Sexual Paraphilias

Sexual attraction to, and arousal by, unusual love objects

Results from early developmental disturbance that created a paraphiliac substitute

May be related to early sexual arousals

Normal lust and arousal were transferred to a less dangerous object, now problematic

Some are harmless and consensual; others are violent without consent

Not voluntary; not chosen; rarely goes away; usually very specific

Ranges from harmless to dangerous

Addictions cannot be controlled by willpower

Punishment does not prevent them; persecutions feed them

Feels like a trance when it is going on

May have these fantasies, and accompanying arousal, many times a day[7]

Eligibility Paraphiliac

This includes any addictive, repetitious, and compulsive arousal by ineligible (forbidden by some criteria) partner

Can be as simple as hair color, religion, or ethnic group

Can be physical only; e.g., only a short, a skinny, or a disfigured partner

Can be aroused by partner from a different social class

Can be as unusual as uniforms, tattoos, or amputees (the turn-on is the stump)

Extreme A4 necrophilia: sexual arousal or acts with a dead partner[8]

---

[6] Masters (1966).

[7] Money (1998).

[8] ibid.

Erectile Disorder
Individual cannot attain or keep an erection until completion of sex.
Possible causes include:
>   Malfunctioning valves in penis
>   Lack of pleasure and lack of excitement during sex
>   Smoking
>   General anxiety or performance anxiety
>   Often a combination of mental and physical
>   Sexual virility is virtually a requirement of the male role, so erectile disorder, impotence, and premature ejaculation are not simply problems of the penis—they become negative descriptions of the man.

Female Orgasmic Disorder
Common in women; individuals do not experience orgasm. Possible causes include:
>   Poor psychological adjustment
>   Negative body image; feels inferior
>   Inexperienced or sexually naïve
>   Dissatisfied with relationship
>   Angry or anxious[9]

Fetishist
Individual is sexually aroused by urges and fantasies of using nonliving objects (clothing, shoes, or toy) instead of a sexual partner
Almost always a timid man who is introverted, withdrawn, and anxious in sexual situations
Nonliving objects are tokens of sin that permit excitement
Objects are usually female symbols, commonly women's underwear
More unusual objects can be shoes and toys
Attraction to object is compulsive and nonvoluntary
Extreme → repeatedly acts on urge and uses nonliving objects instead of a sexual partner[10]

Frotteurist
Individual is sexually aroused by urges and fantasies of rubbing against a stranger's body (usually buttocks) in a public place

---

[9] Knopf and Seiler (1990).
[10] Storr (1964).

145

Usually occurs in a crowded place

Does not want to coerce the other person, only to touch

Fantasizes that the act is in the context of a relationship

Victim is often so unbelieving that she does not protest quickly

Usually a young adult

Extreme → repeatedly acts on urge and rubs against strangers in public places

Guilt

Individual believes sex is bad

Impaired ability to have normal adult relationship

Extent of guilt is partly determined by parents' attitudes

Influenced by society's values

Trouble leaving parents and childhood behind causes trouble becoming independent

Individual is likely to be introverted

Sees people as good (nonsexual) or bad (sexual)

Extreme → guilt prevents falling in love

Extreme → guilt results in rejection of one's own sexuality[11]

Hypoactive

Individual shows inhibited sexual desire

Lacks sexual desire and has no sexual fantasies

Fear and anxiety have turned off sexual drive

Does not seek opportunities and refuses chances to have sexual contact

Few or poor quality relationships

Possible causes include:

> low hormone levels
>
> anger with partner
>
> depression
>
> trouble with sexual orientation[12]

Hypoxyphile

Individual is sexually aroused by oxygen deprivation

---

[11] ibid.

[12] Knopf and Seiler (1990).

Always **Extreme** → Oxygen deprivation is achieved by a noose, bag, or other device around the head and/or throat that cuts off the oxygen supply. The Hypoxyphile escapes before being asphyxiated and achieves orgasm. Accidents often occur and death results.

From the Files

A thirty-two-year-old man who was severely hypoxyphilic had to be institutionalized because he required constant monitoring.

Inferiority
Individual feels undesirable as compared to others

Lacks confidence in sexual identity

Does not identify with society's role for him or her

Often had bad role model in same-sex parent

Often ambitious as another way to be loved

Fantasy and inner world gains importance[13]

Extreme → person will turn away from any competition to be sexual or attractive

Sadomasochism
Condition differs from criminal style because behaviors are consensual

Sadist and masochist live out a fantasy where roles, dialogue, costume, and sex are aspects of the ritual

Bottom (masochist) has a code word to stop the behaviors

Top (sadist) is turned on by altering emotional or physical state of bottom (masochist)

Bottom must trust partner or he or she cannot enjoy the act

Erotic because of focus on forbidden acts

Activities may involve pain

Masochist
Individual is sexually aroused by urges and fantasies of being made to suffer; e.g., humiliation, beatings, rape, bondage, whipping, or cutting

---

[13] Storr (1964).

Sexually aroused by being humiliated, bound, punished, or disciplined

Pain is transformed into sensuous ecstasy

Repeatedly acts on urges and finds others who will perform the range of desired acts

Often suffers from sexual guilt or inferiority

Lives out a fantasy

Strong dependency; wants to be humiliated

Often uses prostitutes

Rare to find serious injury[14]

Sadist

Individual is sexually aroused by games of humiliation, bondage, punishment, and discipline

Sexually aroused by urge and fantasy of inflicting pain on others

Desire to be omnipotent

Strong aggression; wants to render partner helpless

Often uses prostitutes

Extreme ➔ repeatedly acts on urge and causes physical and/or psychological pain to others for sexual stimulation.

There is a category of rapist that is particularly sadistic—individuals who inflict unnecessary suffering on victims. Pain is arousing.[15] Sado-masochistic sex is usually heterosexual or between gay men. It is unusual in the lesbian community.

Symphorophiliac

Individual is sexually aroused by accidents or catastrophes.

Always **Extreme** ➔ arranges a disaster, such as a car crash, to watch and enjoy the erotic excitement. Arranges his/her own disaster to experience daredevil thrill of escape[16]

Transgender

Individual dresses in clothing of other sex

Enjoys being treated as member of other gender

---

[14] Storr (1964).
[15] ibid.
[16] Money (1998).

Not done for sexual thrill

May have two identities and even two names: one male and one female

Usually has no desire to change anatomy

Transsexual

This is a rare condition where a person fully identifies with the other gender

Problem of self-definition

Believes that he or she has been born into the wrong body

Believes that he or she is heterosexual, not homosexual

Occurs more often in men than in women

Begins in early childhood

Body gender is different from gender of inner self

More individuals chose to "cross live" (live as other gender) rather than have surgery

Surgery is reconstruction of genitals and addition or removal of breasts

Postsurgery problems include urinary tract infections, rejection of plastic implants, strictures of newly created vaginas, suicide, depression, sexual dysfunction, and phobias[17]

Transvestite

Individual is involved in cross-dressing

Many people occasionally cross-dress; i.e., wear clothing of other gender to mock rules

Mostly heterosexual males are transvestites; e.g., cross-dressing for sexual pleasure

Keeps a woman's wardrobe and becomes aroused by dressing in the clothes

May be only in private, or sometimes in public; e.g., stockings under a business suit

May be uncertain of masculinity or identify with women

Range of behavior runs from using a piece of underwear occasionally to **Extreme** ➔ full outfits and makeup worn for extended periods of time; i.e., "passing" as a woman

---

[17] Brown and Rounsley (1996).

Voyeur (Peeping Tom)

Individual is aroused by urges and fantasies of watching others
undress or engage in sex

Does not want contact with those he or she observes

Looking provides the excitement

May masturbate while peeping or later while thinking about the scene

Few personal sexual outlets

Peeping may be the only sexual activity

Extreme ➔ Repeatedly acts on urges and watches others undress or
engage in sex

Premature Ejaculation

Male experiences ejaculation before he desires it

Common

Affected by age, frequency of sex, and newness of partner

May have heightened sensitivity in penis

May result from anxiety

Sexual performance may have as much to do with confirmation of
maleness as it does as a sexual release or an intimate expression to his
partner.

Genetic Sexual Types

Androgen Insensitivity Syndrome

Form of pseudohermaphroditism

Externally female and internally male

Has testes inside; no uterus

Genetically male; otherwise nothing masculine in external
characteristics

Discovered at adolescence when "girl" does not menstruate

Does grow breasts and has normal female body (does not respond
to male sex hormone)

May lack sexual hair

Sterile, but disorder runs in families

No masculine behavior; ordinary female roles and behaviors

Hermaphroditism

Characteristics of both sexes are present at birth, internally and
externally

Varies greatly in degree:

      Many have external genitalia that are either male or female

      Some have external genitalia that look ambiguous

Sex assignment is usually done early, so child is reared consistently

Sex assignment is often based on predominant external characteristics

If external characteristics are very ambiguous, sex assignment is made on basis of gonads and hormones

Often sterile

Klinefelter's Syndrome

Males only

47 chromosomes: extra X (47,XXY)

Tall; long arms and legs after puberty

Small testicles; sterile

May develop girl-like breasts, which can be flattened surgically

Can have either lower IQ or superior IQ[18]

Turner's Syndrome

Females only

45 chromosomes instead of 46 (46,XO)

Low hairline and webbed neck

Always short, often 4ft6in

No ovaries; always sterile

No teenage development

Normal, often high verbal intelligence

Seems to be resilient and stable, and copes well

May have space-form perception problems; e.g., cannot copy a hexagon[19]

Traits of Religious Attitudes Toward Sex
Buddhism

Seek perfect morality, wisdom, and compassion

Sexual desire is not emphasized

Monks are celibate

---

[18] Money (1998).
[19] ibid.

Christianity
Sex is exclusively for married couples
Sex outside marriage is a sin
Sex is for procreation
Celibacy is a virtue
Attitudes are becoming more lenient

Hinduism
Many different sects with different customs
Love and sex are of divine origin
Friendship and love are to be practiced between equals
Prohibitions against sex during menstrual period
Rules against adultery
Sexual organs are considered to have a life of their own

Islam
Sexual joy is for males
Women are erotic
Four wives are allowed
Women stay behind curtains
Chief virtue is to avoid excess
Sex is sinful out of marriage, unless with a concubine
Rules of sexual hygiene are found in the Koran
Prohibitions against sex during menstrual period
Must cleanse after menstruation or masturbation

Judaism
Fairly tolerant attitudes
Prohibitions against sex with relatives, animals, or during menstrual
    period
Contraception allowed after two children
Abortion not condemned by most denominations

Taoism
Sex is necessary for general health
Longevity or immortality is attained by sexual activity
Sex with a virgin is particularly prized
Sex is mixing of yin (women) and yang (men)

Sex with love is the way to balance yin and yang
Opposes masturbation in men because semen contains vital energy
Encourages men to satisfy partner and refrain from ejaculation

Traits of Sexual Excitement

Men and Women

Heart rate increases
Blood pressure increases
Body muscles tense—voluntary and involuntary
Sex flush—reddening of the skin, especially neck and chest in light-skinned people
Nipples become erect

Women

Breasts increase in size
Clitoris swells
Vagina lubricates
Labia majora separate
Labia minora swell
Uterus rises slightly

Men

Penis becomes erect
Scrotum thickens
Testes rise closer to body

CHAPTER SEVEN

Love and Marriage

T here is probably no topic more enduring in literature, and in life, than love. Unfortunately, psychology may understand less about love than about hate, and less about long-lasting relationships than about abandonment. In this chapter, I present data on falling in love as well as information on conflict, on falling out of love, and on separation and divorce.

Falling in Love

Traits Associated With Falling in Love

A surge of hope

Dreams of loving and being loved

Hopes of making up for bad aspects of the past

Desire for wholeness

Wish to merge two people into one

Exaggerates vision of loved one's actual characteristics; sees with rose-colored glasses

Emphasis is on the similarities in interests

Sees good characteristics and excludes negative traits[1]

---

[1] Troupp (1994).

Qualities Associated With Being in Love

Loves one's own ideal self as reflected in the other person

The object of one's love holds important values; e.g., kindness, success

Attraction raises desire or presents a challenge

Maintains idealization of falling in love, but sees clearer reality of the other

Confronts limitations of self and partner and survives disillusionment and disappointment

Feels compassion for partner

Tolerates separateness and intimacy

Trust and attachment grow

Makes commitment to maintain love

Envy is tamed and is replaced with admiration

Attitudes of hope and optimism prevail

Love feels like the path out of distress toward enrichment

Lessens feelings of loneliness or isolation[2]

Traits That Distinguish Love and Sex

Love	*Sex*
Always concerned with welfare of the other	May be concerned with other's welfare
Love chooses	Sex is less discriminating
Search is for joy and happiness	Search is for pleasure
Feeling of belonging	Feeling of possessing or belonging
Hard to replace the object of love	Easier to replace the sex object[3]

Choosing a Partner

How do we choose a partner from all the people we meet? The following are theories of mate selection.

Ecology

When people are ready to marry, they will meet an eligible partner close at hand.

---

[2] Reik (1949); Troupp (1994).
[3] Reik (1949).

Similarity

It is easier to be attracted to people who are similar to one's self, particularly in attitudes, personality characteristics, economic characteristics, and race. Also, people are attracted to others who behave as they would in similar situations (e.g., laugh at the same thing). The similarity theory also says that individuals like people who resemble members of their family of origin and who follow the practices of their own childhood. These people make marriages that are meaningful in terms of previous experiences with marriage (e.g., parents).

Complementary Needs

Each person is attracted, consciously or unconsciously, to somebody who can help him or her solve personal problems. The mate completes the partner's personality. Type I occurs when the need, such as achievement, appears in both partners but at different levels of intensity. Type II occurs when different needs are involved; for example, one partner needs to dominate and the other needs to be subordinate. Type III involves needs that are both identical and complementary, such as two people with high needs for sex or achievement who can help each other.[4]

What About Physical Attractiveness?

Often attractiveness is the initial screening device when people meet. People tend to match each other on level of attractiveness which is in the eyes of the beholder. (See *Paraphilias* in chapter six for unusual attractions.) Physical attractiveness becomes less important as the relationship progresses.

Differences

Individuals are attracted to people who are dissimilar from themselves when they widen social networks and leave home. College, travel, military service, and work introduce individuals to people they might not ordinarily meet. Away from home, people feel the excitement of new experiences, have the freedom to learn new attitudes, and enjoy the ability to try new behaviors.[5]

Multicultural relationships are becoming increasingly common in the United States; not Democrats marrying Republicans, but marriages

---

[4] Benson (1971).
[5] Hendrick (1995).

across racial, ethnic, and cultural lines. Diversity makes a relationship exciting, but differences can also cause strain because of lack of understanding. Partners may have been raised with very different expectations as to the roles men and women play, the foods they eat, how to discipline children, or whether the marriage comes before or after family responsibilities. Even simple acts cause people to feel hurt— what to call your mother-in-law, to hug or not to hug, or appropriate dinner table conversation.

Just as parents and children bond, adults attach to each other in some predictable styles. The following three general styles are major varieties of attachment between adults.

Dismissing Attachment
This is a bond marked by extreme self-sufficiency of one or both partners.

Past History
Consistently rebuffed by parents; little affection and little emotional expression

Associates emotional vulnerability with parental rejection

Present Behaviors
Expects people to be untrustworthy and unsupportive

Appears distant, hostile, and irritable

Very self-reliant

Feels misunderstood by others; fears intimacy and high emotions of romantic relationships

Preoccupied Attachment
This is a bond with anxiety and ambivalence about relationships.

Past History
Parents were insufficiently attentive and had mixed feelings about being parents

Received inconsistent parenting and responded by crying and clinging to parents

As a child, believed that he or she was unworthy of love

Childhood was filled with loneliness, doubts, and few friends

Present Behaviors

Love feels like an obsession; wants intense closeness

Displays emotional extremes from ardent attraction to jealousy

May be a compulsive caregiver

Chronically worries about being insufficiently loved, rejected, and abandoned

Discloses too quickly and easily

Wants approval

Secure Attachment

This is a bond where trust and security are present.

Past History

Parents were respectful, accepting, responsive, and sensitive

Love experiences have been happy, friendly, and trusting

Present Behaviors

Feels worthy; has high self-esteem

Expects partner to be responsive and accepting

No serious interpersonal problems[6]

What does she see in him? What does he see in her? The previous types are general; the types listed next are specific attractions or choices that are not healthy. Following are several specific types of undesirable relationships and the needs they satisfy.

Five Types of Don Juans and the Women They Complement

1. The Conqueror

Mama's boy; weak father

Disapproving parents

Has to be in control

A "can do" person; successful, professional, and has a good income

Married or a bachelor, but afraid of intimacy

Sexually proficient; wants sexual needs met

---

[6] Bartholomew (1993).

Needs a conquest; always seeking a woman
Likes his freedom
May use alcohol or drugs for stimulation

The woman he attracts is a daddy's girl who will not make demands. She is young and compliant. She has achieved less than he has in all areas and wants to be cared for. She waits patiently, goes along sexually, and is generally dependent and undemanding.[7]

2. The Charmer
Abandoned son
Good-looking, savvy, and smooth
Subtle, smart, educated, outgoing, and polished
Passionate
Elusive; shows only the best of himself
Reassuring and mysterious
Presents himself as a man who loves women
Wants a princess; ready to be romantic
Does not last long in relationships

The woman he attracts is also lovely and accomplished. She responds to romance and is dazzled by the chemistry between them. She looks more independent than she really is. The romance depends on illusion and fire rather than substance. She wants to get to know him. She is warm and yearns for love, but is better at longing than at loving. When he leaves, she blames herself and grieves.[8]

3. The Adventurer
Mama's boy; unavailable father
Fun loving; preserves freedom
Rebellious to authority; takes risks and breaks rules
Prefers adventure to intimacy; may encourage women to compete
    for him
May take risks with drugs or money
May be married

---

[7] Carpineto (1989).
[8] ibid.

Volatile; out of control

May be successful or a failure, but without responsibility or reality

The woman he attracts is also thrilled by the high-risk game of love and may also be married. She is blatantly sexual and wants the thrills and risks that he offers. The excitement covers up her feelings of low self-esteem and provides her with a sense of identity.[9]

4. The New Age Narcissist

Unempathic parents

Needy and a taker

Expressive, analytical, and reflective

Dependent but hates to admit it; sex is a comfort

Addicted to being understood

Self-centered, self-indulgent, and explosive

Always disappointed by his women

May force her to leave him

The woman he attracts is a healer who responds to the wounds that she senses in him. She needs to be needed. She seems self-sufficient and disguises her dependency. He comes to need her and then hates her because his dependency is intolerable. They see their relationship as meaningful and significant. She keeps trying, even when the relationship has nothing to offer to her.[10]

5. Rescuing Knight

Has been brought up to please others

Expects to do all the providing for his woman

Feels responsible for making her happy

Afraid to disappoint anyone

Suppresses his own needs and keeps aggression under wraps

Anger seeps out against her

The woman he attracts is enchanted by the thought that she can be rescued. She is often in a difficult situation when they meet. She is used to being under the power of others and may have been molded

---

[9] ibid.
[10] ibid.

by a parent whom she adored but who manipulated her. She is confused when she begins to sense his unspoken anger but afraid to leave.

Most people fear romantic involvement to some degree because intimacy involves the risk of getting hurt or rejected. Some people are extreme in their fears. The following traits can be weak or strong, but they are traits that protect *against* relationships.

Barriers to Getting Close to Another Person

1. **Checklist love**—"I must have this, that, and the other" may be a way of avoiding real personal relationships by never straying from your intellectual list.
2. **Sex or love, not both**—Some people can get close either physically or emotionally, but not both because it is too vulnerable, so sex is good and emotions are shut down, or emotionally intimacy is there and sex disappears.
3. **Find the impossible partner**—One way to never risk intimacy is to become involved with a person who is unavailable because of other commitments, such as marriage or work, living elsewhere, or any other factors that make a real relationship impossible.
4. **Freeze-dried love**—Individuals can get together, but once they are, no change is allowed. They are so terrified of change that they close their lives to any people or situations that are new.
5. **"I gave at the office" love**—All intense emotions and commitments have been given to work and nothing is left for another person. The excuse that comes with this fear is often "I'm doing it so I can create a good life when I meet someone or I have to provide for my family."[11]

Jealousy

No discussion about relationship traits, however brief, can be completed without some mention of jealousy. Normal jealousy arises when the fear of losing a loved person or position (job, teacher's pet, star athlete, valedictorian) becomes threatening. Jealousy speaks to a universal desire to preserve anything that is precious.

For some people, jealousy exists all the time—without relationships, without prized possessions, and without impending loss. Jealousy is

---

[11] Callahan and Levine (1982).

an aspect of his or her nature. Jealousy may be kept secret, and others may never be aware of the drama being played out in this person's mind. For these people, rivals do not inspire jealousy; jealousy creates imaginary competitors. The worst torment for a jealous person is to be in doubt, and he or she is always in doubt because they are always suspicious. At its worst, jealousy may slip into paranoia.[12]

One-third of solved murders involve jealousy. Jealousy is linked to family murder/suicides, marital violence, battery, suicide, loss of self-esteem, and divorce. Jealousy is a reaction that ranges from normal → pathological, and feelings are triggered by an event that can range from a simple glance to the discovery of an affair.

General Traits of a Jealous Partner
Perceives a threat, real or imagined; e.g., fears partner will leave
Is predisposed to jealousy as an emotion; begins early in life with the fear of losing love
May have had a parent who was unfaithful
May be unaware of own impulses to cheat and attribute own wishes to partner; e.g., she really wants to go out with other men
Feels inadequate to hold a mate; e.g., impotent or unattractive
Mistakes jealousy for passion and therefore values the feeling
May result from the need for exclusivity in their commitment
Men get jealous about sex; women get jealous about deep emotional connections[13]

Four Types of Romantic Jealousy
Suspicious—suspicions about partner's behavior and fear of losing him or her
Emotional—closeness and expressions of care
Envious—relationships not shared
Betrayal—acts of betrayal[14]

Bachelor
Bachelors tend to be mythologized in several distinctive styles: women haters, emotionally fixated on their mothers, unattractive to women, pining for a lost love, unacknowledged homosexuals, unlucky, play-

---

[12] Gonzalez-Crussi (1988).
[13] Pines (1992).
[14] Patterson, Rapoza, and Malley-Morrison (1998).

boys, or workaholics; any of these types may exist, but research shows that personality traits of bachelors reveal a continuum of qualities from normal to extreme.

Most bachelors expect to marry and say so

Needs autonomy; e.g., "I like my freedom"

Low need for intimacy; e.g., "I don't want a lot of affection"

Not very sexual; e.g., "There's nothing great about sex"

Hard to make decisions; e.g., "I like to keep my options open"

Reluctant to take on responsibility; e.g., "I don't want to deal with someone else's problems"

Fearful; e.g., "What if I make a mistake?"

Fears loss of control over his fate if he marries

Has fears about sex; may not be able to "perform" in a relationship

Reluctant to get involved in other people's lives

Hesitant to become sexually involved with a woman

Finds it difficult to feel dependent on other people

Normal → Extreme

Plans to eventually marry, to → no desire for intimacy

Capable of tender feelings and has friends, to → no friends

Feels very uncomfortable with himself, to → little desire to change

Feels confident about his individual achievement, to → no confidence in himself

Passive, can become → unable to assert any needs

Restrained, can become → isolated, avoids others

Does not want to compromise, can become → angry at women who come too close

Repressed emotionally, can become → emotionally detached: no feelings

May have had serious relationship, to → no capacity to form a relationship[15]

Rituals, the Engagement, and the Wedding

For better or worse, most people find partners and move into formal commitments marked by rituals. Virtually all people in all societies have rituals. The most common rituals surround birth, puberty, marriage, and

---

[15] Waehler (1994).

death, but rituals can also be seen in ordinary activities such as sitting down to eat a meal (e.g., seating arrangements, eating customs, or food). Rituals reflect collective beliefs and values (e.g., Japanese tea ceremony or the Jewish bris [circumcision]) or family values (e.g., the right way to clean the house on Saturday morning). Some rituals are passed along by religion or culture; others develop within families or groups.

Rituals bind individuals to some larger group, whether in marriage or military boot camp. They tell us what behaviors and feelings are allowed, what is too much, and what is not enough. The rituals performed by any character, family, or group provide an inside look at their beliefs, even if it becomes pathological, like silence during mealtimes or compulsive hand washing.

Individuals and families can have any number of idiosyncratic rituals that are inherent in their collective identity; e.g., visiting Grandma on Sunday, opening gifts on Christmas Eve, a new outfit for the first day of school, sex on Saturday night, or who reads the newspaper first.

The following rituals are among the most common.

Traits of the Engagement
A custom that signifies the intention to marry
Allows time to make wedding plans
Opens the relationship to scrutiny of the community
Both parties get feedback from others about what to expect in
    marriage

The engagement ring dates back as least as far as the fifteenth century. The ring was a public pledge that the marriage contract would be honored. The ring itself symbolized the circle of life and eternity. The precious stone may have been partial payment to the bride.

The wedding ring may have signified ownership and/or a gift of value to the bride. The ring is placed on the finger that the Romans believed leads directly to the heart.

The wedding is a ritual that unifies two people in a public, often religious, binding legal commitment. The wedding ritual marks the incorporation of two single people into the clan of married folks. People often create ceremonies that have personal meaning to them; for example, marry on horseback, in balloons, underwater, outdoors in parks, or in houses of worship.

Marriage

Just as individuals grow through a series of developmental stages, marriages proceed through stages, each one having tasks to be mastered. The following chart outlines major tasks and potential problems. More complete descriptions of some stages follow.

Stages of Marriage and Family[16]

Stage 1	*Newly Married*
Tasks	• Shift from family of origin to new commitment
	• Develop intimacy
	• Commit to partner and work
	• Establish basic roles
Problems	• Family of origin and/or in-laws vs. developing family
	• Finding roles for friends and potential lovers who threaten relationship
	• Stress about parenthood
	• Ambivalent about choices that have been made; e.g., work, mate, or home

Questioning (Common Around Age Thirty)	
Task	• Crisis about decisions that will affect life for years to come
Problems	• Restlessness and disruptions; fears about permanence of decisions
	• Doubts about commitments to work and relationship
	• Some marriages end, work changes, and new paths chosen

Stage 2	*Birth of Children*
Tasks	• Solidify relationship to each other
	• Add new role of mother or father
Problem	• May give up the marital role in favor of the parental role

Stage 3	*Settling Down/Individuation*
Tasks	• Settle down
	• Deepen commitments

---

[16] Solomon (1973).

- Pursue long-range goals
- Productivity in children, friends, work, and marriage
- Modify roles as needed to allow some independence to child and to each other

Problems
- Partners have different styles and grow individually
- Distance may develop

Transition — Midlife Transition

Tasks
- Reevaluate life
- Add up successes and failures
- Ponder future goals

Problems
- Conflicts erupt between individual and relationship goals
- Disruptions occur in established patterns
- Conflicts emerge between adolescent children and changing parents
- Differences between partners can lead to estrangement
- Torn between stability and drive to make changes

Stage 4 — Middle Adulthood

Tasks
- Reestablish and reorder priorities/parental role changes
- Allow children to leave/separate
- Resolve conflicts in marriage/work and stabilize or make changes

Problems
- Concerns about aging
- Conflicts about sex, money, and time
- Different ideas about children lead to conflict
- Boredom

Stage 5 — Older Adulthood

Tasks
- Deal with aging, illness, and death
- Integrate losses
- Children grown and launched; relate to them in new ways
- Support partner/modify relationship

Problems
- Conflicts rekindled around loneliness, sexual desire, and intimacy
- Losses of health, friends, and work; depletion

Tasks of the Newly Married

Create one's own definitions of *husband* and *wife*

Clarify expectations about family, work, time, money, and lifestyle

Accept responsibility for one's own happiness

Agree on everyday closeness and distance

Adjust to aloneness

Adjust to conflicts

Adjust to each other in sex, money, food, and habits

Create a vision for the future[17]

Parenting

Many couples take becoming parents for granted, but there are changes that occur in their relationship when a child is born.

Traits Associated With the Transition to Parenthood

Heightened self-awareness; changes in self-perception

Partner/lover self shrinks as parent self grows

Decline in involvement outside the home for women

Increased self-esteem, feeling valuable, and new confidence

New feelings of nurturance, patience, tolerance, anxiety, or anger

Mothers feel less in control of their lives

Stress

Increased sense of responsibility

Awakened appraisal of values and beliefs[18]

Problems Found in New Parents

Too much devotion from one parent pushes the other parent out of
the picture

Severe personality problems in one parent is harmful

Severe personality problems in one parent and the other does not
step in is more harmful

Not flexible in role as a parent; too rigid[19]

Also see traits that surround Adoption in chapter eight.

---

[17] Troupp (1994).

[18] Michaels and Goldberg (1988).

[19] ibid.

Traits of Parents and Their First Born

Child "inherits the kingdom"

Child gets exclusive attention; no sharing for a long time

Child is resentful after new baby, but adjusts and tries hard to be good

Intense relationship

Parents initially in awe of having a child

Parents give everything to the first until a sibling is born

Everything is novel for parents; nothing is taken for granted

An experiment for parents; may be overprotective[20]

Traits of Lesbian and Gay Parents

Percentages of lesbians and gay men who live in couple relationships are similar to the statistics of heterosexual couples. Children, if any, may be from an earlier marriage, adopted, or conceived through artificial insemination.

Traditional in values, careers, and worries about money, power, and balance of responsibilities

Dynamics are more similar to heterosexual parents than different

Nontraditional in gender roles

Worries about discrimination and sexism against selves and children

Secrecy dilutes intimacy and undermines authenticity

Potential isolation, with few role models

Relationship has few definitions and few, if any, legal or community supports

Job is to create a family unlike the family in which they grew up[21]

Not every couple decides to have or adopt children. The percentage of couples who remain childless by choice has risen dramatically in the United States.

Childless Women (By Choice)

People assume that there is a problem when a marriage has no children

Assumption is that every woman wants children

---

[20] Richardson and Richardson (1990); Leman (1985).
[21] Laird (1993).

Prejudice against childless women as neurotic, selfish, abnormal, or
　　hating kids
Feels invisible
Feels stigmatized
Concerns about what a child will do to her life
Fears pregnancy and/or childbirth
Some women see how parents had been limited by birth of children
Very aware of sacrifices made by mother
Parents may have painted bleak picture of parenting
Likes freedom
May have cared for others, younger siblings or mother
Had realistic picture of responsibilities of being a mother
Likes career: can take career risks and can be mobile
Very involved in marriage[22]

Problems in Love and Marriage

Couples argue most often about money, sex, and kids. Here are some of
those problems and others, including Adultery, Alcoholism, Domestic
Violence, and Parenting.

Adultery, General

Some married individuals mutually agree to an "open" marriage where
each is free to pursue other relationships based on a set of agreed-
upon rules. Most couples, however, require fidelity in their marriage
to maintain trust and stability. Although adultery, by definition, refers
to married couples, these dynamics could be applied to any monogamous couple, male or female.

Infidelity most often happens, or is tempting at:
The beginning of a marriage
Just before the marriage takes place; i.e., one last fling
When romance fades in a marriage
When beginning a family
When sex drops off
Midlife, because children leave and individuals feel their mortality

---

[22] Faux (1984).

Why Affairs Happen

Affairs regulate intimacy. Often one partner seeks greater intimacy; the other partner seeks to move away from intimacy.

Some individuals are "in love with love" and are always looking for it

A sign of depression

An attempt to hurt the spouse

A misguided attempt to resolve a marital stalemate

Sexual frustration

Low evaluation of the marriage

Curiosity

Revenge, rebellion, or anger

Boredom

A need for acceptance and recognition

Five Types of Adultery

1. Circumstantial Adultery (Husbands and Wives)

Not planned, an impulsive act

Cannot keep it a secret; tells others

May be an isolated incident

May evoke strong guilt feelings

Often the man or woman is a victim of a "practiced seducer"[23]

2. Conflicted Adultery (Wife Specific)

Adultery is a mistaken attempt to resolve some conflict in the marriage

May be angry with her husband

May want to escape

May be bored

May be unable to voice problems, so she acts on them

Relationship problems contribute to behavior

Relationship may be sexually unfulfilling, either inadequate or exploitative

Marriage may be intolerable, and adultery is a way to stabilize the relationship

---

[23] Caprio (1953).

Infidelity allows her to stay in the relationship; to tolerate the situation by enlisting outside support[24]

3. Philandering Adultery (Husband Specific)

Deliberate and habitual infidelity

Not motivated by love of another woman

Not motivated by the desire for a divorce from his wife

Emotionally maladjusted

Compulsive in adultery

Immature

Lacks discipline when he has conflicts of desire

May be disciplined and successful in other areas of life

Unconsciously wants to boast self-confidence

Rationalizes behavior or makes excuses; e.g., "It wasn't *real* sex"

Many are sexually inadequate[25]

4. Psychic Adultery (Husbands and Wives)

Very, very common to have infatuations and crushes that exist in his or her mind

Behavior remains sexually monogamous

Flirts with others to feel attractive

Fantasies are an outlet for boredom and monotony

Interest in another can be a means to create jealousy in the partner

Flirtations may show the desire to evoke a reaction in the spouse

Attractions makes one's self feel good

Stems from deep instinct toward polygamy

Satisfies rebellious feelings

Fidelity requires self discipline; psychic adultery is a compromise

Often the objects are old friends or former girlfriends/boyfriends/lovers

Chronic flirtation may indicate sexual frustration

Psychic adultery may be rehearsal for physical infidelity[26]

5. Psychopathic Adultery (Wife Specific)

Personality warp that makes her indifferent to ethical considerations

---

[24] ibid.

[25] ibid.

[26] ibid.

Cold

Tends to have older husband

Rarely seeks help because she experiences no conflict or guilt

Other men are a compulsion[27]

Spousal Reaction to Adultery

Feels betrayed and hurt

Feels deceived

Wonders about his or her own judgment

Questions all elements of their life together, past and present

Alcoholism

Traits of Alcoholic Homes

Tense and chaotic

Atmosphere of conflict and uncertainty

Adults behave inconsistently

Fighting overheard by children

Parent disappears or forgets about the child

Isolated from other families; low social interaction

Roles shift, behaviors change, and rules change

Traits of Children of Alcoholics

Anxiety and depression

Predisposition to adult alcoholism

Difficulty developing identity, therefore difficulty with relationships

Too much responsibility because of caring for others

School problems

Mistrustful of self and others

Physical problems of fetal alcohol syndrome or attention deficit
disorder

Types of Adult Children of Alcoholics

Super responsible—leaders, high achieving (all to gain control)

Flexible—adjusts to situations, detached socially, follows instead of
leads, and reactive

---

[27] ibid.

Placater—sensitive to others, sociable, helpful, eager to please, and avoids conflicts

Delinquent—disrupts own life and that of family members, feels bad, and has false confidence[28]

Traits of Adult Children of Alcoholics

Feels different from others

Rigid, serious, distrusting, and in need of control

Merciless on themselves

Lies instead of telling the truth

Trouble finishing projects that they have begun

Excessively seeks approval

Behaves impulsively

Behavior of Married Alcoholic Couples

The Alcoholic Wife is expressive emotionally, laughing, guilty, or depressed. Over time, negative communication increases with less alcohol consumption. When the wife is alcoholic, there is more disruption in the home than when the husband is alcoholic. The amount of her drinking is often influenced by the marital relationship; e.g., she drinks to alter her mood in response to marital difficulties.

The Alcoholic Husband is less guilty than an alcoholic wife. He blames others and denies the impact of drinking on the family. His drinking is less influenced by marriage and family relationships.

An Alcoholic Husband with an Alcoholic Wife show high negative communication between the two and are consistently unfriendly toward each other.[29]

Also see chapter nine for more description of the roles people play in maintaining alcoholic behaviors.

Domestic Violence

Methods of Emotional Abuse

Isolate the partner

Degrade the partner

Sexually abuse the partner

Damage the partner's personal property

---

[28] Black (1992); Woititz (1983).
[29] Haber and Jacob (1997).

The main question outsiders ask when they hear about spousal abuse is, Why does she stay with him? Women *do* leave. Women, not men, initiate the separation. Women do not return.

Traits of Abused Women Who Leave a Violent Home

Whether and when women leave has little to do with the amount of abuse they have endured: Other factors play a greater role in the decision.

Assertiveness

Defend themselves physically

Husbands describe them as becoming "intolerant"

Sufferers of emotional abuse leave before those that undergo physical abuse

Increasingly and intolerably isolated

Husbands have severe personality problems; e.g., narcissism or antisocial behavior

Husbands are degrading

Husbands increase contemptuous comments

Husbands display less humor and more generally negative feelings[30]

Men are also subject to emotional and physical abuse from their wives, but are less likely to report or admit it.

Child Witness to Domestic Violence

The usual scenario is that a child has been exposed to violence in the home and then ignored. Domestic violence is not discussed, and children are rarely removed from the home.

Can come to believe that violence is normal and acceptable

Suffers from impaired emotional development

Desires to escape; may retreat into fantasy

May turn to brothers or sisters

Boys may try to divert parents' attention by "bad" behavior

Girls may try to divert parents' attention by "good" behavior

Some boys behave aggressively as adults; some girls marry aggressive men

Also see *Stalkers* in chapter five.

---

[30] Gortner et al (1997).

Money

Money has many meanings, most of which remain out of awareness. This makes it a perfect lightning rod for conflict.

Arguments about Money may have any of the following roots:

1. **Competition**—Partners use money in the struggle to determine who is more successful.
2. **Meeting needs**—Money becomes the means to gain self-esteem, prove something, feel good, or feel important.
3. **Power**—One partner uses money to gain or keep control over the other person or the marriage.
4. **Distance**—Partners keep money separate as a way to maintain distance; they do not get too intimate or have to negotiate spending.
5. **Old debts**—Present money is needed to pay debts or losses from premarriage days.
6. **Parents**—Taking care of ill or aging parents leads to arguments, especially if parents were difficult during childhood or are unpleasant to the partner.
7. **Keeping up with the Joneses**—Money is used for appearances, for competing with others, and to maintain an image that pleases other people.
8. **Reckless spending**—One partner has a problem with out-of-control or addictive spending.
9. **Miser and spender**—Partners push each other to extremes. When one spends, the other hoards; when one is conservative, the other goes wild.
10. **Second marriages**—Money goes to supporting a wife or children from a previous marriage.

Sex

Of all the negotiations between individuals, sex has the potential to be the most difficult because it remains the most intimate. Sex, like money, is filled with personal meaning and beliefs that go back to childhood and probably remain unexamined. We are bombarded by sex on the screen and in print, but never educated about the sexual aspects of a relationship. Here are *some* of the possible meanings of sex in relationships.

Sexual Traits of Relationships

Sexual attraction is a major component of romantic love but, in long-term relationships, the quantity of sexual activity decreases over time.

Sex can be for procreation—to reproduce (stress increases during pregnancy attempts)

Sex can be relational—to express affection and increase intimacy

Sex can be for recreation—an enjoyable activity with few strings attached

Sex can be circumstantial; e.g., drank too much

      Different beliefs held by the partners increase the conflict

Sex can be coercive; e.g., manipulation, pressure, exploitation, aggression, or rape

Sex can be initiated or refused by verbal or nonverbal messages

Sex becomes a way to communicate closeness, anger, power, affection, interdependence, maintenance of the relationship, love, or nurturance

Conflict often arises from frequency or infrequency of sexual relations

Conflict can arise from negotiating birth control or fear about sexually transmitted diseases

Sexual satisfaction and relationship satisfaction increase with communication[31]

Problems and Triangles

Triangles are repetitive ways of relating among three people. Triangles often occur when two people cannot talk about or resolve some issue and bring in a third person.

Here are some examples that create interesting dynamics. Any two angles of the triangle indicate a possible alliance. The remaining angle indicates the relationship that will suffer.

Separation and Divorce

Why Marriages Fail

Marriages do *not* fail because of marital dissatisfaction or frequency of disagreements as often as they disintegrate from:

---

[31] Hendrick (1995).

He _____ She

Other Man/Woman

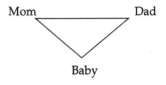

Mom _____ Dad

Baby

The well known "other man/woman" who enters an existing relationship, heterosexual, or homosexual, causes a rift in the partnership.

A shift in the marriage occurs when a baby is born and the relationship between husband and wife changes, often putting the dad on the outside. The alliance between one parent and the child can continue indefinitely.

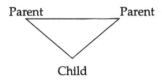

Parent _____ Parent

Child

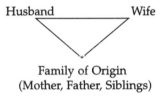

Husband _____ Wife

Family of Origin
(Mother, Father, Siblings)

Another triangle is the alliance of parent against a difficult child to disguise their own problems.

A strong continuing relationship with the family of origin affects a marriage.

Disengagement by one partner from the other
Stonewalling discussions; contempt of the other
Denial; blaming the partner for difficulties

Traits of Marital Arguments
Loud arguments and fights
Silence
Talks about things that don't matter
Attributions of negative traits to partner
Partners emphasize differences rather than similarities[32]

How to Escalate an Argument
Show self-righteousness; e.g., "I am all right, you are completely wrong"
Misunderstand, don't listen, or stop listening
Go for vulnerabilities
Raise new issues; e.g., "And remember when you also did . . ."

[32] Hetherington, Law and O'Connor (1993).

Stages of Marital Conflict

Beginning of Conflict is	Middle	End of Conflict
cued by particular events		
↓		*separate* — both partners withdraw
		or
response is → *avoid* (silence)		*dominate* — one partner "wins"
↘ or	↗	or
engage (discuss)	negotiate →	*compromise* — both give up something
	↓ ↘	or
	or	*agree* — find a creative solution that meets the needs of both
	escalate	or
		improve — changes are made in the relationship that aid future conflict

---

Counterattack or insult

Show contempt or demean

Make it a personality or character issue, rather than behavior

How to De-Escalate an Argument

Listen and show a readiness to understand

Show tact and concern for other's feelings; avoid "red flags"

Draw attention to process; e.g., "This kind of talk isn't getting us anywhere. Let's calm down"

Make a goodwill gesture; i.e., a small concession

Accept the other's feelings; e.g., expressing anger can get it off one's chest

Patterns of Conflict That Lead to Divorce

♦ confronts areas of concern → ♦ expresses feelings about these problems → ■ avoids, withdraws, whines → ♦ gets resentful and angry

or

178

♦ and ■ have little overt conflict ➔ ♦ and ■ later learn that they have different expectations of marriage, children, and family life

Traits of Spouses in a Failing Marriage
Review all that went wrong
Justify some actions and regret others
Replay actual events in one's mind
Create alternative scenes where they could have said or done things
    differently
Develop the "story" of the breakup—history and reasons are differ-
    ent for each partner
        Wrong from the start
        Betrayal, infidelity, and duplicity
        Chronic failings in partner
        Illness, depression, or alcohol
        Lost ability to talk to each other
        Lives take different directions
Attack each other's confidence
Feel reluctant to separate
Often reconcile briefly

From the Files

Jim and Annie had lived together for two years when he announced that he didn't really want to go through with the
wedding plans. Jim could not imagine spending his life with
Annie; she was self-centered and demanding, but he loved her family
and had proposed in good faith. For months while he was wrestling
with this problem, Jim had stayed away from Annie, emotionally and
physically. She felt more and more rejected. The day he moved out, she
answered a newspaper ad placed by a photographer who wanted nude
models. She posed defiantly, hoping that her appeal to someone else
might ease the hurt. It didn't work—and she had to pay a lot of money
to get the photos back.

Traits of Communication in Depressed Spouses
Responds better to other people than to spouse
Communication with spouse is negative and tense

Critical of spouse; disagrees with spouse

Puts down spouse; e.g., intends to hurt, embarrass, or demean

Speaks in a hostile manner; shows irritation

Remains preoccupied with self and unsupportive of other

Disrupts conversational flow; speaks little

Conversation lacks positive statements and congeniality

Wives remain in problem-solving conversations; husbands withdraw from problem-solving conversations

Wives talk more about feelings, including negative emotions, than husbands do[33]

Stages of Marital Separation

Early	*Relief*	*Adjustment*
Distress, fear	Euphoria, confidence	Loneliness, barren world
Sadness, vulnerability	New opportunities	No future with partner
Inability to concentrate, anxiety	Partner is now not needed	Looks for respite from feelings
Shaking, panic	No more fights	Begins affairs, work, activity, travel
Focus on unavailability of partner	"Best thing I've ever done"	
Want information about each other		

Divorce

Fifty percent of U.S. marriages end in divorce and sixty percent of divorces involve children. The process of the divorce and the adjustment afterward is influenced by:

The quality of family relationships prior to divorce

What happened before; e.g., violence

Events after divorce; e.g., financial decline, parents' stress, or peace

Individual adjustment and personality

Events surrounding divorce; e.g., infidelity, violence, cooperation, or court battles

---

[33] Johnson and Jacob (1997).

Postdivorce

Customary routine changes; e.g., father not home for dinner, and
mother leaves earlier

Loss of a family member

Loss of a way of life

Expectations about one's life change

Questions about one's self arise; uncertainty replaces security

Routines break down

Tasks of each family member are overloaded

Children take on more responsibility; daughters often assume care
of younger children

Women's income plummets 40 percent (average)

Loss of income results in lesser schools, poorer housing, poorer
health care, less enrichment

Less contact with one parent, usually father

Children's Reactions to Divorce[34]

Ages 2-3	Ages 3-5	Ages 5-6	Ages 6-10
Toilet training gone	Regression	Wish to restore family	Wish to restore family
Whining	Self-blame	Looks depressed	Loneliness
Irritable		Sadness	Sadness, shame
Separation fears	Crying	Anxiety	Anxiety
Sleep problems			
Clings to comfort objects; e.g., toys, blanket, bottle	Expresses desire for absent parent	Fantasies about saving hurt parent	Feels abandoned
Temper tantrums	Temper	Longing	Awkward socially
Aggression	Aggression	Aggression	School/ behavior problems

Adolescent Reactions to Divorce

Has to figure out how to understand the divorce

Must manage divided loyalties

---

[34] Wallerstein and Kelly (1980).

World becomes a less safe, less secure place

Confused perception of self, especially if accused: "You're just like your mother/father"

May move into pseudomaturity, trying to be on his or her own

May try to manipulate parents into reconciliation

Oldest child in family may take on parenting responsibilities for younger children

Increased responsibilities

Must deal with sexuality issues if parents begin to date

May turn to peers instead of parents

Power struggles with teachers and authorities

Distorts views about marriage

Aggressive behavior

Sadness

Anxiety about the future[35]

Postdivorce Adjustment—Children

Most children are remarkably resilient and emerge as competent. Some suffer early and recover (e.g., poor school grades). Others seem fine and suffer ill effects later.

Get more power; grow up faster; can benefit or harm

Have coercive relationships with parents, especially mother

Fantasize about parents' reconciliation

Fear abandonment by one or both parents

Don't disclose family situation to friends; withdraw socially

Use alcohol and drugs

More sexual activity

Academic problems

Girls show depression; boys behave badly

Lower self-esteem

Problems with relationships with parents, siblings, and peers[36]

Successful Adjustment—Children

Better adjustment correlates with having parents who resolve the divorce issues, because marital discord results in more problems than divorce.

Strong family environment prior to divorce

---

[35] ibid.

[36] Hetherington, Bridges, and Insabella (1998).

Good contact with both parents
Permission for children to express feelings of guilt, anger, or sadness
Support, not punishment, for appropriate expression of feelings
Stable environment; e.g., home, friends, school, and money[37]

Adjustment to Divorce—Children as Adults

Divorce may impact later attitudes toward intimacy and sexuality, so we see:

Earlier marriages; choosing unstable partners
Having children before marriage
Divorce early and often
Feel less secure in loving and being loved
Have not been exposed to negotiating and resolving differences
Have less effective problem-solving skills
Using more negative communication during arguments
Inept parenting

Traits of Continued Relationship Between
Ex-Husband and Ex-Wife

Bonds persist; e.g., money, kids, keys to house, furnishings, or history
Hostility; e.g., bitterness, miscommunication, feeling misused, feeling ignored, or feeling rejected
Conflicting interests; e.g., property, children, visitation, friends, or schedules[38]

Postdivorce Adjustment—Man and Woman

Both are at risk for psychological and physical problems.

Short-Term (Two Years Postdivorce)
Shows Emotional Extremes

Anger; e.g., breaking spouse's windows or following
Depression; e.g., no energy or self-hatred
Impulsive behavior; e.g., casual sex or buying sprees
Anxiety: "Who am I?"

---

[37] Wallerstein and Kelly (1980).
[38] Weiss (1975).

**Short-Term (Two Years Postdivorce) Shows
Disruption in Parent-Child Relations**
Preoccupied with self
Unsupportive of children's feelings
Erratic with discipline
Less likely to know where and with whom children are

Long-Term Possibilities
Alcoholism or drug abuse
Depression
Accidents
Physical illness

Opportunities for Positive Change
Personal growth
Creation of a more authentic life

Postdivorce Adjustment
Women are overrepresented at both the low end and high end of competence and adjustment.

Woman
Identity of wife is gone
Feels permanently overwhelmed
Remains lost; low self-esteem
Worries about child care
Learns to make decisions
Finds new strengths

Even with losses, at two years postdivorce, most women say that they are more satisfied than they were during the year before the divorce: They experience less stress and less conflict.

Man
Feels rootless
Cut out of children's lives
Has less of a social network on which to rely

May seek frenzied social life
Finding a new partner is critical

Remarriage and Stepfamilies

Seventy-five percent of men and sixty-six percent of divorced adults eventually remarry. Fifty percent of divorced individuals remarry within five years. Divorce in remarriages occurs at ten percent higher rates than in first marriages. Remarried wives divorce at significantly higher rates than remarried husbands.

Thirty-three percent of the U.S. population is in a "step" situation and the numbers are increasing. Discomfort with the mix leads to words such as *blended* and *reconstituted*.

Traits of the Stepchild

Boys respond more favorably than girls to a stepfather
Girls have higher stress with stepmother than with stepfather
No biological children enhances bonding for stepfather
One-half of stepfamilies have a joint or "our" child
Kids have "dual citizenship" in two households, two cultures, and two sets of rules
Households may have different foods, languages, and ways of doing things
Tension erupts around comings and goings, or packing and unpacking
Boundaries are less clear (e.g., who sleeps where?) in terms of privacy and property
Conflicting loyalties; e.g., hearing one parent talk against other
Insiders vs. outsiders; e.g., kids living all year round vs. being visitors
Power issues; e.g., "If you aren't nice to me, I'll go live with my father"
Coercive tactics; e.g., "Mom lets me stay up until 11"
Emotional attachments take time; no instant love
Formed by losses in another family; need to mourn
Dreams shattered and need to be altered
Different traditions
Parent-child relationship came before adult-adult relationship
No legal relationship between stepparent and stepchild

Traits of the Stepparent

Stepfathers tend to behave like "polite strangers"

Stepparents try to ingratiate themselves

Stepfathers tend to show less monitoring of children, less closeness, and less control

Disengaged, especially if rejected by stepchild

More abuse by stepfathers than by biological fathers

Stepmothers have difficulty integrating themselves into reconstituted family

Stepmothers are expected to participate more actively in parenting; therefore, they are forced into more confrontations[39]

---

[39] Visher and Visher (1993).

CHAPTER EIGHT

Turn of Events

A thirty-year-old client came into my office for her weekly session and plopped down on the couch. She looked very satisfied—not her recent frame of mind. For months, she had been struggling with making decisions, the meaning of her life, and never having enough control over events— all serious but not unusual dilemmas. "I figured it out," she said proudly. "Life happens along the way." I've always liked her explanation.

No matter that individuals make deliberate, elaborate plans—life happens. This chapter offers characteristics of many normal and unusual events. I list the ways that individuals cope with life's predicaments, whether expected or shocking, normal or traumatic. Many traits are associated, not exclusively with personality, but with age, development, and decisions that we all must make in life.

Even when we cannot know the day of a toddler's first steps, puberty, or old age, we can make general guesses. We expect these events to happen, and we anticipate being able to cope with the changes as they present themselves. Trauma is the opposite. Trauma is a manmade event such as rape, assault, or war, or a natural disaster such as a storm or an earthquake. The event overwhelms the individual or community and sorely taxes the ability to cope. This chapter details some of life's stages, predictable occurrences, and traumatic events.

Stages of Psychosocial Development—Tasks of Life

Age	*Psychological/Social Task*

Birth–First Year   Trust vs. Mistrust

Trust is reliance on sameness and continuity of caretakers and one's self. The result, when trust outweighs mistrust, is the ability to hope.

Second Year   Autonomy vs. Shame and Doubt

Autonomy is gained from a sense of mastery of one's own body and good guidance by parents in making choices. The result, when autonomy outweighs shame, is the sense of mastery.

Third–Fifth Year   Initiative vs. Guilt

Initiative develops with the ability to regulate one's own body. The result, when initiative outweighs guilt, is the ability to cooperate.

Sixth Year–Puberty   Industry vs. Inferiority

Industry develops when a child successfully moves into the wider world.

Adolescence   Identity vs. Identity Diffusion

Identity develops as an adolescent interacts with self and others and begins to figure out: Who am I? and Who am I not?

Early Adulthood   Intimacy vs. Isolation

Relationships with others help create an identity and a place in the interpersonal world.

Middle Adulthood   Generativity vs. Self-Absorption

The ability to nurture others and one's self protects against self-absorption.

Later Adulthood   Integrity vs. Despair[1]

A life that has been led with authenticity and integrity buffers the losses of aging and death.

Birth Order

Whether an individual is the first, only, or tenth child, or one child of a multiple birth, the position influences his or her relation to parents and other brothers and sisters; i.e., the experience of being an only child vs. being the girl with six older brothers vs. being a triplet is significantly

---

[1] Erikson (1976).

different. Also, children born at different points in the family life cycle often have different traits; e.g., a child born when parents have more money or when a mother is depressed. In addition to the family cycle and numerical order, there is also a psychological position (e.g., a favored child or the only son or daughter)—all affect traits.

Traits of the First Born as an Adult

Identifies with parents; likes to be in authority
Disciplined
Good verbal skills
Protective of others
Wants admiration and respect
May appear arrogant; seeks reassurance
Failure is devastating
Finds it difficult to delegate (everyone is a little brother or sister)
High achiever, can lead to ➔ being driven
Tries hard, can lead to ➔ pessimism
Nurturing, can lead to ➔ being overcommitted
Responsible, can lead to ➔ perfectionism or being a worrier
   ➔ Most suicides[2]

Traits of the Only Child as an Adult

Similar to the oldest child
May remain childlike into adulthood
Has high self-esteem
Not used to competition, fears, or failure
Does well in school; good verbal skills
Identifies strongly with parent of same gender
High achiever; expects a lot from life
Has missed having playmates in the family
Lacks negotiation skills
May have trouble with partner when it comes to sharing control
Wants perfection; has trouble settling for less than excellence
Stressed by social situations
Good at using his or her imagination
Males are most likely of all birth positions to remain single[3]

---

[2] ibid.
[3] ibid.

Traits of the Middle Born as a Child and as an Adult

Becomes family mediator

Fewest pictures in the family album

Trouble developing distinctive traits

May be confused about identity

May feel that life is unfair

Not raised feeling special like the oldest or the youngest

Does well in marriage; loyal

Can be secretive

Social and popular

Avoids conflict; does well as a friend, knows how to get along, and can share

Peacemaker or mediator role can become excessive; tries to make everyone happy

Personality is greatly influenced by siblings

Wants to be first ➔ may become competitive or self-destructive[4]

Traits of the Last Born as a Child and as an Adult

Used to a lot of attention; pampered

Had fewer parental expectations and less discipline

Parents were more relaxed

Rules have less meaning; may lack discipline in personal life

May manipulate others to get what he or she wants

Lighthearted; charming

Looks to others for answers; others have broken the ice

Dependent on others; difficult to be self-sufficient

Less career oriented than other birth positions

Great stimulation can lead to extraordinary development

Attracted to creative arts

More likely to follow than to lead[5]

Traits of Twins Throughout Life

Multiple births are a more common occurrence these days because of new techniques of fertilization.

Order of birth, even a few minutes, dictates birth traits of birth order

Usually last born into family

---

[4] ibid.
[5] ibid.

May develop slower than single births

Parents are inconsistent because of the time involved in caring for two

Rely heavily on each other

Fraternal twins may seem more like ordinary siblings than identical twins

Have a great need for closeness and trouble with separations

More well rounded as adults if raised as individuals

May bitterly compete with each other

May have secret language

People born as one sibling in a multiple birth experience attention from others that they attribute to a strange circumstance of birth rather than to any unique quality in themselves. Entering restaurants, going to parties, or walking down the street with the rest of the family draws attention that other people do not experience. They are referred to as "the triplets," and others, often eager to see them as separate individuals, prematurely assign identities to them (e.g., the smart one and the sweet one) and so they feel locked in. Children who have many brothers and sisters may also feel labeled (e.g., "the boys") but they do not have to deal with the "freaky" experience of multiples.

Technology and health care have increased women's ability to have healthy children, and today we expect all our newborns to live. But it was only at the beginning of the 1900s that the highest mortality rates were for women of childbearing age and infants. Reactions to the death of a child are among the most painful and severe of family tragedies.

Stages of Parents' Reactions to the Death of a Child

Early Reactions →	Shock, numbness, physical pain
Disorganization →	Disbelief, inability to concentrate, poor functioning, strong emotions such as anger, sadness, despair, hopelessness
Holding On/Letting Go →	Many memories, reality sets in, daily thoughts, high emotions
Reorganization →	Loss is integrated into ongoing life, memorials, good days exist again

Mourning may never completely end for parents who have suffered through the death of a child.

Friendship Throughout Life

Friendship Traits—Young Children

Focus on common activities; e.g., "We play"

Concrete reciprocities; e.g., "I give him candy, he gives me gum"

Early friends are often based on similarities in social skills

Boys are attracted by similarity in physical activity

Girls are attracted by similarity in attractiveness of personality and social network[6]

Friendship Traits—Middle Childhood

Focus is on understanding; e.g., "A friend is someone who likes you and doesn't hit you"

Loyal and trustworthy

Spend time together

Share interests and share secrets

Similar in social behaviors

Friends are very important and occupy much time[7]

Friendship Traits—Adolescence

Focus on support, dependability, understanding, and acceptance

Reciprocity in intimacy, confidence, and trust

Share interests, experiences, activities, and communication

Similar in aspirations, school-related attitudes, and achievement

Socializing

Support in transition to school, puberty, and dating

Friends are very important and occupy much time (29 percent awake time)[8]

Friendship Traits—Adulthood

Reciprocity in intimacy, confidence, and trust

Look for similarities, ease of communication, experiences, and interests

---

[6] Hartup and Stevens (1997).

[7] ibid.

[8] ibid.

Social and work relationships blend

Husbands and wives share friends

Friends are closely tied to family activities

Support in transitions of marriage, work, childbearing, and family
concerns[9]

Friendship Traits—Old Age

Reciprocity in intimacy, confidence, and trust

Less doing and more letters, favors, phone calls, gifts, and expressions of respect

Support in transitions of retirement, illness, aging, and death[10]

Negative Traits in Friendships of All Ages

Friends encourage negative behaviors

Friends socialize for destructive reasons

Friends engage in destructive activities

Power outstrips negotiation

Competition outweighs cooperation

Influence is out of balance; one is always the follower

No one is allowed to grow beyond the confines of friendship

Conflicts overshadow support[11]

Crises of Adolescence

Adolescent Tasks of Development

Specific traits of children and adolescents at different ages are listed in chapter three. The general tasks of adolescence are outlined below and, following that broad list, some events are described that will complicate the work of growing up.

Adjusts to the physical changes of puberty

Adjusts to the emotional changes of puberty

Establishes effective social relationships

Establishes working relationships with peers

Achieves independence from parents

Prepares for a vocation (see chapter ten for stages of career choice)

Moves toward a sense of values

---

[9] ibid.

[10] ibid.

[11] ibid.

Develops a secure identity, including a sexual identity and a positive sense of self

Coping Strategies of Gay Adolescents

Denial	Denies sexual orientation
Repair	Tries to abolish homosexual feelings and behaviors
Redefinition	Sees behaviors as "just a stage"
Avoidance	Stops behaviors; limits exposure to individuals of the same sex
	Avoids information that might confirm homosexual fears
	Tries heterosexual relationships; becomes antigay
	Avoids facing knowledge through substance abuse
Acceptance	Comes to terms with sexual orientation[12]

Additional Difficulties for an Adolescent Who Is Gay

Some adolescents have none of these problems; others have many of them.

Needs to distance self from peers because they fear that closeness will be misunderstood

Makes sexual contacts without any accompanying social interaction (more likely for males than for females)

Fears rejection from family

Withdraws emotionally from family to minimize possible rejection

Parents threaten abandonment

Parents persuade the adolescent to recant his or her sexual orientation

Forced into therapy to "fix" the sexual preference

Feels guilty or sinful

Sees few role models of lifelong gay relationships

Has few opportunities to learn how to manage sexuality in a positive manner

Feels depressed or hopeless as a result of the barrage of negative attitudes

Becomes truant or drops out of school

Uses alcohol and drugs to numb anxiety and depression[13]

---

[12] Radkowsky and Siegel (1997).
[13] ibid.

Teenage Parents

Teenagers want to become parents to solve problems of wanting love or feeling important. Instead, they create more difficulties for themselves. They face parenting responsibilities, educational and economic instability, family pressures, lack of direction in life, and little support from religion or community.

Traits of Teenage Mothers

Birth rates for teenage women are considerably lower in the 1990s than in most of the twentieth century, but today's young women fair badly economically and emotionally.

Poor and unmarried (75 percent)

Lowered costs of early motherhood because they are alienated from school, have models of unmarried parents, or lack opportunities for career

Little time to individuate and grow; e.g., date, school, work

Lack emotional support and stability; child provides love and closeness

Earlier sexual experiences than women who have children later in life

Poorer psychological functioning; more health problems

Lower levels of marital stability

Additional nonmarital births and more children

Less stable employment, greater welfare use[14]

Traits of Teenage Fathers

Two to three years older than teenaged mothers

Poor

Low education

Work hard early, but have poorer long-term prospects because of education deficits

Provide weak financial child support

Remain involved with children, although not living with the child's mother[15]

---

[14] Coley and Chase-Lansdale (1998).
[15] ibid.

Postpartum Blues

This is the name for a mother's depression that occurs after giving birth to a child. Seventy-five percent of new mothers feel let down in the early weeks after giving birth, but ten to twenty percent suffer severe symptoms.

Occurs in the months following the birth and symptoms can last as long as a year

Whatever the mother's problems were before, they are magnified many times

Fear, panic, and dizziness

Depression

Guilt because the mother thinks she ought to be happy

May result from emotional problems, hormones, role changes, marital problems, or stress

➜ Can reach psychotic proportions with delusions and hallucinations

➜ Can result in infant murder[16]

Transitions

Transitions are periods of discontinuity, when people move from one time of life to another. Some transitions are smooth (high school graduation); most have bumps (marriage). Occasionally, the transition erupts into a full-blown crisis or positive transformation (midlife).

Types of Transitions

Area of Life	Transition Experience (Examples of Life Events)
Personal/Self	Identity crisis, periods of personal development, pursuit of solitary hobbies, times of loneliness, times of freedom
Personal/Family	Decisions about marrying and children, worries about performance as a spouse, empty nest
Personal/Health	Personal illness or injury; adjustment to a physical handicap or recovery from illness (e.g., heart attack, or mastectomy)
Personal/Work	Career decisions, retirement, career changes such as an athlete or homemaker might make, career plateaus or shifts

---

[16] DeAngelis (1997).

Personal/Economics	Financial problems, gambling losses, lottery winnings, inheritance
Interpersonal/Self	Disagreements with friends, breakup of love affair or friendship, meeting new people, travel
Interpersonal/ Family	Marriage or marital problems, joys and troubles being a parent, blended families, aging parents, siblings with problems
Interpersonal/ Health	Sickness or death of family member
Interpersonal/Work	Relationships with boss and subordinates, concerns about a friend or family member's work
Interpersonal/ Economics	Financial problems of friend or family
Community/Self	Public award or recognition, public disgrace, arrest and/or conviction of a crime.
Community/Family	School and plant closings, changes in local laws
Community/Health	Epidemics, contamination of water supply, disaster, hazardous wastes
Community/Work	Public recognition of work, public business failure, running for office
Community/ Economics	Concern about economic policies, taxes, housing[17]

Young Adulthood

Post-traumatic stress disorder can be a result of trauma and has been documented regularly after war, assault, or disaster.

Traits of Relationships With Parents

The twenties are marked by making peace with parents and finding new ways to stay connected. Adults in their early twenties still lean on parents. Late twenties are doing more on their own.

Immature Twenties

Emotional bond with parents
Overwhelmed by intense feelings of rage or dependency
Lash out at parents
Seek to avoid disapproval or anger

---

[17] Schlossberg (1984).

Sees parents in black-and-white terms
Cannot see parents as individuals
Parents involved in minute details
   or
Estranged from parents
Little interest in parents[18]

Mature Twenties

Has an emotional bond with parents
Can discuss feelings
Has strong confidence in own abilities to make decisions
Feels in control of emotional responses to parents
See themselves as best judges
Can risk parents' disapproval
Sees complexities of parents' lives
Can draw a clear line between own lives and lives of parents
Feel proud of parents as role models[19]

Four Patterns of Relating to Parents

Competent and connected (more women than men)
      independent views
      feels empathy
      understand shortcomings
Dependent (more women than men)
      emotionally trapped by parents
      engages in power struggles
Individuated (more men than women)
      feels respected
      enjoys company but maintains distance
      clear boundaries
False autonomy (more men than women)
      pretends indifference
      avoids parents
      resentful and contemptuous[20]

---

[18] Frank, Avery, and Laman (1988); White, Speisman, and Costas (1983).
[19] ibid.
[20] Frank, Avery, and Laman (1988).

Constructing a Family
Adoption

Two to four percent of all families in the United States adopt a child. Many more must deal with infertility and make decisions about adoption.

Traits of Adoptive Parents

Have to grieve infertility

Overvalue the child

Wonder which traits are environment and which are heredity

Early on they fear the return of the birth mother

Normal questions like "Who does she look like to you?" take on
 additional meaning

Traits of Infertile Couples

Difficulty talking about the problem together

Negative, secret thoughts; e.g., "Should I leave him or her?"

Feeling less feminine or less masculine

Before Adoption Process

Loss of dream; terrible disappointment

Shock and denial

Protest and concentration on all methods of pregnancy; sexual
 pressures

Despair when methods fail

Feelings of inadequacy, guilt, or blame; e.g., "If only I started trying
 earlier"

Routine is disrupted

Tears, anger, and confusion

Develop different relationship with his or her own body

Loss of control; e.g., the assumption that one has a choice about
 whether or not to produce a child

Changed attitudes about family

Trauma of deprivation; e.g., difficult to see other babies or go to baby
 showers

Must resolve conflicts and fears

Deciding to Adopt

Loneliness

Painful

Bombarded by other people wanting to solve the problem

Confronts own feelings of inclusion or exclusion; e.g., "Only a baby from my religion"

Tells the family and friends

Women accept the loss of pregnancy

Husband and wife adjust to the loss of biological continuity

During Adoption Process

Rarely enjoy the full celebration; e.g., baby shower (attended to during pregnancy)

Too much or too little time to prepare vs. nine months

Society values biological ties

Mourn the idealized, imagined biological child that "looks like me"

Going public with the decision; hearing horror stories

Reaching out into the community

Decisions about public or private adoption

Involving strangers and public scrutiny (lawyers, adoption personnel in private life)

Judgments made about person; e.g., age, health, income, and marital stability

Anxiety; e.g., "How do we measure up?"

Sometimes rejected by birth mother

After Adoption Takes Place

Satisfaction at passing all the tests

Relief; accomplishment

Joy of becoming parents

Highly valuing the child

Underlying knowledge of grieving birth parents somewhere

Aware of the promise made in adoption of another person's child; "If they knew how wonderful she is . . ."

Begin to emotionally claim the child

Just like all parents, must accept the child as he or she is: "But I don't know what is inherited and what is a result of my parenting"

Caution in interpreting behavior (especially unattractive actions) as hereditary[21]

---

[21] Rosenberg (1992).

Traits of Adoptees
More women than men search for biological parent
Wonders "why was I given up?"
No medical history
No biological family
Tends to search for biological parents after leaving parents' home

Disability
Families With Disabled Child
All members suffer loss
Family ways are disrupted; old ways must be changed
Individuals go through stages: denial, anger, depression, and
    adjustment
Emotions depend on extent and type of disability; i.e., Can child . . .?
Members ride an emotional roller coaster, depending on present
    state of disabled member
Some families find previously unknown resilience
Disabled child may feel the need to please the parents
Parents often expect less from disabled child
Sibling of disabled child may feel guilt for being normal
Siblings try not to cause trouble
20—30 percent of disabled children experience emotional or behav-
    ioral problems; increased stress on all members
Many families become enmeshed, overprotective, or rigid
Some families are unable to resolve conflicts
Some parents involve disabled child in their disagreements

Immigrant Styles of Family Life
Coping Traits of Immigrant Families
Children adjust to values and styles of host country faster than parents
Parents often cling to styles and norms of original culture
Different adjustment rates cause family clashes

Three Types of Family Adjustment
"Kangaroo"
Keeps offspring in a "pouch"
Protect the children in the family pouch
Preserve original culture

See new culture as a threat to children
Preserve original language, dress, and style
Remain segregated
Experience low stress because there is little involvement with outside
Community agrees and supports kangaroo style
Parents maintain confidence and consistency
Children who stray into new culture are guilty of betrayal
Children who identify with new culture risk estrangement and
   scapegoating
Kangaroo works best when new country is undesirable

"Cuckoo"

Raises offspring in the nests of other birds
Rapid assimilation of children into new country
Family disqualifies itself as power
Children are entrusted to formal and informal socialization; e.g.,
   boarding school
Parents maintain old ways
Parents often come to resent new influences
Children later search for lost connections between present and past
Children risk neglect by both parents and society
Family risks cohesion, continuity of generations, and cultural past
Cuckoo works best when new country is seen as better than old

"Chameleon"

Changes color depending on environment
Parents encourage children to live peacefully in both cultures
Children behave and dress like others outside the home
Children may speak original language, or behave differently in home
Family desires to understand new country in order to adjust
Parents allow children to explore values and behaviors of new country
Parents do not expect to change very much
Children learn to negotiate between two worlds
Family maintains contact with old ways
Family maintains cohesion and continuity
Children do not have to choose
Family risks opening up cultural/belief/value/behavior gaps that
   cannot be bridged

Chameleon works best when new country has positive advantages and differences are minor[22]

One of the certainties of life is that, sooner or later, we will deal with loss. It is ironic that the most predictable aspect of life is also one of the most tragic. Losses are not only in the physical world. Some of the most devastating losses are those that occur emotionally, such as betrayal or loss of love. There are many types of losses: illness or injury to the body; loss of material possessions such as a home, jewelry, or money; the separation from, or death of, a loved person; developmental losses such as aging; the loss of an abstraction that has meaning, such as one's homeland; and even an aspect of one's self, such as when we turn out to be people we did not expect to become.

The following chart illustrates the stages of bereavement and the adaptation to the death of a loved one.

Impact (Short Lasting)	Disorganization	Reorganization
Hearing the news	Struggles with changes in roles	Loss is less consuming
Shock, numbness	Family disruptions	Returns to normal activities
Disbelief	Social and economic change	New activities
	Strong waves of emotion	Emotions continue abated
	Anger, sadness, confusion	Well-being returns

People always wonder, "When will I get over the loss?" Never. We go through losses and come out somewhat changed on the other side. We are formed by all our experiences, good and bad, and losses become integrated into our ongoing personalities and into our lives. Many creative people integrate their losses into their work; for example, writers, artists, and sculptors. Creative works are healthy channels to continue to deal with losses. Less artistic people often create memorials, such as charities or scholarships, to commemorate loved ones.[23]

---

[22] Strier (1996).
[23] Edelstein (1984).

Death in the Family

Children's reactions to death depend on age, mental development, personality, life stage, and family influences. The following chart lists reactions by age and development.

Age	Mental Development
0—2	Infants have no concept of death, therefore
	Infants responses are to loss of care, attention, attachment, response
	Infants can respond to parent's grief and feel the isolation, withdrawal, self-absorption, and intense emotion of the adult
3—5	Children conceptualize death as similar to sleep
	Can remember the image of the person
	Think of death as temporary; "I *know* Papa is dead, but when is he coming to visit?"
	Children blur fantasy and fact: "Mom is watching over you" results in the child looking at the clouds for a glimpse of Mom
5—6	Children begin to understand death with loss of a pet
	Still believe that death can be escaped if you are quick
	Life is attributed to organic things; e.g., trees or rocks
7 plus	Understand finality of death
9 plus	Understand that functions cease
	May be less emotional and less responsive than nine to eleven year olds
12 plus	Understanding is similar to adult knowledge
	All things die; life ends
	One's own life eventually ends
	Grieves and shows emotions more like an adult than like a child

Influences on Grief and Bereavement

Personality dictates how feelings will be experienced and displayed. If a person (child or adult) is rigid, sadness will be constricted; if a person is flamboyant, expression of emotion may be quite colorful.

Age and Life Stage—Children express emotions differently at different ages, just as they catch a ball differently. Whereas an adult who hears about the death of a loved one is likely to cry, it is rare for a child under the age of five to weep. Children may seem to lose interest in the death, even of a parent. Don't be deceived by the behavior: The impact is huge and long lasting.

Family Influences—Values and behavior of family members influence adult, child, and adolescent behavior. Families often unknowingly dictate behavior during a crisis. If a child gets the message that everyone is being stoic, he or she will attempt to be silently brave. If Mother faints each time a question is asked, the questions will stop. If an adult must make plans and care for other people's feelings, personal emotions may be intense but behavior will have to be normal.

Stages of Men's Adult Development[24]

Early Adult Transition	*(ages 17—22)*

Bridge to early adulthood; begins adulthood; begins to make adult choices; still vulnerable and immature.

Early Adulthood	*(ages 18—45)*

Peak of biological functioning (twenty to forty); at young end, maximum height, strength, sexual capability, and biological vigor are evident; at older end, visible cosmetic changes (paunch, balding, wrinkles) become apparent but health and capacity remain high; makes major choices in life (e.g., marriage, occupation, residence, style of life); personally, grows from novice lover, husband, worker, and father to responsibility of burdens and being senior; relationships with parents change from son to equal. Relationships with children change (e.g., some empty nesting, youth sees him as senior), burdens of family life peak with children, and financial worries, and then begin to decrease.

Midlife Transition	*(ages 40—45)*

Terminates early adulthood; crucial developmental change, unmarked by any one particular event. Contributions to midlife transition and/or crisis are:
Subtle changes in biology
Declines in quickness, strength, and endurance
Subtle changes in psychology
Loss of youth, alienation, stagnation

---

[24] Levinson et al. (1978).

Faces personal mortality—knowledge that life ends; asks profound question, "What have I accomplished?" Examines fulfilled and frustrated dreams; reappraises life; often, an event that would have passed in another time changes his life course; seen by others as older ("Dad" not "buddy").

Middle Adulthood   (ages 45—60)

Positive outcome to the midlife transition is stability with increased qualities of wisdom, maturity, and reflection.

Late Adult Transition   (ages 60—65)

May be precipitated by retirement; notices bodily decline; must end old ways and modify earlier life structure.

Later Adulthood   (ages 65—80)

Frequency of illness and death of contemporaries; may be pushed out at work by younger generation as out of step; finds new balance of self with society; task of these years is to enhance integrity of life as a whole; makes peace with self and with world.

Old Age   (ages 80pl)

Often dealing with chronic illness; territory of life shrinks in size; makes peace with dying; ultimate involvement is with self.

Stages of Women's Adult Development
Early Adult Transition   (ages 17—22)

Bridge to early adulthood; identity is shaped by relationships and vice versa; worries about both career choices and relationship choices; vulnerable and immature.

Early Adulthood   (ages 18—45)

At early end, biological vigor; at late end, visible cosmetic changes become apparent but health and capacity remain high; makes major choices in life (e.g., marriage, occupation, residence, style of life). Personally, spends much time in relationship to others; e.g., husband or partner, parenting, or being a daughter and a friend. Stress from balancing work and relationships.

Midlife Transition	*(ages 40—45)*

Terminates early adulthood; crucial developmental change, begun less by age than by time of life and what events have transpired (e.g., early child-bearing vs. late, early career vs. late). Contributions to midlife transition and/or crisis include: Biological change, including menopause; facing personal mortality, which is the knowledge that life ends. Accepts the passing of youth. Asks "What have I accomplished?" Examines fulfilled and frustrated dreams; reappraises life. Simplifies life and begins a return to an authentic self, too often lost in lives filled with attention to others.[25]

Middle Adulthood	*(ages 45—60)*

Either feels stuck and continues the path of life that has been followed, or has used the transition to redirect her life in ways that make more sense; accepts changing relationships with children; attends to own interests. May need to care for aging parents.

Later Adulthood	*(ages 65—80)*

Frequency of illness and death of contemporaries; may be pushed out at work by younger generation as out of step; finds new balance of self with society; task of these years is to enhance integrity of life as a whole and make peace with self and with world.

Old Age	*(ages 80pl)*

Often dealing with chronic illness; territory of life shrinks in size; makes peace with dying. Ultimate involvement is with self.

Aging

Traits in later life can be viewed as a mix of character (personality, traits, internal structure), social context (life events), and the changes over time of both character and context. Many people don't change very much as they age. Many people become "more of" whatever they have always been. A forty-year-old woman who has been busy, inflexible, and emotionally restricted all her adult life becomes, in old age, less busy due to physical impairments. Therefore, we see more of her inflexible personality, less tempered by activities. We also see that she becomes increasingly emotionally restricted because she had no

---

[25] Edelstein (1999).

practice behaving differently, and now it is too difficult to change. A woman who has been able to adjust to change through middle adulthood is better able to withstand the losses and declines of aging.

New Traits in the Elderly Emerge When

Bad, damaging childhoods that were covered over lose the cover

Earlier protections are gone

Carefully constructed life patterns that promoted security in earlier days are dismantled

They never learned adult skills that allow change and growth, so they become stuck

They never learned to adapt to change

Choices made in earlier adulthood were limiting and defeating, so in later years they have little to rest on

Never took advantage of intimacy, parenting, work skills, or engagement with social/political/religious opportunities

People are still dependent on early traumas, conflicts, or psychological injuries

Strengths and internal resources were not built

Losses cannot be replaced with satisfying substitutions

Self-image changes based on having to accommodate to the environment rather than changing the environment

Problems for an Older Woman Arise From Her Balance of

Autonomy and dependency

Self vs. others

Problems for an Older Man Arises From

Need to be caring vs. need to assert himself without destroying others

Anorexia, a disorder that we generally associate with young women, has been documented in the elderly. A report from Great Britain describes six cases, all individuals over sixty-five years old, men and women, who suffered from self-inflicted low body weight. Some of them had episodes of anorexia beginning in youth; others suffered only in their later years. The symptoms were food avoidance, conviction that they were fat, fear of weight gain, and some laxative abuse.[26]

---

[26] Wills and Olivieri (1998).

Mother-in-Law

Favorite target in folklore

Myths

Jealous of son's wife

Wicked

Possessive

Domineering

Manipulative

Fears are based on nonblood "mother" who represents all bad feelings (anger, resentment) felt toward one's own mother

Realities

Mother-in-law and daughter-in-law value family

Women feel the need to keep connections

Maintains family ties; "kinkeepers"

Maintains emotional closeness because greater distances loosen relationships

Potential Problems

Both women have dreams and expectations of each other

Both may be satisfied or disappointed

Both want to be good enough

Both worry about making a good impression

Different generations mean changed lifestyles, sexual behavior, customs, sense of power, and/or aggression

May be different in culture, religion, or economics

Daughter-in-law has concerns about passing the test

Differences in personality, warmth, privacy, and behaviors

Daughter-in-law may have unresolved mother issues

Mother-in-law may have no experience with a daughter, may fear losing a son

(also see Naomi and Ruth from the Bible)[27]

Grandparents

Grandparents in the 1880s were always old, with "silver hair" and "dimming eyes," but today more people live long enough to become grandparents. We see a vast age range and a variety of roles. The

---

[27] Arnstein (1985).

average person becomes a grandparent at midlife and may spend as much as four decades in the role. And, with increased divorce, there are also stepgrandparents.

Young Grandmother (25—38 years old)

Because there are many young mothers, there are grandmothers as young as twenty-five years old

Too many roles to carry

Probably still an active mother, a working woman, and wants to have a life

Fears looking old to others; unready for role

May refuse to engage in traditional grandmother role

Easy to fall in the middle between own child and grandchild

Traits Common to Either Grandmother or Grandfather

Often sticks to safe topics; e.g., a "demilitarized zone"

Avoids unsafe topics; e.g., sex, race, or areas of social change

Role depends on health, money, and relationship with own child, as well as personality

Provides stabilizing force in lives of children and grandchildren

Provides buffer against mortality for own children

Mitigate the aloneness of their aging children

Catalyst for family cohesion; e.g., the "excuse" for people to get together

Softens the intensity of modern life

Interprets their child to their grandchild

Mediates for family members

Symbolizes connection across lifetimes

Has time to listen to children and grandchildren

Link to known and unknown past

Always in reserve if help is needed[28]

Traits That Differ Between Grandmother and Grandfather

Grandmother	Grandfather
Attends to interpersonal relations	Attends to tasks
Talks about friendships and family	Talks about education, job, and money

---

[28] Hagestad (1985).

Talks about practical issues	Talks about practical issues
Treats granddaughter and grandson similarly	Concentrates attention on grandsons
Organizes family gatherings	Acts as an advisor, particularly to grandsons
Most involved with daughter's daughter	Most involved with son's son
Sees continuity of life roles	Sees discontinuity of life roles

Six Types of Grandparents
1. Formal
Follow what they regard as proper role

Maintain clearly defined roles

Babysit and indulge grandchildren occasionally

Do not offer advice on parenting

Maintain constant interest in child and grandchild

Want children to have good manners, to be neat and clean, and to be self-controlled

2. Hedonistic
Wants freedom from family responsibilities

No longer interested in being of service to family

Sees grandchildren as nuisances

Grandchildren compete for precious time that could be used for pleasure

Marks a breakdown of the family[29]

3. Fun Seeker
Informal and fun relationship

Joins the child in activities for pleasure

Grandchildren are a source of leisure activity

Authority lines are blurred

Wants the grandchildren to also have fun, making an implicit demand

Wants grandchildren to be happy and get along with others

---

[29] Gutmann (1985).

4. Distant

Emerges for holidays
Contact is fleeting and infrequent
Benevolent but remote

5. Surrogate Parent

Grandmothers usually
Actually takes care of the grandchild in absence of mother
Want grandchildren to try hard, to obey parents, to be good students,
and to behave

6. Wise

Grandfather usually
Authoritarian relationship where skill and wisdom are dispensed
Positions are clear between generations
Children and grandchildren are deferential
Wants grandchildren to be honest, to have good common sense, and
to be responsible[30]

Post-Traumatic Stress Disorder

The term *shell shock* used during World War II was a forerunner of understanding post-traumatic stress disorder. Individuals develop characteristic symptoms after they have experienced a severe trauma. Usually the trauma entails an experience in which the individual witnessed or experienced an event that involved actual death, the threat of death, or severe harm to himself or herself or to another person. A variation of the trauma is learning about the event rather than witnessing it firsthand. Almost always, the person reacts with terrific fear, horror, and helplessness. The most common events that induce this disorder are war and military action; violent personal assault; disasters, whether natural or manmade; accidents; and contracting a life-threatening illness.

Traits of Post-Traumatic Stress Disorder

Flashbacks or reexperiencing of the trauma; e.g., reliving a rape
Terrible dreams
Memories; e.g., visions of war or torture

---

[30] McCready (1985).

Triggers that symbolize or jog a memory of the trauma; e.g., explosion or being followed

Sights, sounds, or smells can trigger reactions; e.g., a song that was playing or the smell of popcorn before an attack

Avoidance of anything associated with the trauma; e.g., the building, street, activity, or people

Memory loss around specifics of the event

Isolated feelings and behaviors; detached (i.e., company of others is painful)

Diminished feelings and emotions; e.g., flat speech, little happiness or sadness, or numbness

Preoccupation with death

Hypervigilant; e.g., always watching and alert

Trouble sleeping

Difficulty concentrating; e.g., mind wanders so work suffers or not paying attention

Jumpiness

Anger, irritability, and easy frustration

Often people refuse to acknowledge or discuss the event so providing help is difficult

Impaired personal relationships because of these symptoms

Trauma is not always an experience of only one person. When a flood, tornado, or other disaster strikes an entire community, trauma and recovery are a collectively shared process.

Traits of Collective Trauma

Loss of community

Loss of ordinary life; e.g., seeing your neighbor or shopping at the neighborhood store

People leave after disasters

Everyone is in the same boat; sympathy, but each is suffering and cannot help others

Difficult to express the sense of loss

Words do not adequately cover the immense nature of the loss

Euphoria at surviving can set in right after the disaster

Early reaction is shock and numbness

Disorientation (confusion, distraction, perplexity) lasts for months
and even years

Feelings of apathy set in

Insomnia can last for weeks; sleep brings nightmares

Depression sets in after shock wears off

Loneliness

Marriages may have trouble; sexual desire may decrease; absorption
in own problems

The old community is idealized

Vulnerability heightened

Loss of feeling safe

Others can share the experiences

Other people understand; group experiences can heal

Most survivors do not have long-term problems[31]

Genocides induce collective trauma of massive proportions. There
have been slaughters in Europe during the Holocaust, and more recently in Central America, Africa, and Bosnia.

Survivors of Holocausts, Strengths
Ability to rally and go on

Willing to work and flexible about types of work

Quick adjustment; astounding resilience

Deep connections to family and relatives

Sensitivity to others; concerned

High functioning

High self-worth

Altruistic

Flexible

Tenacious

Survivors of Holocausts, Problems
Post-traumatic stress disorder

Pervasive depressed mood

Morose; defeated

Guilt for surviving

---

[31] Erikson (1976).

Bodily complaints
Anxiety
Fears of new persecutions
Silent about events
Pessimistic
Never safe from sorrow[32]

---

[32] Whiteman (1993).

Physical Disorders

T he strong and influential relationship between mind and body has become increasingly appreciated, even trendy. Physical problems shape personality, influence behavior, and may have grave psychological consequences. The reverse is also true. Psychological or emotional problems are often displayed through the body.

This chapter includes certain neurological disorders (e.g., amnesia), other disorders that blend psychological and physical difficulties (e.g., substance abuse), and problems that are psychological in origin but have physical consequences (e.g., eating disorders and sexual disorders, malingering, psychogenic amnesia, and dissociation).

Remembering and Forgetting

Remembering and forgetting is taken for granted, like breathing. Only when there are problems in these areas do we recognize the power of memory. Memory means that I recognize my children and remember our muddy hike in the rain forest as well as the hundreds of family stories that are served as expected along with our traditional Thanksgiving foods. Memory for someone else may also include trauma and abuse. What moments are remembered and what events are forgotten create the fabric of mystery and tragedy. To be disbelieved is to shatter our confidence, and to forget is to lose our own experiences.

Amnesia

Amnesia is a (usually) long-term memory disorder due to brain damage (e.g., virus, physical trauma, alcohol, or a tumor). See *Psychogenic Amnesia* (page 218) for psychologically based amnesia.

Intact I.Q.

Selective impairment; not all areas of memory are damaged

Intact short-term memory storage; e.g., can have conversations and remember the present

Impaired delayed memory, e.g., has lost the past

Logical memory impaired

Recognition may be impaired

Can be temporary or permanent[1]

Other Types of Amnesia

Confabulation

Physical, not psychologically based

Brain damage in frontal lobe; e.g., accident or injury

Makes up fantastic recollections

No one believes the story except the person telling it

Dissociative Amnesia

Breakdown in identity

Forgets specific sets of events, but can remember everything else

May be events that are too embarrassing to remember or too painful; e.g., combat related

No physical trauma to the brain; psychological in nature

Reversible[2]

Fugue

Fugue is notable because the person is usually found in a new location, away from home, usually engaged in purposeful activity.

Identified when the person "comes to"

Loss of personal identity

Adopts new identity

Unaware that anything is wrong; psychologically induced

---

[1] Parkin (1997).
[2] Grinker and Spiegel (1945); Janet (1904) was the first to document cases.

Can last for days or years

After fugue, the original identity resumes and the fugue period is
lost

Korsakoff's Syndrome

Due to long-term alcohol abuse or gross thiamine deficiency; this disorder has been seen in prisoners of wars as a result of their diets.

Amnesia (see page 217)

Ataxia—jerking or irregular movements

Gross confusion

Visual abnormalities

Profound memory disorder; e.g., incapable of learning new
information[3]

Psychogenic Amnesia

No brain damage or physical pathology

Psychological cause rather than physical; e.g., witness to brutality

Transient Global Amnesia

Sudden onset of amnesia for a recent period; e.g., the previous month
or year

The attack of amnesia is short, lasting five minutes to several days

Cannot hold new information

Asks same questions over and over

Disoriented about time

No loss of identity

No other impairment

May be precipitated by a change in temperature; e.g., cold shower

Also precipitated by physical stress, eating a large meal, or
intercourse[4]

Dementia Is Another Cause of Forgetting
Dementia

Cognitive deficits and memory impairment

Often progressive and irreversible

Aphasia—impaired language; e.g., cannot name objects

---

[3] Talland (1965); Parkin (1997).
[4] Parkin (1997).

Apraxia—impaired motor abilities, seen in trouble eating, dressing, cooking, etc.

Agnosia—inability to recognize and identify familiar objects and people

Trouble planning and initiating activity

Unable to recall previous events

May have difficulty acquiring new information

May show poor judgment

May be unaware of impairment

There are different causes of Dementia and many have distinguishing traits. The following list includes the types and specific characteristics that can be added to the previous list.

Alzheimer's

Alzheimer's disease is the most common cause of dementia in the United States.

Gradual onset

Slow and progressive; moves through predictable stages

May include personality changes

Slight genetic component, especially early onset

No foolproof tests exist; it is diagnosed by ruling out other causes

Huntington's Disease

Huntington's is an inherited, progressive, degenerative disease of cognition, emotion, and movement.

Twitching and tremors

Lurching gait

Explosive speech

Depression

HIV

Forgetfulness

Slowness and apathy

Social withdrawal

Tremor and loss of balance

        brain injury

        substance abuse

Did you know?
Delusions are primary in some types of dementia.

Other Causes of Dementia
Dissociation
Head trauma
Multiple personality disorder
Pick's disease
Parkinson's disease
Vitamin deficiency

Recovered Memories: True vs. False Memories

There have been bitter debates in psychology about the validity of re-covered memories. News stories have carried accounts, and the courts are processing lawsuits based on later recall of childhood events. Memory plays a vital importance in stories; here are some facts.

False Memories

False memories are events that never occurred. Specifically, an individual has a belief about the past that is *experienced as a memory*, but it never happened. How false memories are created is not only a way to enhance a character, but it is also a novel method of manipulating readers.

How to Plant False Memories

Association—When people are presented with a list of happenings, characters, or words (for example, *nurse, sick person, ambulance, lawyer, medicine bottles,* but not *doctor*) their recall may include *doctor* because it is natural to associate *doctor* with the other words on the list.

Mixing—When people are given unknown (made-up) names that are later mixed in with well-known names, they may assume the unknown name is a person who is well known; for example, " I enjoy those women writers, especially Jane Austen, Virginia Woolf, Abigail Bronk, and Lillian Hellman."

Retelling—People retell stories and drop out certain details that they were given and add others that are more consistent with their own experiences. This is idiosyncratic; i.e., based on the content of someone's experience. For example, a four-year-old city boy hearing the story of the "Boy Who Cried Wolf" might repeat the tale with a big animal and a child calling "Mom!"

Post-event Information—After a genuine event occurs, another person can introduce elements into the remembering which will be recalled as fact. For example, Ben and Tom see an auto accident. The police officer interviewing Ben later asks, "Did the car stop at the stop sign?" (there was no stop sign). Later, Ben will have more difficulty and less accuracy than Tom in recalling whether there was a stop sign. Reports of events can be distorted by misleading information given after the event took place.[5]

Implantation—A psychology experiment convinced a fourteen-year-old boy that he had been lost in the mall at a young age. His older brother, a researcher, told him a series of stories about his childhood, all of which were correct except for getting lost in the mall. Asked to recall the stories, initially the fourteen-year-old did not remember the fictitious event, but after five days, the boy began to generate memories of the event. Weeks later, asked to recall and rate his memories on vividness and accuracy, the mall story came out ranked very high. People can construct memory reports for entire events that never occurred, and these reports can be very convincing.[6]

Differences between true memories and false memories are hard to detect and the rules are unreliable. Here are a few guidelines that may help the creation.

True Memories
Memories can often be externally validated
Masturbation fantasies may contain some reality-based information; the rest is imagination
Lives may include repetition of trauma; e.g., early sexual abuse may influence later behaviors, such as prostitution or promiscuity
Memories are convincing and psychologically recognizable
Emotions are aroused in the listener[7]

False Memories
Memories are rarely entirely, massively repressed

[5] Lampinen, Neuschatz, and Payne (1998).
[6] Loftus and Ketcham (1991); Loftus (1993).
[7] Friedman (1997).

Most horrible incidents of childhood are remembered

Therapists, books, movies, or other individuals may unwittingly induce memories in susceptible people. Recall can spread like a contagious disease under the right conditions with easily influenced people.

Memories of Childhood Abuse

Abuse of children has probably existed in all times, social groups, and cultures. In the 1980s, at first in the United States and then spreading to other countries, adults reported apparent "recovery" of previously unknown abuse, usually sexual. A recovered memory is the emergence of a recollection of abuse of which the individual had no previous knowledge. Recovery is different from the normal, everyday memory retrieval we all experience through active recall or simple remembering. For example, a thirty-five-year-old client had always known that he was brutally beaten as a child, although he rarely talked about it and avoided thinking about it. However, talking about it in therapy where he felt safe, he even recalled the color of his pajamas on the day he stayed home and was beaten badly enough to require hospitalization. He was *recalling* and *retrieving* memories, not *recovering* them.

Some individuals who reported recovered memories have since retracted the accusations; some have even sued their therapists for planting false memories. Planted false memories seem to have several characteristics in common: recovered-memory abuse was reported to have started at a much earlier age than never-forgotten abuse; accusations were usually nonspecific; and accusations arose in the context of therapy.[8]

Retrieval of Memories

Sodium pentothal was considered a "truth drug" in the 1920s. Until recently, this notion of getting truth from drugs has been discredited. Occasionally drugs can help to recall one event known to have occurred at a specific time, but even then, researchers checking these reports have found many, many fantasies.

Hypnosis is another method of memory retrieval, but it is also unreliable, although subjects have the utmost confidence in their productions.

---

[8] Brandon et al. (1998).

For believers, hypnosis not only produces memories but also reveals past lives and alien abductions.

Traits of Genuine Hypnotic Trance

Person is in a state of relaxed wakefulness

Trance can make a person more compliant, but not always

Can rarely induce an individual to share experiences or do acts that the person would not do while awake

Can alter mood

Can alter perceptions and memory

Can help recover some memories that are otherwise unavailable

Can take a person to an earlier age to remember specific events (age regression)

Events that are recalled may not be accurate

May exaggerate a person's confidence in the validity of memories

Good uses in treatment of cigarette smoking and overeating

Used for disorders of self-control

Used as anesthetic during surgery

Used to reduce acute pain

Used (often unwisely) in treatment of multiple personality disorders to reveal other personalities

> Psychological distress isn't the only cause of anxiety and depression. Illnesses and medications can cause reactions. Hyperthyroidism may cause anxiety. Many medications may heighten anxiety and depression.

Pseudophysical Disorders

Pseudophysical problems are a collection of disorders that are physical problems with emotional causes and/or consequences. These disorders are not based in any known physical problem, yet the individual's body is telling him or her that pain or hurt exists. An individual feels pain, so he or she is convinced that some medical condition is undetected.

There are people who suffer one or more physical disorders that have no basis in the physical body; i.e., no known medical condition. Could some of them have conditions that have not yet been diagnosed or even discovered? Sure, but many are dealing with problems that seem to have their basis in mental or emotional disturbances rather than bodily upsets. The following types represent the different possibilities. Medically, these disorders are referred to under the rubric of *somatoform* (*soma* = body) disorders.

People who suffer from somatoform disorders have a very difficult time because family and professionals imply "It is all in your head," adding anger and distress to the situation. Some psychologists have come to believe that the brain has produced, for that person, some translation of psychological pain and has sent the message to the body. The body carries the emotion in the way that it knows best: physical symptoms. The body pays the price for some internal disturbance. It is easy for a person to say, "I had a lousy day and it gave me a headache," but it stretches the ability of most of us to imagine, "I hate my job and feel so trapped that I have gone blind" or "I am in such grief over my husband's death that I will faint several times a day." It happens.

Somatoform

General Traits of All Somatoform Disorders
Physical symptoms that cannot be found to be the result of a medical
   problem after extensive physical testing
Psychological factors can be established as important in the begin-
   ning or maintenance of the disorder
The individual is suffering and may be unable to function well in
   life, work, or love
The problems are not intentionally faked
Runs up huge medical bills with visits to doctors and repeated tests

The following are types of Somatoform disorders.

Hypochondriasis
(See *Hypochondriac Style*, page 91, for the complete style)
Terribly, unreasonably fearful of having diseases
Preoccupied with self
Overly attentive to one's body
Overestimates physical symptoms
Likes visiting doctors and likes the relationship with them

Rarely goes for psychotherapy; prefers medical attention

Unfortunately, severe disorders like multiple sclerosis, brain tumors, syphilis, and lupus, because of vague symptoms, may appear, at their outset, to be hypochondriacal concerns

A Special Type of Hypochondriasis

Flamboyant Complainer (similar type to Flamboyant *but* dominated by physical problems)

Usually women

Begins in early adulthood, before thirty years old

Complains about continuing, various problems; e.g., stomach pain, sexual symptoms, vomiting, diarrhea, or loss of sensation in a part of the body

May have severe symptom; e.g., blindness or paralysis

Complaints are always dramatic and overstated

Seeks treatment often and from many practitioners

Anxiety and depression are usually everpresent

May have suffered physical problems as a child

Conversion

Conversion disorder is so named because symptoms are converted from the psychological turbulence to the physical. This disorder mimics known pathology (e.g., stroke, heart attack, or hearing or speech problems) but has no underlying damage. For example, after many tests and much worry, the heart checks out fine.

Freud wrote about hysterical blindness and paralysis, a condition where an individual (he said women only) becomes incapacitated without a physical basis. He treated people with hypnosis and was temporarily able to relieve the symptoms. This disorder is unusual and dramatic.

Traumatic event precipitates symptoms; e.g., financial loss or abandonment

Symptoms are blindness, paralysis, and loss of sensations in the body

Symptoms often suggest brain lesions

Symptoms may allow the individual to avoid unpleasantness; e.g., can no longer work

Annie, 32, became my client after her doctor found no physical cause for fainting spells that occurred several times a day. She was in excellent physical condition, and the physicians could not come up with an explanation for her problem. In our first couple of meetings, she told me the following story. She had fallen in love in high school, married the young man after college, and had three sons in the next eight years as her husband built his computer company and made quite a bit of money. They bought a large home near both sets of parents and were having a fine, almost storybook life. Two years before she came to my office, her husband was crossing the street and was killed by a drunk driver—no warning and no time to say good-bye. She missed him terribly, but the way that she adapted to his loss was to freeze time—she continued her life just as they had lived it together. Their income allowed her to maintain the same style of living: She kept the same house, followed the same routines, enjoyed the same activities, and saw the same friends and family. She added nothing, and her husband was the single missing piece. Annie worked to keep everything the same.

What changed? I wondered what broke the pattern and caused symptoms now, two years later. The answer was that she met a man! He slowly came into her life: He was friendly, easy, with no pushing. But now he was suggesting more than friendship—a love relationship, maybe marriage. She cared about him. If she hadn't, it would have been easy to get rid of him. We came to the conclusion that she was just beginning to mourn the death of her husband. He was truly gone and she was alive. The fainting may have been a hope of reunion or an identification with him—joining him in temporary death. The symptoms disappeared in two months as we talked. This was the easiest, most satisfying experience I have had working with somatic disorders. Most are very difficult and hard to resolve. The earlier the symptoms are detected and understood, the better the outcome. After years, the symptoms are entrenched, and it may be impossible to change.

Symptoms usually only last hours or days, although some have been
    known to linger
May be noticeable because of the lack of concern displayed by the
    individual
Rare in the United States; strangely, more common in Iceland
Very difficult for physicians to diagnose, and errors are very common

Factitious

Factitious disorders differ from the other disorders in one very significant way—the symptoms are consciously and intentionally produced.
    Intentionally produced symptoms
    Needs to occupy the role of a sick person
    Dramatic, vague, and inconsistent
    Has a history of surgeries, procedures, or medical evaluations

Variations of Factitious Disorders

Munchausen's Syndrome is a variation in which the individual actually does some harm to his or her own body to get treatment.

Munchausen's by Proxy Syndrome is child abuse where the adult
intentionally causes symptoms in a child: symptoms are gone when
adult is not around, illness cannot be explained, and a fast onset.

Faking is also intentionally produced but with a clear goal of avoiding work or prison, or getting a reward of money.

Body Dysmorphic Disorder

Another strange body disorder that is getting more interest these days
is called *Body Dysmorphic Disorder.*
    Preoccupied with an imagined defect in appearance
    Defect can range from wrinkles to the shape of a body part
    Reality sometimes shows a slight defect; e.g., a wrinkle or a funny-
        shaped finger
    Attention to, and preoccupation with, the defect is highly
        exaggerated
    Can become delusional in proportions
    Usually begins in adolescence
    No amount of talk or reassurance helps
    May avoid social events; work or relationships may suffer
    This disorder may flare up when stress runs high and confidence is

low, and may be worse for people who tend to be obsessive or compulsive

The extreme version of a Body Dysmorphic Disorder can result in an Appearance Addict.
Willing to go to extremes to "fix" the problem
Excessive concern with physical appearance
Looks for defects in appearance
Overdramatizes a mole, spot, or hair
Often imagines the defect or exaggerates a small flaw
Often uses plastic surgery to correct appearance

Sleep Problems

We take sleep for granted, but there are estimates of staggering numbers of individuals who have different forms of sleep disorders. The impact of a sleep disorder can range from mild to severe. Most people know occasional sleep problems, which are annoying and produce fatigue or a bad mood the next day. Severe disorders can have a much greater impact on personality, mood, and the ability to function.

Insomnia
Cannot get to sleep
Cannot get the quality of sleep that allows an individual to feel rested

Narcolepsy
Sleep attacks that cannot be resisted; e.g., falling asleep at the wheel of a car

Nightmares
Sleep is repeatedly disrupted by being awakened with details of very vivid dreams

Sleep Terror
Screams or cries during sleep
Cannot be easily awakened
Cannot be easily comforted

Occurs in children, ages four to twelve

Occurs in adults, ages twenty to thirty

Sleepwalking

Gets up and walks about

Cannot be awakened

Has a blank stare

May talk and hold a conversation

Usually occurs in the early portion of the night

Substance Abuse

The following substances are among the most popularly abused in the United States: cocaine, hallucinogens, marijuana, and alcohol.

Cocaine

Cocaine comes from a plant probably native to Peru but now grown widely in the mountains of South America. It had been cultivated by the Indians and was regarded as sacred. By 1885, cases of cocaine addiction were being reported around the world.

Cocaine is extracted from the coca shrub with kerosene and evaporated into a paste where it exists as a free basic substance. Hydrochloric acid is added, which converts the substance to a salt that is then recrystallized into powder.

When snorted, coke reaches the brain in three to five minutes. When converted into its freebase and inhaled from a pipe, it reaches the brain in six seconds. When made liquid and injected, coke reaches the brain in fourteen seconds. Cocaine stimulates the central nervous system. "Street" coke (*blow, toot, lady,* and *snow*) varies in purity from 90 percent in the kilograms down to 10 percent in grams.

Possible Effects of Cocaine

1. Stimulation of the brain. Produces a "high" by increasing the action of the brain's alerting system.
2. Anesthetic effects by blocking transmission of impulses in the sensory nerves.
3. Elevates blood pressure and heart rate, constricts blood vessels, causes sweating, decreases skin temperature, produces bowel movements and diarrhea, decreases ability to gain and maintain

an erection but increases ejaculation when it is achieved. In greater doses, coke may dilate pupils, elevate body temperature, and increase respiration rate.

4. Produces euphoria, increases activity, dulls feelings, and reduces conflict.
5. Short-lived effects. Decreases, depending on mode of use, in forty-five to sixty minutes.
6. Psychologically very habit forming, and physical dependence is now identified.

Common Progression of Cocaine Use

Introduced to "snorting" at a party → Uses when others provide drug → First purchase → Keeps a gram for weeks → Uses until cocaine is gone → Buys more than originally intended → Self-medicates side effects with other drugs → Tries new ways to administer (e.g., intravenous or freebase) → Finds occasions for use → Uses at work → Irritable or depressed when cocaine is not readily available → Needs more to reproduce original high → Attempts to control use → Attempts to stop for varying lengths of time → Uses consistently for several days and then crashes.

Psychological effects from use can be Paranoid psychosis.

Hallucinogens (Psychedelics)

LSD is manufactured from lysergic acid found in ergot, a fungus. It is colorless, odorless, and tasteless. LSD is used in tablets, capsules, as a liquid, and intravenously. Mescaline is made from peyote cactus and is similar to LSD but not as strong. Mescaline is smoked or swallowed as capsules or tablets.

Psychological and Cognitive Symptoms of Hallucinogens
Several different emotions at once
Mood swings
Altered perceptions
Abnormal sensations; e.g., *hear* colors and *see* sounds
Impaired thinking
Altered self-awareness
Altered sense of time

Physical Symptoms of Hallucinogens
Dilated pupils
Elevated body temperature
Increased heart rate and blood pressure
Sweating and loss of appetite
Sleeplessness, tremors, and dry mouth
Dependence
Heavy use may result in brain damage, impaired memory, mental
confusion, and difficulty with abstract thinking.

Marijuana (Cannabis Sativa)
The illegal drug most used in this country
Greatly increased used in grade school children; average age of first
use is 13.5 years old
More than five million Americans smoke marijuana at least once a
week
Parents may find it hard to make rules about marijuana because they
also used it
Green, gray, or brown mixture of dried shredded flowers and leaves
of hemp plant
Hashish (hash) is the stronger drug made from same plant
All forms of cannabis are mind-altering drugs
All cannabis contains THC (delta-9-tetrahydrocannabinol) as the
main active ingredient
Marijuana is stronger today than it was in the 1960s
Older slang terms include: *pot, herb, grass, weed, Mary Jane, reefer,* and
joint
Newer terms include *Aunt Mary, skunk, boom, gangster, kif,* and *ganja*
Street names denote different strains; e.g., "Texas tea" or "Maui
Wowie"
Names change from city to city
Most marijuana is rolled into cigarette paper and called a *joint* or *nail*
Some marijuana is smoked in a pipe or a water pipe called a *bong*
Marijuana is sometimes mixed into food or brewed into tea
Newer use is to cut open a cigar and replace tobacco with marijuana,
a *blunt*[9]

---

[9] U.S. Department of Health and Human Services (1995).

Psychological and Cognitive Symptoms of Marijuana Use
Dizzy; trouble walking
Silly; giggly for no reason
Very red, bloodshot eyes
Difficulty remembering events that just happened
Sleepy as the effects fade
Loss of motivation
Hungry
Decreased concentration
Funny odor on clothes and hair[10]

Physical Symptoms of Marijuana Use
Increased heart rate and pulse
Bloodshot eyes
Dry mouth and throat
Irritates lungs
Impaired coordination
Impaired reproductive systems; i.e., loss of fertility

Traits of a User Over Time
Withdrawn
Careless grooming
Fatigue
Psychological dependency
Changes in habits; e.g., loss of interest in sports
Changes in sleeping and eating patterns
Uses eyedrops and incense
Impaired memory for recent events
Poor reaction time and bad judgment of distances lead to car crashes
Poor judgment may result in risky sex
Timing and coordination is impaired, so sports performance suffers
Disputes are ongoing about whether prolonged use causes depression and/or mental illness[11]

Traits of an Individual Likely to Use
Belongs to a family where other members use drugs and/or alcohol

---

[10] ibid.
[11] ibid.

Hangs out with others who use
Becomes dependent on the drug
Needs to cope with anxiety, anger, stress, or boredom[12]

Alcohol Use and Abuse
Social Drinker
May or may not like the taste
Drinks to be friendly
Can choose whether to drink or not
May drink regularly or sporadically
No damage done to functioning, personality, or relationships

Heavy Drinker
Frequent use of alcohol
Quantities taken are sufficient to cause intoxication
Binges at parties or on weekends
Excessive
May continue for life, or may cut back with age

Alcoholic
Excessive
Drinking interferes with social life or economic functioning
No consistent control over the start or end of drinking
Relies on alcohol
Chronic and repetitive
Ill effects on health
Disrupts family
May drink alone
May begin first thing in the morning
Experiences blackouts
Experiences amnesia
Has irrational fears and resentments
Has regular hangovers or nausea
Feels self-disgust
Lies about drinking

---

[12] ibid.

Activities are controlled by the availability of alcohol

May spend extravagantly[13]

General Traits of Alcoholics

In denial—does what she or he says she or he will not; denies what has been done

Manipulates others to protect continued drinking

Deflects criticism of the drinking and resultant behavior

Blames others for failures of responsibility

Blames someone or something for out-of-control drinking

Tries to control levels of drinking by manipulating environment and people

Wants help on own terms

Puts others on the defensive

Plays on sympathies of others

Situations worsen

Patterns seen at work and at home

Shame and fear make person cover up, control, and hide

Downward spiral of problems and crises

Coerces others into covering up and protecting[14]

In the alcoholic's environment, we find people who take the following roles.

Enabler

Helpful

Compelled to rescue friend

May suffer own guilt or anxiety

Wants to relieve friend of unbearable tension

May be meeting own needs without realizing it

Can be a member of any helping profession who does not recognize alcoholism; e.g., clergy, doctors, lawyers, or social workers

Never carries out threat to stop

Can be as compulsive to rescue as alcoholic is about drinking[15]

---

[13] Clinard (1963).
[14] Reddy (1984).
[15] ibid.

Victim
Responsible for getting the work done
Protects alcoholic from consequences by coverup
Never carries out threat to reveal
Usually co-worker or person at work[16]

Provoker
Veteran player
Hurt and upset by repeated episodes
Endures and accepts broken promises
Always outwitted and undermined
Keeps life going
Displays bitterness, resentment, hurt, and fear
Controls, forces, sacrifices, and adjusts but never gives up
Does not want to fail the alcoholic
Adjusts to all the crises
Always upset; never knows what to say without adding guilt and
    bitterness
Never carries out threat to leave
Usually spouse or partner[17]

Substance abuse affects anxiety
Intoxication from alcohol, cocaine, hallucinogens, and cannabis heightens anxiety. Withdrawal from alcohol, cocaine, and sedatives may also cause anxiety.

Eating Disorders
Anorexia
The essential nature of anorexia is a refusal to maintain minimally normal weight, fear of gaining weight, and a distorted image of the body. Anorexia usually begins in adolescence; some people recover completely, while others struggle with the disorder for years. Hospitalizations are common to help stabilize weight. There are a surprising number of deaths each year. Some theories about anorexia suggest that young girls are afraid of increasing sexuality and want to remain children. The American culture is also preoccupied with weight and encourages thinness, adding to the

---

[16] ibid.
[17] ibid.

strain for girls and women. Both anorexia and bulimia are increasingly being diagnosed in boys and men.

Weight loss is achieved by starving

Excessive exercise

Self-induced vomiting and/or use of laxatives

Always feels fat

Cannot see accurate reflection of body image

Always thinking about eating or not eating

Preoccupied with food

Very concerned with approval of others

Feeling good depends on weight at the moment

Losing pounds, not eating, is considered an accomplishment

Very restrained emotionally

Tries to control the environment

Anorexia Family Characteristics

Early mother-child difficulties that result in separation problems

Enmeshed

Overprotective

Rigid

Trouble resolving conflict

Bulimia Traits

Feelings of helplessness; nonassertive behavior

Low self-esteem

Fears of growing up

Has not learned to manage tension; does not know how she or he feels

Desires to be perfect; wants to please

Binges typically followed by induced vomiting, laxative use, starvation, and/or too much exercise

Feels ashamed of body; shame hides behind masks of independence, smiles, or lies

Sometimes bulimic women have been traumatized, raped, or molested when they were younger; many blame themselves

Concerned with appearances

Seems unemotional; emotions (e.g., anger), are hidden

Typically has a normal weight and above average intelligence, is

middle class, ambitious, and motivated, and appears to function
well

May have begun with a diet

Actions are not under control

Physical hints include

     swollen glands

     broken blood vessels in the eyes

     bruises on the backs of hands

College-age women commonly display a few of these symptoms

More women than men suffer with eating disorders[18]

From the Files

Kristie remembers her parents fighting. She always felt that she should do something and tried to distract them and protect her frightened younger sister. Kristie first thought that being good would give her a peaceful home. That didn't work. Then she brought home top grades, got into the school plays, and stuck with the popular kids, even when she didn't like them. Kristie learned two things during those years—that she had no control over the situation at home and that growing up certainly looked awful.

By the time I supervised Kristie's case, she was a nineteen-year-old college woman who resolved to eat nothing all day. She went to class, drank black coffee, and managed to function until she walked back to her apartment in the late afternoon, passed the grocery store, and loaded up on ice cream, cookies, chips, and peanut butter. The items never made it to the kitchen shelves because Kristie sat on the floor and ate most of it (binging) without thinking. Then, ashamed, she felt stuffed and disgusted. Sweating, unable to stop herself, she stuck her fingers down her throat and vomited and was finally relieved. Some days, she has forced herself to throw up as often as five times.

Family Characteristics Can Include

Little expression of feelings except for high conflict, anger, and marital discord

Low cohesion

---

[18] Johnson and Flach (1985).

Discourages independent and assertive behavior

Competitive one-upmanship

Relatives with alcohol problems

High achievement expectations but low emphasis on intellectual, recreational, and cultural activities

Similar to normal families about rules and control

An individual can be trapped by a family that expects much from the young person but discourages the independence, free expression, and intellectual pursuits necessary to achieve results.[19]

Communication Disorders

Dyslexia

Always begins in childhood but may go undetected until later and can range from unnoticed to severe

Reading aloud is distorted; e.g., letters and words omitted or letters and words substituted

Reading is slow, with problems understanding material that has been read

May also result in writing problems

May be part of a larger problem of delayed language development

Shows anger from frustration, and may have other behavior problems

Language Disorder

Cannot properly express himself or herself

Limited speech and/or limited vocabulary

Strange word order

Speaks in a simplistic fashion

Mutism

May be no speech

Can be voluntary; person may have ability to speak

May speak in certain situations (e.g., at home) but not in others

---

[19] Johnson and Flach (1985).

Stuttering
Speech is not fluent
Begins early in life; i.e., between two and seven years old
Usually ends by age sixteen
Worsens with anxiety

Sexually Transmitted Diseases
Twenty-five percent of Americans contract a sexually transmitted disease.

Chlamydia
Most common and most invisible sexually transmitted infection in
 the United States
74 percent of women and 25 percent of men have no symptoms
Damages sex and pelvic organs; can cause sterility
Parasite infects the cervix (women) or urethra (men) and spreads
Can cause Reiter's syndrome in men (eye infections, urethritis, or
 arthritis, and can be permanently disabling)
Can be cured

Symptoms of Chlamydia

Men	Women
Discharge from penis	Discharge from vagina
Pain or burning while urinating	Pain or burning while urinating
Abdominal pain, fever, and nausea	Abdominal pain, fever, and nausea
Inflammation of the rectum	Inflammation of the rectum
Swelling or pain in the testicles	Inflammation of the cervix
	Spotting between periods or after intercourse
	Excessive vaginal bleeding
	Painful intercourse

Symptoms appear in seven to twenty-one days, if they appear

Chlamydia is spread by oral sex, vaginal and anal intercourse, during pregnancy from birth canal to fetus and, rarely, from hand to eye.[20]

Herpes

Thirty million Americans have one of the two forms of genital, sexually transmitted herpes: simplex virus-1 or simplex virus-2. There are 500,000 new cases diagnosed each year. Herpes virus remains for life, even if it is inactive (which is true of approximately one-third of all infected persons).

Symptoms vary greatly from individual to individual

Contagious just before sores appear, during sores, and until it is completely healed

May have tingling or itching sensation just before sores appear

Recurring rash with clusters of blisters; painful or itchy sores

Sores develop scabs, heal, and then disappear

Appearance on vagina, cervix, buttocks, penis, mouth, or anus

Primary outbreak results in pain and discomfort around sores

Primary outbreak may also include fever, headache, and a rundown feeling

Recurs with stress

Herpes is spread by:

Contact with the active herpes virus

Touching and sexual intimacy (includes kissing)

Vaginal, oral, or anal intercourse

Rarely, during childbirth

Contagious from the time that sores are present to complete healing with no scabs

Human Immunodeficiency Virus (HIV)

Weakens the body's ability to fight disease

Can cause AIDS (acquired immune deficiency syndrome), the last stage of HIV infection

Leading cause of death for Americans between ages twenty-five and forty-four

Forty thousand infected each year, with no cure

---

[20] Moglia and Knowles (1993).

Symptoms of HIV

Constant, unexplained weight loss

Diarrhea and lack of appetite

Swollen glands or lymph nodes

Continuing fever, chills, and night sweats

Dry cough or shortness of breath

Fatigue, persistent fevers, night sweats, or dry cough

Light-headedness, headaches, or mental disorders

Thick, white coating on tongue or mouth (thrush)

Severe or recurring vaginal yeast infections

Purplish growths on the skin

Chronic pelvic inflammatory disease

HIV is spread in blood, semen, vaginal fluids, breast milk, during childbirth, during breast-feeding, by sharing contaminated needles for injecting IV drugs, in transfusion of contaminated blood products, or by vaginal, oral, and anal intercourse.

Syphilis

Venereal disease gotten from sexual intercourse, anal sex, or oral sex

Symptoms show up one to twelve weeks after sex

Men have symptoms; many women do not have symptoms

Symptoms

Skin sores, small or large, on penis, vagina, mouth, throat, breasts, anus, or fingers

Lymph glands near the throat may be swollen

Symptoms disappear for six to eight weeks, and then new symptoms appear

Sick all over, like the flu; e.g., fever, aches, poor appetite, sore throat, or headaches

Skin rash over the body, in the mouth, hands, and sex organs

Symptoms disappear again; without treatment, years pass until:

Disease moves to brain, spinal cord, and heart and results in blindness, crippling, and insanity

Pregnant woman can give syphilis to baby during pregnancy

Women can have miscarriage or child with birth defects

Sexual Dysfunction

Roots of Orgasmic Dysfunction (Women)

Learned to hide sexuality

Cultural taboos

Lack of sexual knowledge

Trauma

Fear of own performance

Worry about partner's performance

Religious orthodoxy

Disappointment/dislike of partner

Homosexual preference

Guilt

Lack of mutuality with partner

Unmet requirements of sexual needs

Holds romantic desire; denies sexual desire[21]

Roots of Impotence (Men)

Urologists estimate that thirty million American men suffer from erectile dysfunction and the number is rising.[22] Causes of impotence usually have several, but never all, of the following traits.

Continuous Impotence

Sleeping in mother's bed until adolescence

Sexual abuse

Inappropriate sexual display from mother

Washing or touching by mother

Religious orthodoxy

Misinformation or lack of knowledge

Wife/partner who is equally unknowledgeable

Sexual taboos

No prior sexual activity

Lack of confidence

Homosexuality during the teen years

Denial of homosexual desire

Traumatic experience with prostitute

Drugs or alcohol

---

[21] Masters and Johnson (1970).

[22] Sleek (1998).

Intermittent Impotence
High or exaggerated expectations about his own performance
Increased life expectancy; i.e., dysfunction triples between the ages
of forty and seventy
Prior problems with premature ejaculation
Distracted, fatigued, or angry
Humiliation
Performance anxiety
Father so dominant that confidence in masculinity is destroyed
Religious orthodoxy
Sexual failures that were psychologically damaging
Immaturity
Early homosexuality
Medication for other problems; e.g., drugs for diabetes and
hypertension
Physical disorder; e.g., diabetes, vascular problems, or
hypertension[23]

Ordinary, Temporary Arousal Inhibitions
Occurs in most men and women at various times
Use of alcohol
Fatigue, stress, boredom, illness, or anger with the partner
Anxiety about impressing a partner
 Fear of inability to please
 Fear of sexual dysfunction
 Lack of self-esteem
 Poor body image
 Becomes self-conscious; a spectator
 Monitors, grades, or compares performance to imagined
  others

Causes of Sexual Dysfunction in Men
Physical problems
Lack of sexual drive; lack of sexual interest
 Psychosis
 Disturbed relationships

---

[23] Masters and Johnson (1970).

Withdrawal from relationships
Depression
Anxiety
Withdrawal from intimacy
Phobic response to women
Phobic response to sex
Underlying homosexuality

Erectile Dysfunction (Impotence)

Cannot have an erection with his partner
Cannot sustain an erection to permit intercourse
Had been able to have erections and presently cannot
Can have an erection during masturbation
Occurs increasingly after age sixty
Becomes very frustrating to both gay and straight men
Fears rejection by partner
Makes excuses and covers up
Avoids sex
May be fear of making partner pregnant
May be guilt or shame
Can be physical or psychological in nature

Premature Ejaculation

Ejaculates before he wants to
Unable to control response to stimulation
Up to 30 percent of men experience early ejaculation at some period
Feels guilty and anxious
Worries about not pleasing partner
May avoid sex[24]

Sexual Dysfunction in Women
Vaginismus

Painful or impossible intercourse due to muscle contractions
May be result of fear
May occur after trauma

---

[24] Doleys, Meredith, and Ciminero (1982).

Dyspareunia
Pain during penetration in intercourse
May be hormone imbalance
May result from intercourse attempts before arousal

Arousal Dysfunction
Cannot become aroused
Cannot enjoy sex play
Has sexual desire
Can be physical or psychological in nature

Inhibited Orgasm
Common in women; uncommon in men
May not know about orgasms
May be able to reach orgasm during masturbation
May not find orgasm important
May not have had intercourse long enough
Insufficient stimulation
May decide to fake orgasm
May result from shame or guilt

Sexual Disorders of Children
Organic conditions
> Sexual ambiguity of genitals
> Early puberty
> Late puberty

Gender Identity Confusion
Precocious Sexual Interest
> Preoccupied with sex
> Molestation of other children

Masturbatory problems
> Compulsive masturbation
> Public masturbation

Fetishes (common in children)[25]

Alternative Healing Practices
In addition to the commonly used treatments for physical disorders, holistic practices and Chinese techniques are becoming very popular.

---

[25] ibid.

Americans are spending their own money because insurance covers few holistic treatments, and people want to try alternatives. Some of the most popular treatments are the Alexander Technique, Sacrocranial, Chinese Herbs, Acupuncture, and Acupressure. Also, there are lesser known types of massage, such as Hellerworks, Reflexology, and Rolfing. Further out are occult practices and mystics.

Occult Practices and Mystics

Alchemist

Secluded

Practices transmutation; i.e., changing metals into gold

Contemplates nature

Can be men or women

Emblem is the tree and the serpent

Mystic

Contemplative

Struggles with ordinary dilemmas of selfishness, idleness, and hatred

Always remains a novice and always learning

Tries to go beyond words or intellect

Wishes to remain in place of mystery

Attempts to be in the moment

Goes forward without a clear way

Occult Practitioner

Fashions one's self as an instrument to understand the universe

Develops skills of occult ritual magic

Uses visualization and psychic sensitivity

Types of Mystical Methods[26]

Astrology

Cabala—mystical writings of early Jews to know God

Chiromancy—reads the hand for character and the future

Divination by moles—reads moles on face

Metopascopy—reads lines on the forehead

---

[26] Knight (1996); Seligman (1997).

Physiognomy—reads character by facial expression and traits
    silky hair = timid, pointed chin = mutilated body, small
    eyes = envy or malice
Tarot Cards
More unusual are reports of Anomalous Healing, or miracles.

Anomalous Healing, or Miracles
Miracle is that which provokes awe
Sudden
Healing or cure occurs within days
Healing is complete
The healing process takes a normal course but is speeded up

Healed Client's Experience
Altered state of consciousness, similar to falling in love
At the moment of healing, a vision of a holy figure appears
Red-hot heat is reported
Balls of white light are seen
States of unawareness; dazed
Feels peace
Feels strong emotions
Feels connected to the healer at a deep level

Career Traits

Career Choice

Work is an important element in most people's lives and, when things are going well, generally enhances self-esteem. For many individuals, the choice of a career represents an extension of their personality; for example, an actor. Career also represents a preferred lifestyle, such as a race car driver.

Identification with adults in childhood often influences career directions, if not the job itself. I have often told my students that, as a psychologist, I am following in my mother's footsteps—she did her informal counseling at the kitchen table and everyone loved her. I'm probably not as good at it as she was, but I have turned her way of life into a well-paying occupation. Admiration for a parent or another adult can be very formative, knowingly or unknowingly. The favorite English teacher at school has launched many avid readers and fine writers.

Identification works in reverse as well. Years ago I treated a young man who wanted to become a police officer. Why? Because as a child he was tied up and physically abused. He wanted to be in a position where no one would hurt him and he could protect others.

Psychoanalytic theory has ascribed unconscious motives to career choice but, although it makes sense intuitively, the theory has not stood up well to research. Still, it is fun to think about unconscious motivations for our character's choice of work. For example, psychoanalytic theory would suggest that aggressive impulses might be gratified by a career choice such as a butcher, murderer, or a surgeon. In two out of three choices, the aggression is sublimated, or channeled appropriately into socially acceptable work. Stretch this idea further and we have little Timmy, fascinated by his stream of urine, becoming an engineer who builds waterways or canals.

Career Problems
Certainly, we can see work motives and problems that come from childhood and may be conscious or unconscious. The student who is driven to succeed to compete with a successful father is one example. The other side of that same equation could be the student who is afraid to succeed because success would feel like the destruction of a mother who had not achieved her goals. Avoidance of success could also come from the fear that a parent's love would be lost, or that the child would suffer real or imagined retaliation from the parent who has been surpassed.

Success at Work; Failure at Home
Traits that are very successful on the job may fail miserably at home. The aggressive, powerful cop may be intimidating at home, much to the dismay of his wife and children. The exceptional dealmaker in business may drive her family crazy with activities. The magnificently detailed conference planner may ruin friendships with his overattention to the details of everyone's lives.

Definitions
In the following lists, the traits are those that have been found in people in these professions; many are healthy personality traits, and some are problems. Not everyone has a disorder but, to be realistic, problems are included because these are the emotional difficulties that have been found to be associated with particular careers.

Definitions of psychological syndromes used in the lists:

Alcohol dependence or abuse = evidence of physical work, personal, interpersonal, or legal problems related to compulsive, excessive, and/or sustained drinking.

Anxiety = sustained periods of fearfulness, apprehensiveness, agitation, or panic with no adequate cause.

Adjustment reactions = problematic but reversible periods in response to stress. Reactions are usually out of the range expected and associated with an inability to cope. Usually there are symptoms, such as depression, work paralysis, or anxiety. A cause triggers the reaction, and the response passes.

Drug dependence or abuse = evidence of physical work, personal, interpersonal, or legal problems related to compulsive, excessive, and/or sustained drug use.

Depression = at least one sustained period of severe depression, marked by sad mood, sleep problems, appetite changes, lack of energy, dread, social withdrawal, dark thoughts, or suicidal preoccupation or attempts.

Mild depression = moodiness, unhappiness, and general pessimism with no obvious cause.

Mania or "highs" = at least one sustained period of elation, grandiosity, too much energy, poor judgment, racing thoughts, insomnia, and excessive buying or sprees.

Mild mania = major moods swings, heightened well-being, irritability, no sleep, and high energy.

Psychosis = at least one sustained episode with hallucinations, delusions, inappropriate reactions, incoherent communication, or bizarre behaviors, with an impaired ability to care for one's self. See descriptions of *Schizophrenia* in chapter four for more complete details.

Stages of Career Development

Period	Age	Dynamics of Career Development
FANTASY	CHILDHOOD	Play with no realities of ability or time; tries on roles such as cowgirl, police officer, parent, or movie star
TENTATIVE	11-18	
Interest	11-12	Recognizes need for work direction; sees/identifies with parents' work, and concentrates on enjoyment
Capacity	12-14	Begins to evaluate his or her ability and looks around at others
Value	15-16	Thinks about his or her role in society; notes differing lifestyles, perspective broadens, and they wonder how to use their talents
Transition	17-18	Has some independence; feels the need to make some realistic moves about direction; thinks about financial rewards; may seek new surroundings to try out ideas

REALISTIC   18-24

Exploration	Has narrower interests but fearful of wrong choice
Crystallization	Involved; knows what he or she likes and does not like; commitment grows
Specification	Selects path; some never arrive here[1]

The many diverse traits listed in the following sections are those that have been shown to be associated with people in these fields. No one person possesses all the traits, and people possess many traits that are not listed here. Also listed are the ways that people in certain careers tend to run into trouble, either with personality disturbance, mental illness, or substance abuse.

Traits of People in Forty-Six Careers

Accountant
Self-controlled
Makes a good impression
Introverted, quiet, and serious
Judgmental, demanding, and reserved
Responsible, introspective, and orderly
Quiet; wary of impulse
Plans ahead
Combats disorder
Likes to give advice
Conformist
Conventional[2]

Actress/Actor
Some lack identity
Desire to exhibit one's self; satisfies exhibitionism in a healthy way
Desire to be admired
Expressive
Vulnerable to stress
Self-observation leads to self-criticism and overidentification with roles

---

[1] Roe (1956).
[2] Granleese and Barrett (1990).

Self-esteem gained from applause
Narcissistic satisfaction from entrancing an audience
Ability to concentrate
Good observing skills
Remembers emotion
Can copy or mimic characters
Recognizes specific talent fairly early
Problems with alcohol and drugs
Emotional problems of mania or anxiety
Higher suicide rate than other fields[3]

Artist, General
Needs some isolation
Also needs others to stimulate and share ideas
Has inner drive
Makes "babies" with art productions
Creative
Strong in emotional expression
Relates to other people indirectly though art
Dislikes structure
May show little self-control
Asocial[4]

Architect
Solid citizen
Very creative and sensitive to beauty
Talented into old age
Flexible
Independent of social constraints
Little worry about making a good impression
Aggressive
Goal oriented
Follows own ethics and values
Reliable, outgoing, and resourceful
Ability to delegate

---

[3] Roe (1956).
[4] ibid.

Early adjustment problems
Some depression or anxiety[5]

Peter changed his job after he was sent to Spain for a month. Why? Change becomes more possible during times of discontinuity; e.g., being fired, life events intervene and broaden people's views, they learn more about themselves, they meet others who expand their thinking, or they realize some talents and/or limitations.

Astronaut
Agreeable; i.e., willing to cooperate with others on a team
Patient; low irritability
Gullible
Somewhat subordinate; e.g., concerned with needs of co-workers
Not egotistical and not arrogant; modest
Able to share concern for others; effective interpersonally
Not very open to new ideas; sticks with accepted ways of doing things
Not fussy or whiny
Perfectionistic[6]

Researchers expected to find low impulsiveness and high perfectionism and endurance in this group. Some traits were found but they were not of statistical significance.[7]

Athlete: General Traits of Professional/Champion
Emphasis is on the physical body rather than emotions
Independent
Used to doing battle with other men and/or women
Plays to win; competitive
Highly aggressive
Uncontrolled affect (emotion)
High general anxiety

---

[5] Dudek and Hall (1991).
[6] Rose et al. (1994).
[7] ibid.

High aspirations
Self-assured
Ability to concentrate on desired objectives
Unusual concern for physical power and physical perfection

Certain personalities gravitate to certain sports; for example, men seeking high sensation from sports play pool, water ski, and racquetball. Low-sensation-seeking males prefer jogging, weightlifting, or hiking. High-sensation-seeking women seek whitewater rafting, windsurfing, or kayaking. Low-sensation-seeking women prefer sailing, handball, or ballet.[8]

Boxer
Quick ascent at an early age, and often a quick descent
Usually born into lower socioeconomic classes; rage is the way out
Adheres to rigorous training
May fast or exercise vigorously to make weight
Disciplined, with notable exceptions such as Mike Tyson
Can control pain
Likes to inflict hurt; aggressive
Physical and direct—the world is a physical place
Primitive rage becomes art; anger is ennobled[9]

Bookkeeper or Bank Teller
Conventional
Likes rules
Self-controlled
Honors others who have power and status
Likes structure
Likes order[10]

Coach
(See chapter eleven)

Comic
Willing to sacrifice dignity

---

[8] Furnham (1990).
[9] Oates (1987).
[10] Roe (1956).

Trades on self-degradation
May have masochistic or sadistic tendencies
Observant
Critical nature channeled into work

Corporate Businessperson, Newcomer

Loyal
Accepts authority
Conforms to prescribed behaviors
Understands that there is no room for eccentrics
Has to be "the right person" and able to fit in
Knows that corporate men reproduce themselves
Trustworthy
Dedicated[11]

Corporate Businessman, Top Echelon

Lives in a closed circle
Little room for novelty
Every activity is tinged with corporate position
No distance between work and play
Hardworking
Learned how to play the game
Often charismatic
Attuned to image and importance of appearances[12]

Corporate Wife

Very traditional couples still exist in top ranks of U.S. executives
Her value is in adaptability, attractiveness, discretion, and social
    graces
Has little freedom to refuse role
No private acts; all behaviors reflect on husband's position
Makes sure nothing comes between husband and work
Raises beautiful, well-mannered children
Maintains well-appointed home
Works in charity
Smiles and enjoys all meetings and trips

---

[11] Kanter and Stein (1979).
[12] ibid.

Entertainment is important because activities bind people personally
Knows her place; accepts importance of image
Is the clue to husband's personal side
Confirms husband's image and message
Prevents scandal
Is her husband's instrument of communication
Looks, talks, and dresses tastefully—no extremes
Entertains easily, quickly, informally, or extravagantly
Remains up-to-date on current events and business
Stays in the shadow of her husband
Hides opinions
Plays down her own ability[13]

Corporate Woman
Torn between conflicting values
Understands that big corporations are still men's arena
Tries to balance values and family with corporate work culture; ambitious
Wonders whether the success is worth the cost
Must find a way to fit in
Learns to show little emotion[14]

Chemist/Biologist
Investigator
Thinker
Not a doer
Likes organizing
Asocial; neither drawn to people or away from them
Does not have strong need for close contact[15]

Engineers
Objective
Likes technical hobbies; e.g., chess
Smart

---

[13] Kanter and Stein (1979); Morris (1998).
[14] Sampson (1995).
[15] Roe (1956).

Not persuasive
Mechanically gifted[16]

Farmers/ Truck Drivers
Realistic
Skilled
Strong
Masculine
Like dealing with concrete problems
Not sensitive[17]

Dancer
Unhappy; anxious
Hypochondriacal
Obsessive; dependent
Achievement motivated
Struggles with feelings of inferiority and self-contempt[18]

Top players in individual sports, such as riding, swimming, fencing, or track and field tend to be:
Dominant and aggressive
Adventurous and self-sufficient
Stable and normal
Unsophisticated
Introverted

Top players in team sports are:
Neurotic
Sophisticated
Extroverted
Guilt prone

Fencer
Reserved
Aggressive

---

[16] ibid.
[17] ibid.
[18] Marchant-Haycox and Wilson (1992).

Autonomous
Experimental
Creative

Mountain Climber
These traits also apply to other high-risk sportsmen and women
Stable
Sensation and thrill seeking
Underestimate risk
Impulsive
Seeks stimulation
Extroverted and adventurous
Highly sensitive to reward; low sensitivity to punishment[19]

Superior Athletes, General
Extroverted
High pain threshold
Sensation seeking
Assertive and competitive
Fast reactions
Low anxiety
Strong genetic component to athleticism
Tough minded and self-confident[20]

Football Player (American)
Team's high arousal adds to success
Anxiety increases as playoffs get closer
Less depressed than general population
More fatigued
Vigorous
Submissive to authoritarian rules
Accepts standards of harsh discipline
Likes rigid control of life *off* the field
Values obedience
Narrow-minded
Conventional and conservative

---

[19] Goma (1991).
[20] Furnham (1990).

Likes group activities
Emphasizes mental aspects of the sport
Bold
Different positions emphasize different talents[21]

Funeral Director
Social
Likes to be helpful
Ordered
Likes systematic activities
Avoids mechanical and scientific pursuits

Golfer
Solitary and individualistic
More similarity to tennis than any other sport
Players are never tackled or blocked, and don't get bad calls
Controls one's own fate
Cannot usually explain why play was good or bad
Confident
Able to concentrate
Attends to his or her own rhythm
Expensive sport for pro and amateur; all pay to compete
Can play into the sixties
Nerves are significant because of slowness of the game
More sedate than other sports; e.g., pro players travel with families
    and there is little nightlife
Unprotected, by gear or speed, from other people or anxiety[22]

Kept Woman
Young and good-looking
Fill the fantasies of the men that keep them
Exaggerated expressions of self-worth may hide insecurity
Fears rejection
Wants male approval
Feels important through gifts and being desired, especially by married men

[21] Freudenberger and Bergandi (1994).
[22] Feinstein (1995).

May have good job and respected employment
Seduced by a lifestyle better than anything she could pay for
Has time to be free and alone
Must make herself available and on call
Limited time makes activities more exciting
May be angry, self-centered, or manipulative
Relationship prevents commitment
Feels controlled; trying to take control
Previously unresolved difficulties in relationships
Does not allow others to know her beyond her beauty
Manipulates with sex
Convinces herself that she has power
May have been sexually abused or violated in the past

Rationalizes; e.g., "I'm special," "He prefers me to his wife," or "We are always on a honeymoon."[23]

Manipulator
Shrewd
Polished
Calculating
Always thinking of an angle
Able to read others well
Stays removed from people and situations
Knows how to get things done
Ambitious
Plays life close to the chest
Manages groups well
Smooth; not fussy

Martial Artist, Woman
Seeks development of self
Martial arts are empowering
Develops willingness to face challenges
May be a road back to bodily comfort
Increases body awareness

---

[23] McRay and Schwarz (1990).

Teaches discipline, physical and mental
Learns to take self seriously[24]

These qualities may be similar for men, but research documents traits of women.

Medicine Man or Women
Understands problem as disharmony between client and universe
Shares the same values as his or her clients; e.g., importance of clan
Performs ceremonies that are symbolic reenactments of events gone
    wrong in the past that are now set right
Dependable and stable
Leader of the clan
Occupies high position
Careful and shrewd
Uses power of suggestion to achieve results

Musician
Cynical and resigned
Introverted and unadventurous
Reserved and sober
Apprehensive and tense
Imaginative
Emotionally sensitive
Likes to create noise
Perseveres
Good manual skills

When psychological traits and disorders have been found in musicians, they tend to appear in the following patterns.
Brass players are more extroverted and happy-go-lucky.
String players are more neurotic than other musicians.
Pop musicians have psychological problems.
Opera singers are extroverted and conceited.[25]

---

[24] Wiley (1992).
[25] Marchant-Haycox and Wilson (1992); Galligani, Renck, and Hansen (1996); Moss, Panzak, and Tarter (1992).

Mystic

Contemplative
Struggles with ordinary dilemmas of selfishness, idleness, and hatred
Always remains a novice and always learning
Tried to go beyond words or intellect
Wishes to remain in place of mystery
Attempts to be in the moment
Goes forward without a clear way

Occult Practitioner

Fashions one's self as an instrument to understand the universe
Develops skills of occult ritual magic
Uses visualization and psychic sensitivity

Pool/Billiards Hustler

Manipulates impressions to create false images
Deceives opponent ("sucker" or "fish") about level of skill to get a
    game
Feigns less competence originally
Restrains from making difficult shots
Lets opponent win on occasion
Wants a series of games, not just one
Looks at spectators as future opponents or as bettors
Good skills in assessing people
Disciplined; can refuse tempting shots
Courageous
Has stamina
Not easily rattled or upset
Flexible
Keeps opponent on hook with close calls

Police Officer

Observant of behavior
Investigative
Desires excitement
Must be healthy, strong, and agile
Not easily excitable
Cannot be ruled by anger

Idealistic at beginning of career
Willing to make decisions
Comfortable with physical force and firearms
Willing to take action
Used to directing and controlling; e.g., traffic, demonstrations, and
    emergencies
Wants to serve community
Wants respect from others
Uniform draws attention to self

Politicians
Enterprising
Good verbal skills
Manipulative
Likes to dominate
Wants power
Wants status[26]

President
(See chapter eleven)

Real Estate, Investment, or Insurance Salesperson
Likes face-to-face contact
Personally persuasive
May be mildly exploitative in relationships
Likes work
Resourceful
High energy
Interest in people is not personal
Not interested in routine selling

Real Estate Sales/Investments/Auctioneer/Insurance Sales
Likes face-to-face sales
Personally persuasive
Exploitative
Likes work

---

[26] Roe (1956).

High energy
Interest in people is not personal[27]

Salesperson
Sees through the eyes of the other person
Able to find out what the customer cares about; e.g., money, happiness, or family
Uses information that he or she hears to relate to the sale
Asks questions; does not make assumptions
Interested in others
Knows his or her product
Knows his or her competition
Likes being own boss
Likes making own hours
Likes meeting new people
Highly self-motivated
High energy
Likes being involved in the community
Sees sales as freedom
Sales Approach
Prospecting—everyone is a possible sale; likes people who make things happen
Setting the stage—enjoys and perfects the performance
Closing the deal—asks for the order
Servicing the account—maintains relationships with customers

Scientists, Social
Grew up in an overprotective home
Oriented toward people
Close with family[28]

Scientists, Physical/Biological
Grew up in cool, demanding home
Not oriented to people
Achievement oriented
> Eminent scientists

---

[27] ibid.
[28] ibid.

Childhood homes often disturbed by divorce and/or death
Distant from family
Psychosexual problems
Dedicated to work[29]

Shadow Mom
Women who mother other people's children
Provide nurturance that has been missing; e.g., talking or calls
Entertains; remembers birthdays; listens
Shapes the child
Voluntary love, not obligatory
Provides a healthy subversive influence; e.g., can share misdeeds[30]

Social Worker
Protective
Encouraging
Likes to exert influence
May be provocative
Skilled interpersonally
Seeks situations with other people
Attends to others
Supportive
Shys away from physical skills
   Feminine
More concerned with people than with ideas
Generally outgoing
Likes work
Practical
Intelligent
Slightly inhibited
Slightly compulsive[31]

Teacher
Likes children

---

[29] ibid.
[30] Schmich (1998).
[31] Roe (1956).

Traits of Steroid Users

May induce psychosis or organic problems that can lead to violence,
suicide, or homicide
Aggressive, especially verbally
Unprovoked rage attacks
Hostile, especially toward wives and girlfriends
Impulsive; needs stimulation; hates monotony
Begins using in early twenties, peaks in mid twenties to thirty
Used mostly by body builders and athletes
Guilty; disagreeable[32]

Likes security; stable
Socially at ease
Sensitive to the opinions of others
Curious
Cooperative, patient, with a good disposition
   Feminine
Responsible and efficient[33]

Tennis Player, Female
Task oriented more than people oriented
Competitive; deliberate
Uncomplicated and unpretentious in approach to others
Very well trained
Emotionally stable; high ego strength; high confidence
Low anxiety and low depression
Domineering
Intelligent
Younger players are more conservative; older ones are more radical[34]

Therapists/Guidance Counselors
Service oriented
Attends to others
Prizes personal relationships

---

[32] Galligani, Renck, and Hansen (1996); Moss, Panzak, and Tarter (1992).
[33] Roe (1956).
[34] Gondola and Wughalter (1991).

Wants to connect with people rather than ideas
Slightly compulsive
Verbal and intelligent
Mildly extroverted

Trades for a Woman

Skilled trade careers include auto repair mechanics, carpenters, plumbers, electricians, computer technicians, and heating and air conditioning technicians. Federal legislation in the early 1970s opened the door for women to work in skilled trades and in organized labor shops.

Higher pay than traditional women's jobs, including during training
Goes against traditional sex role attitudes
Family is often not in favor of masculine job, so she creates a supportive inner circle
Someone, man or woman, serves as a strong role model
Faces ridicule from men
Feels overwhelmed
Has to overcome employer skepticism
May go against her self-image
Individualistic; e.g., "I don't care what anyone else says"
Enjoys autonomy
Has a history of pattern-breaking experiences
Wants to earn good money
Likes physical activity
Has a strong sense of herself; satisfied with who she is and what she does
Believes that she has the ability to do the job; e.g., "I was born with it"
Enjoys being successful in a man's world[35]

Writers/Painters

Create in order to heal their parents or old wounds in themselves
Abstract thinkers
Fear mediocrity
Disregard routine problems
Not adaptable

---

[35] Greene and Stitt-Gohdes (1997); Galligani, Renck, and Hansen (1996); Moss, Panzak, and Tarter (1992).

Driven toward achievement
Creative thinkers
Sensitive
Not aggressive[36]

Writers

Writers often drink alcohol, especially after forty
Depression in younger writers
Problems with anxiety and drug use
Creative
Has to tolerate aloneness
Has to let go of work
Families with mental illness and creativity
Higher rates of bisexuality or homosexuality[37]

Poets

Higher suicide rates than other fields
Problems with mania, psychosis, and depression
Drug and alcohol use

---

[36] Roe (1956).
[37] Ludwig (1992).

Group Influences

I would never belong to any group that would have me as a member." In spite of Groucho Marx's disclaimer, humans are sociable. We belong to groups all our lives, beginning with family. Some groups we can see, such as tall people; other groups are carried around inside, such as religion or being a writer. From birth to death, we live and work in groups—families, schools, sports, work, religious, hobbies, beliefs, and interests.

Family is perhaps the most powerful group, the one that creates us and travels along in our heads—the values, tastes, and rituals developed in our families of origin remain strong. We are rarely alone. Family influence can be seen easily—almost any woman, when taken to a dress department, could tell you what outfit her mother would have picked out for her, even if her mother is long dead. Almost any man can repeat his father's instructions about how to take care of a car.

Other groups exert influence also; professional allegiances are obvious. Writers always listen for material, and skaters choreograph moves in their heads whenever they hear a good piece of music. Tragedy, too, creates group membership as soldiers or survivors of disaster can testify. Groups *create* some traits and also *evoke* traits in people. Only in group settings do certain traits emerge because it is necessary to have a gathering of people for the traits to be displayed and observed (e.g., reactions to authority or singing too loud in church).

We carry our group memberships around with us all the time,

whether they are family, professional, or tragic. Whatever groups we deeply belong to, we take with us.

Whether individuals choose membership in a group, such as the Democratic Party or the KKK, or individuals are born into a group, such as being Puerto Rican, male, or poor, belonging carries ways of thinking and behaving. At their worst, groups reduce intellectual richness, critical judgment, and rational decision making. Irving Janis, in his book, *Victims of Groupthink*, analyzes the best and worst of these processes in several examinations of political decisions.

This section explains general characteristics of groups, of group membership, and of specifics associated with selected groups.

Family Types

The group with which we are most familiar is the family, an often strange, tightly bound collection of individuals.

Three Basic Family Types

I describe three basic family types: Closed, Random, and Open. The traits are based on how these families try to achieve their goals. The following dimensions allow you to construct families or family members based on how they conduct themselves in the course of everyday affairs as well as in unusual situations.

Families are neither entirely closed to outside influences nor entirely open. Families can be constructed and examined with regard to the following variables: Space, Authority, Goals, Emotional Tone, Time, Energy, Crises, and Flaws.

Closed Families	*Random Families*	*Open Families*
Closed families do not tolerate strain or deviance because the closed family cannot tolerate a change to its equilibrium. The closed family believes that family interests come before individual goals.	Random families encourage change because the random family thrives on disequilibrium.	Open families mix change and constancy. They permit strain and deviance but restrain excess through negotiation and management of closeness and distance.
Space is fixed, meaning that traffic (locked	**Space** is dispersed, and each person develops	**Space** is moveable, meaning that traffic is

doors, supervised trips, privacy, secrecy, parental control of media, unlisted phone numbers) coming in and out are regulated. The family remains distinct and apart from the larger community.

Authority is tightly maintained by the parents (we "run a tight ship") who are the main links or bridges to the world and regulate friends, requests, or interactions.

Values are tradition, fairness, propriety, family unity, responsibility, discipline, little waste, strength, perseverance, and self-sufficiency.

Goal—Stability

Emotional Tone—Stable intimacy and nurturance, staying composed.

Time that is valued is the past, and newness is not accepted. Schedules are important, whether they provide for waking, dinner, chores, or the age to marry.

his or her own patterns. Entering and leaving family space is not regulated. The family members sometimes feel invaded. Members choose voluntarily who and what to mix with.

Authority is dispersed, and individual freedom can be maintained at the expense of others. Authority is relinquished on the justification of "do your own thing."

Values are freedom, genuineness, voluntary action, no coercion, individual decision making, spontaneity, creativity, and discovering potential.

Goal—Adaptation to individual's and family's needs

Emotional Tone—Exploratory intimacy and nurturance, being original.

Time that is valued is equally the past, present, and future, depending on interest. Little in the way of a family schedule; for example, no fixed mealtimes or bedtimes. Schedules are fixed by individuals, and plans may be dis-

regulated by consensus, so the family is brought into the larger community, and outside culture comes into the home. Space may include varieties of activities, people, and pets.

Authority is shared, and individuals bring in guests and information as long as others are not caused discomfort. All members serve as links or bridges to the world. Individuals can have freedom as long as family guidelines are not violated.

Values are change, variation, fairness, freedom with limits, family cohesion, limited experimentation, personal responsibility, openness, developing talent, and autonomy.

Goal—Free exploration

Emotional Tone— Adaptive intimacy and nurturance; share and do, not withhold.

Time that is valued is past, present, and future, especially the present. Variations are accepted within a range of family comfort. Schedules are guidelines rather than blueprints. The family tries to synchronize members in

	carded without completion.	order to pursue goals, but the plan is open to modification.
Energy is steady, and activities are well planned with little deviation. Energy is directed toward clear goals, and excessive emotion is discouraged.	**Energy** fluctuates as individuals pick up and put down activities. Tomorrow can be very different from today; energy can be high, and tasks are attended to but not for long.	**Energy** is flexible; members demand variation and are allowed to tap new sources, such as different music. Too much variety can lead to members spreading themselves too thin and activities become inefficient.
Crises are met primarily by suppressing the individual. When suppression fails, sometimes a severe schism may erupt. Less often, a successful rebellion occurs.	**Crises** occur often because members tend to fly in different directions. Crises are often not resolved, and effects are often unchecked. Resolution, albeit temporary, may come from one family member imposing leadership on the others.	**Crises** that are minor become frequent occurrences and are preferred to constraint. Energy runs high and low. Open discussion is the route to crisis resolution.
Flaws of this family are lack of escape or relief, insularity, members are poorly equipped to live in a big, heterogeneous world, or individuals violently leave.	**Flaws** are seen when unconnected members dissolve in chaos, no vital connections exist, and individualistic members compete, so family becomes irrelevant.	**Flaws** are obvious as members detach, there is no resolution of conflict, no standards, and members withdraw so the family fails.[1]

Like any group or organization, the family is a system that interacts with the outside world; e.g., members go to school, work, meet outsiders, and reproduce. A family is not permanent; i.e., people are born or brought in and they leave. A family grows and matures, sustains challenges to its structure, is torn down, and is rebuilt throughout the lifetimes of its members.

Group Development

These traits exist on a continuum and are neither good nor bad. They simply help to define the behavior of any group.

---

[1] Kantor and Lehr (1975).

Traits of Groups

Autonomy	functions independently of other groups.	depends on other groups
Cohesiveness	functions as a tight unit.	members are independent
Control	highly regulated behavior of members	low regulation of members
Flexibility	rigidly structured procedures. . . .	informal procedures
Tone	pleasantness predominates	unpleasant-feeling tone
Homogeneity	members have similar characteristics	members are diverse
Intimacy	highly familiar with each other's lives.	lack details of lives
Participation	much time and effort given to group	little effort goes to group
Permeability	group permits easy access	others cannot be members
Polarization	one goal for all members	individual goals predominate
Potency	group has power over members	little power over members
Size	large number of members	few members
Stability	group stays the same over time . .	group changes
Stratification	clear hierarchy of status.	no differentiation[2]

Conflicts Engendered by Group Membership

The basic conflict on entering any group is "How much of myself do I surrender in order to belong?" Whether a young bride wants to fit in with her husband's family, a police officer wants to be accepted by the other cops, or an immigrant moves to the United States, the basic conflict is the same. The answer to the question depends on the individual. If a person surrenders all, then he or she belongs wholeheartedly but gives up individuality (e.g., Nazi soldiers). If a person gives up little of themselves, they retain individuality, but never fully belong to

---

[2] Borgatta, Cottrell, and Meyer (1971).

the group or take on the group's norms, values, and beliefs (e.g., the family black sheep).

Members want to participate and belong but preserve his or her own identity. Just the right amount of self and other is not static and shifts over time, depending on many factors, including personal needs, time of life, other commitments, and interest. For example, a young woman might be a devoted sorority sister during college, but remain group-free for years afterward. A man may not be interested in group membership until he joins a company that intrigues him.

Stages of Group Development

Groups grow and develop. Like individuals, infant groups have much to learn and work ineffectively. In adolescence, groups, like people, rebel, trying to find an identity; hopefully, in maturity, groups settle down and get some work done before they die. Groups can be compared to families where individuals have distinct personalities but also have reactions to authority, whether it be a boss, parent, or teacher. Common negative reactions to authority are submissiveness, rebelliousness, or withdrawal. Common negative reactions to peers in groups are destructive competitiveness, emotional exploitiveness, or withdrawal.[3]

The following table provides some ideas about phases of groups, the dynamics, and the members' personal crises.

Stages of Group Development

Phase One—Coming Together

Members take on the same roles in the group as they usually do outside; e.g., someone makes introductions and someone else tries to assume leadership.

Individuals rely on existing leadership, are dependent on a leader, and are preoccupied more with leader than with peers.

People look for orientation, rules, and how to do it.

Members must decide whether they want to join and give up some individuality in favor of a group cohesiveness. If they give up too much individuality, they feel like sheep; if they give up too little, they remain outside.

Mood—anxious; wants security.

---

[3] Bennis and Shepard (1965).

Phase Two—Defining the Task

Members create, or are given, a task and determine how the job is to be accomplished.

Mood—temporary relief.

Phase Three—Unrest

Newness wears off and members do not feel as agreeable as previously.

The group members struggle with individual rights and want to take back some of their personal autonomy.

Members are disenchanted with leader and with each other.

Control takes on importance, and members try to figure out where they belong in the hierarchy.

The task continues, although emotions are higher.

Mood—hostile.

Phase Four—Cohesion

Members begin to feel like a team.

Members look for commonalities among them; less preoccupied with leader and more interested in each other.

Mutual involvement helps sense of "we-ness."

Group norms are established.

People discuss the task, or work. They give and receive opinions.

Phase Five—Interdependence

Emotions and task come together as members operate together, take responsibility, and believe in the subculture they have created.

Task problems are solved as a working team.

Group as a Whole

Each group takes on a life of its own, has a Group Mentality, and creates a Culture that is different from the sum of the individual members.

Group mentality is the collective and unanimous opinion, willpower, and desire of the group at a particular moment. Group mentality develops as the group functions as a unit. Group mentality may never be in the awareness of the members, and it may be in conflict with opinions, willpower, or desires of individual members, producing anger or discomfort in them.[4]

Group culture develops from an interplay of group mentality and individual desires. It includes group structure, leadership, task, and organization.

When groups are good, they are creative and can generate more ideas than an individual. When groups are bad, people may behave less competently, make strange alliances (often unconscious), projections take over, and scapegoating occurs.

Group Transformation

Group transformation can be seen simply in a classroom during the school year—the students meet, find friends, assume certain roles, bond or not, have conflict, and end. More complex groups can be observed in families over the years as infants are born into the family, everyone grows and ages, some leave, and others enter. Certain persons lead and others follow; some are central and others are peripheral. Those who marry in are treated in certain ways. Holidays and rituals are observed and, over the years, as membership changes and the family grows, the group is transformed, whether they like it or not, peacefully or through conflict.

A small mom-and-pop restaurant has a cook/boss, a waitress/wife, part-time hired help, and ten tables, and they are in business. If they succeed, others are brought in (e.g., cashier, accountant, wait staff), work becomes more specialized (e.g., a pastry chef), the physical setup changes (they add the storefront next door or redecorate), and conflict results because change is rarely accomplished smoothly. So the mom-and-pop atmosphere, where the boss knew and guided everything, is now divided among different people with diverse agendas.

Traits of Intergroup or Intragroup Conflict

Groups interact with other groups—one football team with another or one software company with its competitor—and that can lead to Intergroup Conflict. When the conflict is among members of one group (siblings, for example) it is Intragroup Conflict. When people get along, we don't have any conflict to write about.

---

[4] Bion (1959).

A Change—Some members or some groups believe that they are worse off and others are better off than they were before the change occurred. A common example these days is restructuring a company or blending a stepfamily.

Unfair Trading—Someone or some group gives up more than they get.

Reactions—Hostility is heightened as members or groups react to each other's behavior in ways that create a continuing negative spiral.

Stalemate—A group or members cannot make a decision because it is pushed or pulled in two directions at the same time, producing disorganization and self-hatred.

Traits of Leaders and Members in Groups

People in groups take on roles for which they have some attraction. A meek, shy woman is not likely to emerge as the leader. Roles reduce anxiety; scripts make it easy to know how to behave, but become one-dimensional. The constriction requires other aspects of one's self to be put aside. Women are often expected to assume caretaking or nurturing roles; young people are often expected to behave like children, even when they are capable of far more; men are often expected to tackle physical tasks and be aggressive. The following characters exemplify roles that emerge in groups.

Leaders
Charismatic Leader
Visionary, inspirational, and influential
Articulates a vision
Refers to distant rather than proximate goals
Has high expectations of followers' performance
High confidence; dominant
Willing to exploit others
Shows disregard for the rights and feelings of others
Self-aggrandizing
Narcissistic—inflated self-importance, seeks admiration, and is
    intolerant of criticism

Aggressive

Likes control over others or control over the environment

Transforms needs and values of followers from self-interest to collective interest[5]

U.S. Presidential Personality

Must lead through inspiration rather than control of the country

Needs ability to exercise intense influence over beliefs, values, performance, and behavior of others through his own beliefs and behaviors

His charisma remains only as long as followers agree

Some charisma comes with the office; the rest comes with the man

Effective presidents have high need for power with lower need to please others

Ability to understand the needs and wishes of those he leads[6]

Women Business Leaders

Like going into a "man's world"

Greater expression of feelings

More use of intuition in problem solving

Increased emphasis on personal relationships

Stress collaboration, teamwork, and empathy

More likely to share power

Supportive, confirming, and participatory

Most had close relationships with parents and had mothers who worked

Played a sport in their youth; i.e., understand competition, winning and losing

Had male role models[7]

Male Leaders Emphasize

Autonomy

Strength and self-confidence

Uses more rational and confrontational strategies; more directive

Competitive rather than collaborative

---

[5] House and Howell (1992).

[6] House, Spangler, and Woycke (1991).

[7] Parker and Ogilvie (1996); Sachs, Chrysler, and Devlin (1992).

Roles of Group Members

Roles are scripts unconsciously followed by different members of any group. The group uses roles to isolate a conflict in one person, who then plays it out. The rest of the group then feels at ease because each of them is spared the feelings contained in the one individual. For example, during a meeting of the hospital staff, a young nurse begins crying because of a death on the unit. Others comfort her, but are secretly glad that they did not break down. Or a high school boy cracks jokes during an anxiety-filled discussion on birth control. He is thrown out and the tension is relieved. Or a cop crosses the line when he is interrogating an attractive female prisoner, and other cops know that they have thought about doing the same thing but stopped themselves.

The following are some of the roles assumed by group members.

Hero

Champion; wants to lead and be noticed; ready to go out front

Seducer

Seduction can be sexual, power, or money; the goal is the same: wants to bewitch others

Silent

Long periods of quiet; keeps opinions to himself or herself; gets attention through silence

Taskmaster

Someone always reminds the group to get back to work; appreciates the task and wants to reach solutions

Clown

Jokes, relieving tension through silliness and often taking the group away from more serious matters

Victim

"Poor me," even if those words are never said aloud: tries hard but sees everyone else as getting the rewards; everyone else looks stronger

Oppressor

Likes to dominate; wants his or her own way; not interested in demo-cratic action; treats high-status people with much more respect than low-status individuals

Conciliator

Tries to manage a compromise; doesn't take a position, except to bring people together and avoid conflict

Combatant

Easily angered; sees a fight as the answer; likes action; finds it hard to sit still

Nurse

Usually a woman who tends to everyone's needs; never angry; con-cerned about others; often gets resentful that he or she is not highly valued; hides feelings of anger, jealousy, or competition

Young Turk

Someone is eventually ready to compete for leadership, just like the myth of Oedipus, where the son finally dethrones the father

Innocent

Young person usually; can ask questions and be naïve

Scapegoat

The scapegoat represents, and repents, for the weaknesses of the group. Scapegoating is found in the book of Leviticus. Early Hebrew tribes selected a goat to atone for their sins. The goat was separated from the tribe and carried the sins into the wilderness. Rumor has it that a member of the tribe followed the goat and tossed it over a cliff to make sure the animal did not return home lugging the sins along on its back.

These days, scapegoats do not fare much better. Scapegoating is the most dramatic behavior of a group in exploiting an individual. The group isolates one person as the source of conflict or bad feelings and, rather than share responsibility, the group consciously or uncon-sciously keeps the individual isolated in that role. Usually the group has deposited unwanted feelings (e.g., guilt, incompetence, or rage) into one individual. Then the group acts as if this person is the only one who has feelings of anxiety or is incompetent. Some undesirable feeling is localized in one individual. Tacit agreement maintains the strict roles. The group treats him or her as one-dimensional and may need to expel that individual in order to feel comfortable. The group exerts powerful influence on the individual even if he or she does not want to play the role. The short story "The Lottery" by Shirley Jackson is a marvelous example of scapegoating.

Traits of Scapegoating
The group

> Searches for a *likely* scapegoat to contain unwanted feelings
> Deposits unwanted feelings (e.g., guilt, incompetence, or rage) into one individual
> Maintains the person containing the guilt, rage, etc.
> Consciously or unconsciously keeps the individual isolated in that role
> Exerts powerful influence on the individual even if the role is unwanted
> Acts as if this person is the only one who has the unwanted feelings
> Does not share responsibility
> May need to expel that individual in order to feel comfortable

Tacit agreement maintains the strict roles
Scapegoating occurs in families, classrooms, work, children's camps
Roles are interdependent; leaders need followers and nurses require patients

Traits of Specific Groups
Juries
Voir dire (to see, to tell) is the interview process in which lawyers question assembled prospective jurors. Lawyers are attempting to determine their fitness to serve on a particular jury.

Lawyers are looking at
1. is juror predisposed to side with authority
2. will juror conform to wishes of others

3. is juror open/flexible or closed/rigid

Prosecution Lawyer Prefers:	*Defense Lawyer Prefers:*
authoritarian leanings	democratic leanings
juror conformity	individuals willing to dissent
closed or rigid outlook	people who consider conflicting information[8]

The jury is a small group and therefore subject to small-group processes as well as some dynamics unique to the judicial system.

Traits of Juries
80 percent of the time, judges and juries agree on the decision

Results, guilty or not guilty, of the first ballot are usually (90 percent) identical to the final result

Jury foremen are not necessarily the most influential people

Often the first person nominated is selected; prior juror experience is a factor; those who sat at the ends of the table were chosen more often than those who sat in the middle; people seldom seek the position of foreman

Minority members are reluctant to speak up without an ally

Male jurors talk more than female jurors

Low confidence leads to conformity

Deviants get a lot of attention until they are seen as intractable; then they are ignored

Jurors are more lenient with defendants who are physically attractive because they are seen as "better" people than those who are unattractive (unless attractiveness facilitated the crime); height does not influence juries; young people fare worse than older people; obese people fare worse than thin people

> In assessing monetary damages, male genitals were valued about three times as highly as female genitals[9]

Sorority or Fraternity
Greek group on college campus

---

[8] Simon (1975).
[9] ibid.

Juries on Film

Adam's Rib (1949)

Anatomy of a Murder (1959)

Breaker Morant (1979)

The Caine Mutiny (1954)

Compulsion (1959)

In the Name of the Father (1993)

Inherit the Wind (1960)

Judgment at Nuremberg (1961)

Philadelphia (1993)

Rashomon (1952)

To Kill a Mockingbird (1962)

12 Angry Men (1957)

Witness for the Prosecution (1957)

A group of men or women united in brotherhood or sisterhood

Goal is to promote fellowship

Members are under pressure to conform and impress each other

"Actives" (full members) live together in a supervised house

Students go through a series of open houses and parties, culminating in a "bid"

Pledges are individuals who have received and accepted bids to join

Hazing is more of an activity in fraternities than in sororities. Hazing includes any activity that intimidates, exhausts, or distresses participants. The activities have a possibility of injury, and certainly of embarrassment.

Brothers do to others what was done to them

Shows manliness

Ritual of belonging, joining, and bonding

Brothers want submission and obedience from pledges

Brothers seem unified, all in agreement

Norms of behavior are suspended

Single members or dissenters are not tolerated

Weak president may allow cruelty to get out of control

Individual responsibility is lost to the group

Sadistic brothers have opportunity to rule
Behaviors seem like tradition, not out-of-control impulses[10]

In Cortland, New York, a lethal paint mixture was used to apply the fraternity's letters to the backs of pledges. Two pledges were hospitalized with kidney failure.

Coach
Simplistic, conservative, and dictatorial
Cannot be thin-skinned or shy
Failures are witnessed by all
Works under pressure
Leader; aggressive; highly organized
Persistent, inflexible, and dogmatic
Unlike other teachers, ignores teaching journals but attends coaching clinics

Sports Teams and the Relationship to the Coach
Strong allegiance to the coach
Listens to coach's rules about hair, dating, and bedtimes
Receptive; listens to coach's ideas
Looks for support and feedback from coach
Trusts the coach and follows instructions, especially new players
Accepts assignments
Lives with coach's resolution of conflict

Building a Cohesive Sports Team
Cooperation
Players accept roles
Optimal size allows many to have chance to play
Stable membership
Communication
Conflicts are resolved

Self-Help Groups
Self-Help Groups are groups that form based on a common problem/situation/experience; for example, depression, grief, or alcoholism. The

---

[10] Nuwer (1990).

members help each other rather than relying on a professional leader or therapist.

Advantages of Self-Help Groups
Receipt of emotional and social support
Each member identifies with the others
Each helps facilitate the group's progress
Feels like a mix of expectations of family with aspects of formal
  professional help
Some have behavior change as the goal
Some have adaptation and coping as the goal
Open communication and links with others
Modeling from others who had similar experiences

Many self-help groups are discussion groups. Others are based on the principles of Alcoholics Anonymous.

Alcoholics Anonymous
Twelve Steps
1. I am powerless over alcohol and life has become unmanageable
2. A greater power can restore sanity
3. I decide to turn my will and life over to a care of God as I understand Him
4. Make a searching and fearless moral inventory
5. Admit to God, to self, and to another person the extent of my wrongs
6. I am ready to have God remove my character defects
7. I ask God to remove my shortcomings
8. List persons harmed and become willing to make amends
9. Make direct amends wherever possible, except where it would injure them or others
10. Continue to take a personal inventory and admit wrongs promptly
11. Seek contact with God through prayer and meditation
12. Carry the message to others and practice these principles in all affairs

Male Secret Societies

Neither positive nor negative; can be Masons or literary society

Voluntary, not coercive or deceptive like a cult

Special dress, language, ritual, and structure

Opportunity for safe male bonding

Temporary isolation from women

May be created to defend a way of life

Group is predictable, stable, and satisfying

Provides a place to be gregarious

Weaknesses of members are minimized or disguised

A culture is created within the larger society, often differing from majority

Secret society stimulates aggression against outside culture

Secrets create boundary between inside and outside[11]

The Significance of the Millennium

There are people who believe that the world will end (the apocalypse) or disasters/wars/destruction will occur. When people believe that the end of the world is close, their behavior is significantly influenced. People who tend to believe will look for signs that indicate the end of the world is fast approaching; e.g., documents, weather, or earthquakes.

Possible reactions to a belief in the apocalypse

1. Freedom to protest the effects of modern life in a violent fashion
2. Leaders who use certain aspects of modern culture (some technology tool) as a powerful and cohesive group technique to adapt to culture
3. Powerful group bonding, drawn together in the face of disaster; e.g., food accumulation or housing plans; may study documents together

If the world ends, there is no need to read further. Taking a more optimistic view, let's examine the rich implications for fiction after the deadline passes.

1. Groups must deal with the setback of being incorrect. Some groups will fade and disband.

---

[11] Tiger (1969).

2. Some groups will detach themselves from the beliefs and return to normal time.
3. Other leaders will revise their calculations and reset the clock to a future date.
4. Still other leaders or groups will reshape their message and continue.

Cults

As we approach the turn of the century, we can expect to see more cult activity.

We have drifted away from age-old beliefs, and cults fill the vacuum. People want answers to the questions that have always made us uneasy—living and dying, life's meaning, and time and space. Individuals need to replace chaos with tranquility, need to belong, and flee from a frightening, complex world that requires unwanted responsibility and choices.

A Cult is a group of individuals who follow a living, usually male, leader. The group leader makes extreme claims about his person or abilities; for example, he is God's agent, all-knowing, or has the absolute truth. Membership in the cult requires complete acceptance of the leader's claims, complete obedience to the rules, and complete loyalty to the leader.

Cult Members

Who joins cults? Recruits are similar to other people; no particular factors predispose certain individuals to cult membership.

Idealistic students who want to believe in something
Middle and upper middle class
Lonely; alienated; disenchanted
Depressed
Weak relationship with father and need for authoritative figure
Need direction and discipline; uncertain; trouble making decisions
Searching for *the* answer to their own problems and those of society
Want acceptance
May have fragile internal world; at extreme, can border on psychotic
Recruited by cult rather than seeking cult[12]

---

[12] Kaslow and Sussman (1982).

Steps of Recruitment to a Cult:

Student invited by a new friend to have dinner
and discuss a favorite "cause."

Warm greetings; "love-bombed" by praise; self-esteem is bolstered.
As recruiters learn about the individual's relationships,
they begin to intentionally act like family members.

Invited to a free weekend at a lodge or camp where songs, talk,
and esprit de corps set a warm tone. A personal companion is
assigned and everpresent. Lectures, bombardment with messages,
pressure to conform and induced states of euphoria through diet and
sleeplessness make the person pliable. There is no persuasion
at this time and no requests for money.

Contact with parents and friends is cut off, diminishing support.
Pressure continues and individuals are robbed of self-reflection.
Loss of ability to think independently is the result.

Members can be remade in a new, controlled cult image
that becomes self-sustaining.

The individual has gained a purpose and has direction without
making decisions. The cult becomes the perfect family with a father
figure (leader) and noncompetitive siblings (other members).[13]

Once Recruited, Cult Dynamics Include

Members dominated by group thought
Encapsulated environment
No outside or contradictory information is allowed
Communication is restricted

---

[13] ibid.

Decisions are made for members

The spirit is seduced—misused faith

Members are subjected to repetitive lectures, chants, and rituals

Psychological pressure applied

Inquiries are discouraged by making the questioner feel guilty

New identity is created for members

Submission to authority is required

Financial contributions are made to cult

Charismatic leader, not democratically elected, rules

Fear and hatred of nonmembers; "we" vs. "they" mentality is encouraged

Food or sleep deprivation[14]

Parents are stunned and bewildered, and feel that they have been abandoned for the "new" family

Cults differ from other groups or communal lifestyles because, in other groups:

Potential converts are fully aware of the identity of the group

No deception is practiced

Families are supported as a way of carrying on the group's identity

---

[14] ibid.

Nonverbal and Verbal Communication

Nonverbal Traits

There is more to an authentic character than personality, speech, behavior, and career. There is also the world of nonverbal communication, where a shrug, a smile, or silence communicates information effectively. *How* something is said changes the meaning of *what* is said. Tone, such as defiant or apologetic, conveys important information about personality. Gestures may indicate the opposite of words. Tapping toes often mean anxiety even when voice does not convey nervousness. Involuntary movement such as tics, blushing, or frowns convey more than words alone. Emotions can be seen in one's stance; hopelessness and despair may be conveyed more clearly in posture than through words.[1] The stone statues created by sculptress Kathe Kollwitz after her sons died in World War II convey grief better than most written accounts.

The traits that follow are those that have been subject to research and have some accuracy. A warning! I have noticed over the years that there is a tendency for people to give great weight to nonverbal communication, as if crossed arms were the key to a locked-up heart. Be cautious—gestures can have multiple meanings (e.g., tilting the head may have meaning or not, or can be manipulated for a certain effect).

---

[1] Bruch (1974).

Faces

Artists, authors, and moviemakers all rely on appearance to communicate character. An excellent movie can be spoiled by a character who does not look like the person we constructed when reading the book. We all look for descriptions of characters and are disappointed when the character is sacrificed in favor of the plot.

Description alone can put ideas into the readers' minds. For example, individuals whose features deviate from the norm (e.g., very wide eyes or very thin lips), are perceived to also have more extreme character traits. The meaning of a specific interaction is heavily influenced by tone of voice and facial expression, whether sincere, sexy, or serious.[2]

First, we will analyze faces. Faces can be constructed along three dimensions: *structural*, such as size and shape, color, or skin; *diagnostic*, such as blushing or muscular movements; and *artificial*, such as hairstyle or makeup.

Different cultures tend to identify the same facial expressions as signifying basic emotions, such as surprise, anger, happiness, or sadness.

People's assumptions may be true or false when they read faces. Following are some common misperceptions.

What do people assume about certain traits?

Facial Trait	*Faulty Assumption*
People who always look the same; e.g., relaxed	Stable disposition
People who change appearance; e.g., hair length goes from long to short; messy to neat; glasses to lenses	Inconsistent personality

Conclusion: Changing appearance conveys change in character.

Short nose	Weak, compliant, gullible
Baby face (round face, large round eyes, high eyebrows, small nose, and small chin)	Nonaggressive, nonthreatening
Baby-faced men and women	Honest, warm, dependent, affectionate

Conclusion: When baby-faced people act assertively, it will be compelling, because it is unexpected, just as compliance is from a mature-faced individual. In court, baby-faced people are less likely to be found

---

[2] Zebrowitz (1997).

guilty of an intentional offense, but if they are judged guilty, the penalty is stronger.

Blond hair	Weak, fun, delicate, simple
Dark hair	Less fun, intelligent, complex
Light coloring/blue eyes	Naïveté, warm, submissive
Women wearing makeup	Popular, sociable, talkative
More cosmetics used	Sex-role stereotypes
Stylish hair	Reliable, warm, caring
Low eyebrows	Angry
Fine hair, short necks, and flabby ears	Low intelligence
Receding chin	Weak
Bald men	Timid, naïve, weak, submissive
Bearded men	Mature, dominant, educated
Eyeglasses	Less attractive but intelligent

Facial Trait	*Usually Valid Assumption*
Lighter skin	Female
Bigger nose, higher bridge, and flared nostrils	Male
Sloped forehead	Male
Deeper eyes	Male
Larger jaw	Male
Prominent cheekbones	Female
Smile that does not include the eyes	Fake smile
Use of makeup, and frequent head movements	Extroversion
Friendliness; smiling, self-assured expression	Extroversion
Refined appearance and short hair	Conscientiousness
Blue eyes	Shyness in children[3]

Lack of eye contact is often assumed to mean that the person is lying, but good liars often maintain more eye contact and smile less often

---

[3] ibid.

than truth tellers. Facial expressions are more easily controlled than people like to believe. Voice and body are harder to fake.

What Makes a Face Attractive?

Straight profile rather than jutting or receding features

Orderly face—equal distances from hairline to brow, brow to just under nose, just under nose to tip of chin; eyes not too wide or too close

Symmetry of features rather than asymmetry

Youthfulness

Large eyes, high cheekbones, full lips, small nose, and light skin (women)

Rounded rather than angular facial structure

Smooth, healthy, and free of marks or blemishes

Exaggerated attractive features; e.g., very large eyes

Large chin (men)

Beauty is associated with goodness, and people who are seen as attractive are also thought to be kinder, warmer, stronger, more interesting, sexually responsive, modest, sociable, and outgoing. Attractive women, more often than men, are also considered vain, egotistical, snobbish, and materialistic. Attractive people often have more influence on other people than unattractive people.

For typically masculine jobs that are high in prestige and power, such as managerial positions, attractive women are rated less favorably than unattractive women. But attractive women are rated more favorably for stereotypically female jobs (e.g., clerical positions). Attractive men are always ranked more favorably than unattractive men in work opportunities. Attractive people also receive lighter sentences in courtrooms, but are underdiagnosed when seeking medical care.[4]

When we learn a face, we rarely forget it. One study showed that people were able to identify faces taken from their own yearbooks as opposed to faces taken from other yearbooks with almost perfect accuracy *after fifty years.*[5]

The ability to recognize people of other races is weaker than the ability to identify individuals of one's own race.

---

[4] ibid.
[5] Bahrick, Bahrick, and Wittlinger (1975).

Aging can be described by distinguishing characteristics of the face, for example: leathery skin, crinkled and open-pored skin texture, facial pouches, sagging skin, a double chin, and a generally more infantile appearance.

Appearance of the Face for Six Emotions[6]

Emotion	Brows	Eyes	Lower Face
Surprise	Raised brows Long wrinkles in forehead	Wide-open eyes White shows above the iris	Dropped mouth No stretch or tension in lips Lips parted
Fear	Raised and drawn brows Flattened brows	Hard stare Tension in lower lids	Corners drawn back Lips stretched
Anger	Pulled together Strong wrinkles	Tightening of lids Squinting	Lips pressed or open Teeth may show
Disgust	Brows down, not drawn together Vertical creases	Lower lids raised	Cheeks raised Upper lip may rise Tongue may be visible Lips may pull down
Sadness	Brows drawn Inner corner raised Bulge above brow	Eyes glazed Drooping lids or tense upper lids	Trembling lips Lip corners turn down
Happiness	No distinctions	Relaxed or lower lids raised Crow's feet seen	Corners raised Lips may be open slightly

Body Actions

In a group, a person tends to orient his or her body to one other person or a small group of others who are of interest. Head and eye movements also take in the person or group. Disinterest can be seen when body posture or head and eyes are searching elsewhere.

---

[6] Ekman (1971).

In a group, a person may signal his or her intent to speak by leaning forward, by putting a prop, such as a pencil, out in view, by looking at the faces of the others to gather them, or he or she may utter sounds to signal the group.

Coalitions (e.g., partners or lovers), often sit next to each other in a group. Their movements may echo each other; for example, head nodding to reinforce the other person's comments. Even when spouses are not together in a group, in the United States they reestablish contact with an exchange of a glance every twenty to thirty minutes.[7]

Speakers often use their hands to depict an action that occurred or an object they wish to describe.

Gestures can be used in lieu of speech; e.g., a wink, showing the middle finger, or a wave.

Attraction Gestures, Unconscious
High muscle tone; sagging disappears (watch the bodies of people meeting on a beach)
Skin color has great variability, from flush to pallor
His or her hand strokes head and hair
Rearranges clothing
Holds gaze with the other person
Smiles; touches lip or neck
Licks lips, puckers lips, and presents neck
Man buttons his coat or tugs on his socks
Woman crosses her legs, exposing more of her thigh
Woman may place her hand on her hip or stroke her leg
Woman slips in and out of her shoe

Language, customs, religion, and appearance are obvious traits of distinctiveness, but there are even more subtle differences that have the potential to cause trouble. The following list gives you an idea of some differences in communication that will be different depending on the character's culture.

Diversity in Nonverbal Traits
How close to stand when speaking: What does close mean? What does far mean?

---

[7] Scheflen (1974).

Is shaking hands an appropriate greeting? A kiss? A kiss on both
cheeks?

What does touch mean? On the face? On the arm or back?

What does eye contact mean? Looking down? Looking away?

What do different positions in posture mean?

How loud do people talk? What does it mean to whisper? To shout?

What does women's clothing signify? Show of legs or face, jewelry,
or color choices?

Posture

Posture is less subject to censorship than either voice or facial
movements.

Physical proximity More eye contact Torso tilting toward the other → Leaning forward toward the other	Communicates a more positive attitude to the other person

Reclining position instead of straight Leaning sideways → Relaxed hands Asymmetrical placement of arms and legs	Communicates information about the relationships; e.g., more relaxed with intimates and those of lower status

Relaxed posture →	Communicates a subtle show of intimacy

Warning Off, Distancing, or Silencing Gestures

Inattentiveness

Frown or deadpan expression

Finger to lips

Gaze shifts away or body shifts away[8]

---

[8] ibid.

Signals During Interaction With Others

Listener covers his or her mouth	belief that speaker is lying
Rubs nose	plans to censor speech or lie
Puts finger in his or her mouth	needs reassurance
Blows air out of mouth	cannot take in all the information that is being said
Sits on the arm of a chair	wants attention and to be dominant
Sitting, hands locked behind his or her head	overconfident; "know it all"
Picks imaginary lint off his or her sleeve	disapproves of the attitude expressed or the opinion spoken, but will withhold his or her own opinion

Zones of Comfort

1. Intimate zone = 6–18 inches: entry is for those who are emotionally close
2. Personal zone = 1½–4 feet: entry is for social functions
3. Social zone = 4–12 feet: entry is for strangers, workmen, or unfamiliar people
4. Public zone = over 12 feet: for addressing a large group of people

These zones are very different in countries other than the United States (e.g., Japanese and Danes stand closer than North Americans; people from the country stand farther apart than people from the city; bosses feel freer to stand closer to subordinates than vice versa). Other interesting occurrences involving space can been seen in public bathrooms, locker rooms, and elevators where people try to keep some distance between them. On the other side of manipulating space, police move into personal space when exerting authority, particularly when they are asking questions.[9]

Nonverbal Traits of Privacy

Children are permitted greater leeway of space than adults
Looking away invites disengagement and provides privacy

---

[9] Pease (1984).

Holding a gaze invites engagement and less privacy

Individuals walk around a group, rarely through it

Certain areas of the body may be glanced at (breasts, genitals), but staring invades privacy

The same way that walls and doors create privacy in a room, body position or objects create privacy in other places; e.g., at the beach[10]

Dress
Traits of Dress

Clothing may define important aspects of a character without words. The following representative ideas will help you think of others.

Trait Revealed	Piece of Clothing
Protection	armor
Proclamation/affiliation	gang beret
Self-definition	hairstyle, hair color, tattoos
Sect; e.g., Amish	black, simple clothing, broad hat
Religion; e.g., Hasidic	black suit for men, beard, hat
Gang; e.g., Hell's Angels	insignia, leather
Subculture; e.g., hippies	bell bottoms, beads, hairstyle
Values	religious medal, expensive watch
Temporary identity	apron, disco outfit
Peer culture	torn T-shirts, college sweatshirt[11]

Traits of Power in Dress

Walking stick

Tools; e.g., keys or medical bag

Uniform; e.g., pilot or police
        badges, insignia, weapons

Sword

Gold

Crown

Unity of outfit from head to toe—continuity of fabric increases size, makes a commanding presence

---

[10] Ashcraft and Scheflen (1976).
[11] Rubenstein (1995).

Loose-fitting garments have power because they convey impersonal distance[12]

Traits of Power in Behavior

A lot of eye contact

Sitting at the head of a table in a group setting

Lowering one's eyebrows

Use of expansive and relaxed body movements

Erect posture

Powerful gait—rapid, forward leaning, arm swing, and picking up of feet

Loud voice; low pitched voice

Control of conversation[13]

Traits of Insignificance in Dress

Clothes too big

Clothes too small

Cheap look[14]

Traits of Invisibility in Dress

No bags

No distractions or extremes

Hair covered or bland

Loose clothes

Longer clothes[15]

Traits of Seductiveness in Dress

Clothes hint at body

Unexpected elements (draws awareness)

Emphasis on curves or muscles

Harmony of outfit (the whole is greater than the parts)

Glamour

Exotic or foreign

Fabrics that cling

---

[12] ibid.
[13] Zebrowitz (1997).
[14] Rubenstein (1995).
[15] ibid.

Vulnerable or soft appearance
> childlike
> woman in big brother's hand-me-downs

Traits of Helplessness in Dress
Ripped clothing
Body exposed[16]

Traits of Success in Dress
Dark-color suit = authority
White shirt = intelligence[17]

Women's Clothing Styles
Classic styles of dress (i.e., simple, conservative, and tailored lines) are seen as dominant and sophisticated, but not approachable.
Romantic styles of dress (i.e., curved lines and feminine) are seen as submissive and approachable.
Natural styles of dress (i.e., informal, casual, comfortable, with minimal ornamentation) are seen as unsophisticated.[18]

Mistakes in Men's Dress
Jacket or pants too short
Wrinkles at the arm hole
Pleats or pocket pulled open
Tight waist
High or low rise in the pants
Too much color[19]

Names
Names can be unusual (e.g., Tamalika) or unconventional because of their spelling (e.g., Lynda or Barbra) as compared to the conventional American-European names that used to be the only options in the "Name Your Baby" books. Times have expanded tolerance, but uncon-

---

[16] ibid.
[17] Molloy (1998).
[18] Zebrowitz (1997).
[19] Pooser (1990).

ventional names continue to exert a subtle but persistent effect on the perceptions of others in business, social, or professional situations.

Unconventional Names

Work was judged less favorably in school
Ranked less attractive in beauty contests
Less desirable qualities attributed to person
Seen as less successful
Seen as less popular
Seen as less warm
Seen as less moral
Men were seen as less masculine
Women were seen as less feminine[20]

Verbal Communication

Teaching student psychologists, I often remind them that *what* someone says is only part of the discussion—*how* they say it and *what they omit* are also very significant.

Everyone has unique patterns of communication, but men and women have some distinctions that can be used to enliven character and dialogue. The following comparisons illustrate the edges of communication patterns. Most people have more flexibility in their communication than the extremes set out below and fall closer to the center.

Self-Disclosure

This is the willingness to talk to another person honestly.

Mutual disclosure leads to greater intimacy
Women tend to disclose more than men
Levels of disclosure change when moods change; e.g., during anger

Male and Female Traits of Communication

Female	*Male*
Asks questions to show interest in the topic or person speaking.	Asks questions to gain more information about the person or topic.
Talking about problems provides a relief.	Talking about problems feels like he is dwelling on the negative.

---

[20] Mehrabian and Piercy (1993); Mehrabian (1990, 1992).

Sharing one's own complaints is meant to show closeness and support.	Thinks that sharing complaints does not create solutions.
Provides background and detail because she wants to be understood.	Too much detail feels like justification—make your point.
Continuing to discuss problems demonstrates support.	Continuing to discuss problems is useless—make a decision.
Can be indirect or subtle; sometimes apologetic.	Says what he wants directly.
Believes that talking about a relationship brings people closer.	Believes that simply talking is useless, unless things can be changed.
Enjoys discussion of emotion and relationship.	Feels inept discussing emotion and relationships.

Words Used by Men and Women to
Describe Their Feelings About Relationships

Affectionate	Afraid	Agitated
Alone	Angry	Annoyed
Bitter	Bored	Cautious
Cheerful	Content	Cooperative
Critical	Daring	Desperate
Destroyed	Devoted	Disagreeable
Discouraged	Enraged	Fearful
Free	Friendly	Frightened
Furious	Glad	Happy
Hopeless	Hostile	Hurt
Impatient	Irritated	Jealous
Kind	Lost	Loving
Lucky	Mad	Mean
Meek	Miserable	Nervous
Obliging	Offended	Outraged
Panicked	Patient	Peaceful
Pleasant	Polite	Powerful
Quiet	Rejected	Resentful
Sad	Safe	Secure
Shaky	Shy	Sociable
Strong	Stubborn	Sympathetic
Tense	Terrified	Thoughtful
Timid	Trapped	Turned on
Understanding	Unsociable	Upset
Vexed	Warm	Weak
Wild	Worrisome	

CHAPTER THIRTEEN

The Big Index

T he aim of this chapter is to make the preceding twelve chapters even easier to negotiate. There are five sections: *Styles* lists the main styles described in the previous pages; *Traits* includes emotions, personality characteristics, behaviors, and attitudes; *Careers* lists careers alphabetically; *Physical Disorders and Physical Symptoms*; and *Criminals* lists the types of criminals. You can enrich characters with details of their specific traits. For example, your character is a young woman boxer with bulimia. Look up boxing in the section on *Careers*. Look through *Traits* for references to anger and aggressiveness. Check out eating disorders in *Physical Disorders and Physical Symptoms*. Maybe your boxer has a criminal friend, a minor character who will help her in some way. Look through the section that lists *Criminals* styles and consider forgery or another talent for the friend. These details will lead you to other ideas.

Styles, Adult Normal

Styles, Adult Problems

Anxious/Nervous Style 83-86
Black-and-White Style 86-87
Delusional Style 99-100
Depressed Style 87-90
Grief 90-91
Hypochondriac Style 91-93
Manic Depressive Style 90, 99

Multiple Personality Style 100-101
Narcissistic Style 93-94
Obsessive Style 94-98
Psychopathic Style 103-104
Schizophrenic Style 104-107
Suspicious Style 101-103

Styles and Symptoms, Child Problems

Adolescent (adolescence) 43, 86,
    106, 124, 166, 205
  development 58-66
  disorders of 68, 78, 81
  end of 66-67
  gay 194
  reactions to divorce 181-182
  suicide 82-83, 89
  tasks of development 188, 193
Anxiety 69-70
Attention-Deficit Hyperactivity 74-76
Autism 76-77
Bed-wetting (enuresis) 70-71, 137

Conduct Problems 77-78
Defiance 71-72
Depression 78
Gender Identity Disorder 78
Mental Retardation 79-80
Mutism 80, 238
Obsessiveness 72-73
Overattachment 73-74
Self-cutter 81-82
Suicide 82-83
Twins 190-191
Unpopular child 55

Traits (Emotions, Personality Characteristics, Behaviors, and Attitudes)

abandonment 92, 114, 154, 194, 225
  fear of 22, 41, 86, 89, 182
abuse (abusive) 18, 41, 43, 87, 119,
    122, 123, 127, 128, 134, 138,
    143, 186, 216, 222, 227, 248
  definition of 124, 131, 142, 222,
    242, 260
  sexual 72, 109
  spouse 122, 131, 174
academic 17, 182
  work 83
acceptance 47, 192, 194, 287

  need for 170, 287
  social 123
accident prone 21
achieve 36, 42, 61, 189, 249, 261
  achievement 156, 163, 192, 238,
    257, 264, 268
  underachiever 26, 78, 158
action(s) 12, 22, 34, 55, 68, 95, 102,
    121, 179, 200, 212, 229, 237,
    263, 280, 290, 294-295
adopt 168, 199, 200
  adoptees 201

Careers

Physical Disorders and Symptoms

human immunodeficiency virus,
HIV 240, 241
syphilis 241
sleep terror 228-229
sleepwalking 229
substance abuse 81, 86, 110, 184, 194,
208, 216, 218, 219, 235, 250, 251
cannabis 106, 231, 235
dependence 233
surgery, unusual 149, 227

sweating 85, 143, 229, 231, 238, 241
tremors 219, 231
twitch 30, 74, 219
venereal disease 241
vitamin deficiency 220
vomiting 47, 73, 84, 143, 225
self-induced 235-237
weight
gain 60, 83, 235, 254
loss 208, 235, 241

Criminals

arsonist 109-110
career professional 111
confidence 111-112
delinquent 114-115
forger 112-114
gambler 115
kleptomaniac 115-116
late blooming 116
looter 116-117
murderer 131-132
argument 132
domestic 132
erotomaniac 132-133
extremist 133
female 133
incidental 134
inheritance 134
passionate 135
product tampering 135
professional 135
psychotic 136
serial offender 137-138
sexual 136-137
simmering 138-139

visionary 139
occasional 117
organized crime 139
pedophile 125-126
pyromaniac 117-118
sexual crimes 123-131
abuser 124
exhibitionist 123-124
nymphophile 125
pedophile 125-126
psychopath, sexual 127-128
rapist 128
acquaintance 128-129
angry 129
exploitation 129
group 129
power-reassurance 130
sadist 130
sexual 130
skyjacker 118
stalking 118-120, 135
violent 120
white-collar 121-122
wife batterer 122-123

BIBLIOGRAPHY

Abel, Gene and Osborn, Candice. *The Paraphilias*. Psychiatric Clinics of North America, 1992. 15, 675-687.

Abrahamsen, David. *The Mind of the Accused: A Psychiatrist in the Courtroom*. New York: Simon and Schuster, 1983. An account of specific, famous murderers and the psychiatrist's investigation of insanity.

Achenbach, Thomas M. *Developmental Psychopathology*. New York: John Wiley and Sons, 1982. 35.

American Psychological Association practice directorate "Psychological Series: Essential to America." February, 1995.

Ames, Louise Bates, and Haber, Carol Chase. *Your Seven-Year-Old: Life in a Minor Key*. Gesell Institute of Child Development. New York: Delacorte Press, 1985.

Ames, Louise Bates, and Haber, Carol Chase. *Your Eight-Year-Old: Lively and Outgoing*. Gesell Institute of Child Development. New York: Delacorte Press, 1989.

Ames, Louise Bates, and Ilg, Frances. *Your Three-Year-Old: Friend or Enemy*. Gesell Institute of Child Development. New York: Delacorte Press, 1976.

Ames, Louise Bates, and Ilg, Frances. *Your Four-Year-Old: Wild and Wonderful*. Gesell Institute of Child Development. New York: Delacorte Press, 1976.

Ames, Louise Bates, and Ilg, Frances. *Your Five-Year-Old: Sunny and Serene*. Gesell Institute of Child Development. New York: Delacorte Press, 1979.

Ames, Louise Bates, and Ilg, Frances. *Your Six-Year-Old: Loving and Defiant*. Gesell Institute of Child Development. New York, Delacorte Press, 1979.

Ames, Louise Bates; Ilg, Frances; and Haber, Carol Chase. *Your One-Year-Old: The Fun-Loving, Fussy 12- to 24-Month-Old*. Gesell Institute of Child Development. New York: Delacorte Press, 1982.

Ames, Louis Bates; Ilg, Frances; and Baker, Sidney. *Your Ten- to Fourteen-Year-Old: Middle Childhood*. New York: Dell, 1989.

Arnstein, Helene. *Between Mothers-in-Law and Daughters-in-Law*. New York: Dodd, Mead & Company, 1985.

Bibliography

Ashcraft, Norman, and Scheflen, Albert. *People Space*. New York: Anchor Press/Doubleday, 1976.

Athens, Lonnie H. *The Creation of Dangerous Violent Criminals*. Chicago: University of Illinois Press, 1992.

Bahrick, H.P.; Bahrick, P.O.; and Wittlinger, R.P. "Fifty Years of Memory for Names & Faces: A Cross-Sectional Approach." *Journal of Experimental Psychology: General* 104 (1), 1975, March 54–75.

Bartholomew, Kim. " From Childhood to Adult Relationships: Attachment Theory and Research." In *Learning About Relationships: Understanding Relationships Processes*, 30–62. Edited by S. Duck. London: Sage Publications, 1993.

Baumeister, Roy. *Evil: Inside Human Cruelty and Violence*. New York: W.H. Freeman and Company, 1997.

Bennis, Warren G., and Shepard, Herbert A. "A Theory of Group Development." Human Relations 9, 1965: 415–57.

Benson, Leonard. *The Family Bond: Marriage, Love and Sex in America*. New York: Random House, 1971.

Ben-Yehuda, Nachman. *Deviance and Moral Boundaries: Witchcraft, the Occult, Science Fiction, Deviant Fiction and Scientists*. Chicago: University of Chicago Press, 1985.

Berger, Ronald J. "Female Delinquency in the Emancipation Era: A Review of the Literature." *Sex Roles* 21, 5–6, Sept. 1989: 375–99.

Berman, Ellen, and Lief, Harold. "Marital Therapy From a Psychiatric Perspective: An Overview." *American Journal of Psychiatry* 132, 6 (June 1975): 583–92.

Bion, Wilfred. *Experiences in Groups*. Basic Books, 1959.

Black, Claudia. *It Will Never Happen to Me*. Denver, CO: M.A.C. Publications, 1992.

Borgatta, Edgar F.; Cottrell, Leonard S., Jr.; and Meyer, Henry. *On the Dimensions of Group Behavior in Groups and Organizations*. Edited by Bernard Hinton and H. Joseph Reitz. CA: Wadsworth Publishing Co. Inc., 1971.

Bornstein, Robert, and Bower, Raymond. "Dependency in Psychotherapy: Toward an Integrated Treatment Approach." *Psychotherapy* 32 (Winter 1996): 520-34.

Brandon, Sydney; Boakes, Janet; Glaser, Danya; and Green, Richard. "Recovered Memories of Childhood Sexual Abuse: Implications for

Clinical Practice." *British Journal of Psychiatry* 172 (April 1988): 296-307.

Brown, Mildred L., and Rounsely, Chloe Ann. *True Selves: Understanding Transsexualism*. San Francisco: Jossey-Bass Pub. 1996.

Bruch, Hilde. *Learning Psychotherapy*. Cambridge, MA: Harvard University Press, 1974.

Burns, Rex. "Characterization." *The Writer* (May 1988): 11–14.

Calhoun, George; Jurgens, Janelle; and Chen, Fengling. "The Neophyte Female Delinquent: A Review of the Literature." *Adolescence* 28, 110 (Summer 1993): 461–71.

Callahan, Roger, and Levine, Karen. *It Can Happen to You: The Practical Guide to Romantic Love*. New York: A & W Publishers, 1982.

Caprio, Frank S. *Marital Infidelity*. New York: The Citadel Press, 1953.

Carpineto, Jane. *The Don Juan Dilemma*. New York: William Morrow & Company, 1989.

Cattell, Heather Birkett. *The 16PF: Personality in Death*. Champaign, Illinois Institute for Personality and Ability Testing, 1989.

Charlton, William. "Feeling for the Fictitious." *The British Journal of Aesthetics* 24 (Summer 1984): 206–16.

Chatman, Seymour. *Story and Discourse: Narrative Structure in Fiction and Film*. Ithaca: Cornell University Press, 1978.

Clifford, C.A.; Murray, R.M.; and Fulker, D.W. "Genetic and Environmental Influences on Obsessional Traits and Sumptoms." *Psychological Medicine* (November, 1984): 791–800.

Clinard, Marshall B. *Sociology of Deviant Behavior*. New York: Holt, Rinehart and Winston, Inc., 1963.

Cole, Sonia. *Counterfeit, Counterfeit*. New York: Abelard-Schuman, 1956. Detailed, easy-to-read accounts of various forgers, their craft, and methods of detection.

Cohan, Steven. "Figures Beyond the Text: A Theory of Readable Character in the Novel." *Novel: A Forum of Fiction*, Fall 1983, 5–27.

Coley, Rebekah Levine, and Chase-Lansdale, P. Lindsay. "Adolescent Pregnancy and Parenthood." *American Psychologist* 53 (February 1998): 152–66.

Curtis, George C.; Magee, W.J.; Eaton, W.W.; Wittchen, H.-U.; and Kessler, R.C. "Specific Fears and Phobias." *British Journal of Psychiatry* 173 (1998): 212–17.

DeAngelis, Tori. "There's New Hope for Women With Postpartum Blues." *APA Monitor*, September 1997: 22–23.

Dodson, Fitzhugh, and Alexander, Ann. *Your Child: Birth to Age*. New York: Simon & Schuster, 1986.

Doleys, Daniel M.; Meredith, R.L.; and Ciminero, Anthony R., eds. *Behavioral Medicine: Assessment and Treatment Strategies*. New York: Plenum Press, 1982.

Douglas, John E.; Burgess, Ann W.; Burgess, Allen; and Ressler, Robert K. *Crime Classification Manual*. New York: Lexington Books, 1992.

Douglas, John E., and Olshaker, Mark. *Journey Into Darkness*. New York: Scribner, 1997.

Douglas, John E., and Olshaker, Mark. *Mindhunter: Inside the FBI's Elite Serial Crime Unit*. New York: Scribner, 1995.

Douglas, John E., and Schlesinger, Louis B. "Distinctions Between Psychopathic, Sociopathic, and Anti-Social Personality Disorders." *Psychological Reports*, 47: 15–21.

Dudek, Stephanie, and Hall, Wallace B. "Personality Consistency: Eminent Architects 25 Years Later." *Creativity Research Journal* 4, 3 (1991): 213–31.

Edelstein, Linda N. *Maternal Bereavement: Coping With the Death of an Older Child*. Westport, CT: Praeger, 1984.

Edelstein, Linda N. *The Art of Midlife: Courage and Creative Living for Women*. Westport, CT: Bergin & Garvey Trade, 1999.

Ehrenberg, Tamar. "Female Differences in Creation of Humor Relating to Work." *Humor* 8, 4 (1995): 349–62.

Ekman, Paul. "Universals and Cultural Differences in Facial Expressions of Emotion." In *Nebraska Symposium on Emotion*, 207–83. Edited by James K. Cole. Lincoln: University of Nebraska Press, 1971.

Erikson, Erik. *Childhood and Society*. New York: W.W. Norton & Co., 1964.

Erikson, Kai T. *Everything in Its Path: Destruction of Community in the Buffalo Creek Flood*. New York: Simon and Schuster, 1976.

Esau, Truman G. "The Evangelical Christian in Psychotherapy." *American Journal of Psychotherapy* 52, 1 (Winter 1998): 28–36.

Faux, Marian. *Childless by Choice*. New York: Anchor Press, 1984.

Feinstein, John. *A Good Walk Spoiled: Days and Nights on the PGA Tour*. Boston: Little, Brown, 1995.

Flannery, Raymond B., Jr. *Violence in America*. New York: Continuum, 1997. An account of biological, sociological, and psychological factors that cause violent behavior.

Fraiberg, Selma. *The Magic Years*. New York: Scribner, 1959.

Frank, Susan; Avery, Catherine B.; Laman, Mark. "Young Adults' Perceptions of Their Relationships With Their Parents." *Developmental Psychology*, Sept. 1988, Vol. 24 (5): 729–37.

Friedman, Stanley. "On the 'True-False' Memory Syndrome: The Problems of Clinical Evidence." *The American Journal of Psychotherapy* 51, 1 (Winter 1997).

Freudenberger, Larry, and Bergandi, Thomas A. "Sport Psychology Research in American Football: A Review of the Literature." *International Journal of Sport Psychology* 25 (Oct.–Dec. 1994): 425–34.

Furnham, Adrian. "Personality and Demographic Determinants of Leisure and Sports Preference and Performance." *International Journal of Sports Psychology* 21 (3) (July–Sept. 1990): 218–36.

Galligani, Niklas; Renck, Annika; and Hansen, Stefan. "Personality Profile of Men Using Anabolic Androgenic Steroids." *Hormones and Behavior* 30 (2) (June 1996): 170–75.

Garber, Stephen; Garber, Marianne Daniels; Spizman, Robyn Freedman. *If Your Child Is Hyperactive, Inattentive, Impulsive, Distractible. . . .* New York: Villard Press, 1998.

Gardner, Richard. "Toward a Definition of Stereotypes." *The Midwest Quarterly*, Summer 1985: 467–98.

Geis, Gilbert, and Stotland, Ezra, eds. *White-Collar Crime: Theory and Research*. Pacific Grove: Sage Publications, 1980.

Gold, Steven N., and Heffner, Christopher L. "Sexual Addiction: Many Conceptions, Minimal Data." *Clinical Psychology Review* 18, 3 (1998): 367–81.

Goma, Monserrat Freixanet. "Personality File of Subjects Engaged in High Physical Risk Sports." *Personality and Individual Differences* 12, 10 (1991): 1087–93.

Gondola, Joan C., and Wughalter, Emily. "The Personality Characteristics of Internationally Ranked Female Tennis Players as Measured by the Cattell 16PF." *Perceptual and Motor Skills* 73 (3, pt. 1) (Dec. 1991): 987–92.

Gonzalez-Crussi, Frank. *On the Nature of Things Erotic*. New York: Harcourt Brace Jovanovich, 1988.

Gortner, Eric; Jacobson, Neil S.; Berns, Sara B.; and Gottman, John M. "When Women Leave Violent Relationships: Dispelling Clinical Myths." *Psychotherapy* 34 (Winter 1997): 343–52.

Graham, John R. *MMPI-2 : Assessing Personality and Psychopathology.* New York: Oxford University Press, 1990.

Granleese, Jackie, and Barrett, Timothy. "The Social and Personality Characteristics of the Irish Chartered Accountant." *Personality and Individual Difference* 11, 9 (1990): 957–64.

Greene, Cherry, and Stitt-Gohdes, Wanda. "Factors That Influence Women's Choices to Work in the Trades." *Journal of Career Development* 23, 4 (Summer 1997): 265–78.

Greene, Roger L. *MMPI-2/MMPI: An Interpretive Manual.* Boston: Allyn and Bacon, 1991.

Griffith, Richard M.; Miyagi, Otoya; Tago, Akiro. "Universality of Typical Dreams: Japanese vs. Americans." *American Anthropologist*, 1958. 60: 1173-79.

Grinker, Roy, and Spiegel, J. P. *Men Under Stress.* New York: Hill, 1945.

Grossman, Dave. *On Killing.* Boston: Little, Brown, 1995.

Gutmann, David. "Deculturation and the American Grandparent." In *Grandparenthood*, 173–82. Edited by Vern L. Bengtson and Joan F. Robertson. Beverly Hills: Sage Publications, 1985.

Haber, Jon Randolph, and Jacob, Theodore. "Marital Interactions of Male vs. Female Alcoholics," *Family Process* 36 (4) (Dec. 1997): 385–402.

Hagestad, Gunhild O. "Continuity and Connectedness." In *Grandparenthood*, 31–48. Edited by Vern L. Bengtson and Joan F. Robertson. Beverly Hills, CA: Sage Publications, 1985.

Hartup, Willard W., and Stevens, Nan. "Friendships and Adaptation in the Life Course." *Psychological Bulletin* 121 (3) (May 1997): 355–70.

Hatch, Marjorie. "Conceptualization and Treatment of Bowel Obsessions: Two Case Reports." *Behavioral Research Therapy* 35, 3 (March 1997): 253–57.

Hawthorn, Jeremy. *Multiple Personality and the Disintegration of Literary Character: From Oliver Goldsmith to Sylvia Plath.* New York: St. Martin's Press, 1983.

Hendrick, Susan S. *Close Relationships.* Pacific Grove: Brooks/Cole, 1995.

Hetherington, E. Mavis; Law, Tracy; and O'Connor, Thomas. "Divorce: Challenges, Changes, and New Chances." In *Normal Family Processes*, 208–34. 2d ed. Edited by Froma Walsh. New York: The Guilford Press, 1993.

Hetherington, E. Mavis; Bridges, Margaret; Insabella, Glendessa M. "What Matters? What Does Not? Five Perspectives on the Association Between Marital Transitions and Children's Adjustment." *American Psychologist*, Feb. 1998. Vol. 53 (2): 167–84.

Himber, Judith. "Blood Rituals: Self-Cutting in Female Psychiatric Inpatients." *Psychotherapy* 31, 4 (Winter 1994): 620–31.

Holmes, Guy; Offen, Liz; and Waller, Glenn. "See No Evil, Hear No Evil, Speak No Evil: Why Do Relatively Few Male Victims of Childhood Sexual Abuse Receive Help for Abuse-Related Issues in Adulthood?" *Clinical Psychology Review* 17 (1) (1997): 69–88.

Holmes, R.M., and DeBerger, J.E. "Profiles in Terror: The Serial Murder." *Federal Probation*, 49, (3) (Sept. 1985): 29–34.

Holtzworth-Munroe, Amy, and Stuart, G. L. "Typologies of Male Batterers: Three Subtypes and the Differences Between Them." *Psychological Bulletin* 116 (3) (Nov. 1994): 476–97.

Hopwood, J.S., and Snell, H.K. "Amnesia in Relation to Crime." *Journal of Mental Science* 79 (1933): 27–41.

Horton, Andrew. *Writing a Character-Centered Screenplay*. Berkeley: University of California Press, 1994.

House, Robert J., and Howell, Jane M. "Personality and Charismatic Leadership." *Leadership Quarterly* 3, 2 (Summer 1992): 81–108.

House, Robert J.; Spangler, William D.; and Woycke, James. "Personality and Charisma in the U.S. Presidency: A Psychological Theory of Leader Effectiveness." *Administrative Science Quarterly* 36 (3) (Sept. 1991): 364–96.

Hubbard, David G. *The Skyjacker: His Flights of Fantasy*. New York: Macmillan Company, 1971.

Jacobs, David M. *The UFO Controversy in America*. Indiana: Indiana University Press, 1975.

Janis, Irving. *Victims of Group-Think*. Boston: Houghton Mifflin, 1972.

Janet, Pierre. *Neurosis et Idees Fixes*. 2d ed. Paris: Felix Alcan, 1904.

Johnson, Craig, and Flach, Anna. "Family Characteristics of 105 Patients With Bulimia." *American Journal of Psychiatry* 142, 11 (Nov. 1985): 1321–24.

Johnson, Sheri, and Jacob, Theodore. "Marital Interactions of Depressed Men and Women." *Journal of Consulting and Clinical Psychology* 65 (1) (Feb. 1997): 15–23.

Journal Watch for Psychiatry. Massachusetts Medical Society, vol. 3, no. 4, April 1997.

Kanter, Rosabeth Moss, and Stein, Barry. *Life in the Organization.* New York: Basic Books, 1979.

Kantor, David, and Lehr, William. *Inside the Family.* New York: Harper & Row, 1975.

Karson, Samuel, and O'Dell, Jerry W. *A Guide to the Clinical Use of the 16PF.* Champaign: Illinois Institute for Personality and Ability Testing, 1976.

Kaslow, Florence, and Sussman, Marvin. "Cults and the Family." *Marriage and Family Review* 4, 3/4 (1982).

Knight, Gareth. *The Practice of Ritual Magic.* New Mexico: Sun Chalice Books, 1996. Describes the skills of ritual magic.

Knopf, Jennifer and Seiler, Michael. *ISD: Inhibited Sexual Desire.* New York: William Morrow and Co., 1990.

Kopelman, Michael D. "The Assessment of Psychogenic Amnesia." In *Handbook of Memory Disorders,* 427–50. Edited by A.D. Baddeley, B.A. Wilson, and F.N. Watts. Chichester: Wiley, 1995.

Korn, Richard R., and McCorkle, Lloyd W. *Criminology and Penalogy.* New York: Holt, Rinehart, and Winston, Inc., 1963.

Krug, Samuel E. *Interpreting 16PF Profiles.* Champaign: Illinois Institute for Personality and Ability Testing, 1981.

Laird, Joan. "Gay and Lesbian Families." In F. Walsh (ed). *Normal Family Processes.* New York: Guilford Press, 1993. 282–328.

Lampinen, James; Neuschatz, Jeffrey; and Payne, David. "Memory Illusions and Consciousness: Examining the Phenomenology of Tone and False Memories." *Current Psychology: Developmental, Learning, Personality, Social* 6, 3/4 (Fall 1997/Winter 1998): 181–224.

Leman, K. *The Birth Order Book: Why You Are the Way You Are.* New York: Dell, 1985.

Lemert, Edwin. "The Behavior of the Systematic Check Forger." Social Problems, 1958; 6: 141–49.

Levin, Jack, and Arluke, Arnold. *Gossip: The Inside Scoop.* New York: Plenum, 1987.

Levinson, Daniel; Darrow, Charlotte; Klein, Edward; Levinson, Maria; and McKee, Braxton. *The Seasons of a Man's Life*. New York: Ballantine, 1978.

Loftus, Elizabeth. "The Reality of Repressed Memories." *American Psychologist* 48 (5) (May 1993): 518–37.

Loftus, Elizabeth, and Ketcham, Katherine. *Witness for the Defense*. New York: St. Martin's Press, 1991.

Ludwig, Arnold M. "Creative Achievement and Psychopathology: Comparison Among Professions." *American Journal of Psychotherapy* XLVI, 3 (July 1992): 333–56.

Ludwig, Arnold M. "Mental Illness and Creative Activity in Female Writers." *American Journal of Psychiatry* 151, 11 (Nov. 1994): 1650–56.

Mann, Coramae Richey. *When Women Kill*. New York: State University of New York, 1996.

Marchant-Haycox, Susan E., and Wilson, Glenn D. "Personality and Stress in the Performing Arts." *Personality and Individual Difference* 13, 10 (1992): 1061–68.

Margolese, Howard O. "Engaging in Psychotherapy With the Orthodox Jew." *American Journal of Psychotherapy* 52, 1 (Winter 1998): 37–53.

Masters, R.E.L. *Sex-Driven People: An Autobiographical Approach to the Problem of the Sex-Dominated Personality*. CA: Sherbourne Press, Inc., 1966.

Masters, William, and Johnson, Virginia. *Human Sexual Inadequacy*. Boston: Little, Brown, 1970.

McCready, William. "Styles of Grandparenting Among White Ethnics." In *Grandparenthood*, 49-60. Edited by Vern L. Bengtson and Joan F. Robertson. Pacific Grove: Sage Publications, 1985.

McDavid, Joshua D. "The Diagnosis of Multiple Personality Disorder." *The Jefferson Journal of Psychiatry* 12, 1 (1994): 29–43.

McRay, Leslie, and Schwarz, Ted. *Kept Women: Confessions From a Life of Luxury*. New York: William Morrow and Co., 1990.

Mehrabian, Albert. "Interrelationships Among Name Desirability, Name Uniqueness, Emotion Characteristics Connoted by Names and Temperament." *Journal of Applied Social Psychology* 22 (Dec. 1992): 1797–1808.

Mehrabian, Albert. *The Name Game: The Decision That Lasts a Lifetime*. MD: National Press Books, 1990.

Mehrabian, Albert, and Piercy, Marlena. "Positive or Negative Connotations of Unconventionally and Conventionally Spelled Names."

The Journal of Social Psychology 133, 4 (Aug. 1993): 445–51.

Merckelbach, Harold; de Jong, Peter J.; Muris, Peter; and Van den Hout, Marcel A. "The Etiology of Specific Phobias: A Review." *Clinical Psychology Review* 16, 4 (1996): 337–61.

Michaels, Gerald Y., and Goldberg, Wendy A., eds. *The Transition to Parenthood*. Cambridge: Cambridge University Press, 1988.

Millon, Theodore. *Disorders of Personality: DSM IV and Beyond*. New York: John Wiley and Sons, Inc., 1996.

Moglia, Ronald Filiberti, and Knowles, Jon. eds. *All About Sex: A Family Resource on Sex and Sexuality*. New York: Three Rivers Press, 1993.

Molloy, John. *John T. Molloy's New Dress for Success*. New York: Warner, 1998.

Mones, Arthur. "Oppositional Children and Their Families: An Adaptational Dance in Space and Time" *American Journal of Orthopsychiatry* 68 (1) (Jan. 1998): 147–56.

Money, John. "Myths and Misconceptions About Sex Offenders" *Canadian Journal on Human Sexuality* 7 (1) (Spring 1998): 77

Morris, Betsy. "It's Her Job Too." *Fortune Magazine*, February 1998: 65–78.

Moss, Howard B.; Panzak, George L.; and Tarter, Ralph E. "Personality, Mood, and Psychiatric Symptoms Among Anabolic Steroid Users." *The American Journal on Addictions* 1, 4 (Fall 1992): 315–24.

Muris, Peter; Merckelbach, Harold; and Claven, Michael. "Abnormal and Normal Compulsions." *Behavior Research Therapy* 35, 3 (March 1997): 249–52.

Nuwer, Hank. *Broken Pledges*. GA: Longstreet Press, 1990.

Oates, Joyce Carol. *On Boxing*. Dolphin/Doubleday: New York, 1987.

Osipow, Samuel H. *Theories of Career Development*. New Jersey: Prentice-Hall, 1973.

Parker, Patricia S., and ogilvie, dt. "Gender, Culture, and Leadership: Toward a Culturally Distinct Model of African-American Women Executives' Leadership Strategies." *Leadership Quarterly* 7, 2 (1996): 189–214.

Parkin, Alan J. *Memory and Amnesia: An Introduction*. Great Britain: Blackwell Publishers, 1997.

Patterson, Marcus; Rapoza, Kimberly; Malley-Morrison, Kathleen. An Examination of Four Subtypes of Jealousy. American Psychological Association 103rd Annual Convention, CA, 1998.

Pease, Allan. *Signals: How to Use Body Language for Power, Success and Love*. New York: Bantam Books, 1984.

People Magazine, March 23, 1998.

Pines, Ayala M. "Romantic Jealousy: Five Perspectives and an Integrative Approach." *Psychotherapy* 29, 4 (Winter 1992): 675–83.

Pooser, Doris. *Successful Style*. Menlo Park, CA: Crisp Publications, 1990.

Powers, Diane C. Stalking: A Form of Disordered Attachment and Mourning Variant. An unpublished dissertation, 1977.

Quarantelli, E.L., and Dynes, Russell R. "Property Norms and Looting: Their Pattern in Community Crises," Phylon, Summer 1970. Vol. 31 (2) 168–82.

Quay, Herbert C., and Werry, John S. (eds). "Residential Treatment." In *Psychopathological Disorders of Childhood*. 2d ed. New York: John Wiley and Sons, 1979.

Radkowsky, Michael, and Siegel, Lawrence. "The Gay Adolescent: Stressors, Adaptations, and Psychosocial Interventions." *Clinical Psychology Review* 17, 2 (1997): 191–216.

Reddy, Betty. "How We Help the Alcoholic Drink." *Illinois Bar Journal* (September 1984).

Reik, Theodor. *On Love and Lust*. New York: Farrar, Strauss & Cudahy, 1949.

Revich, E., and Schlesinger, L.B. "Murder: Evaluation, Classification, and Prediction." In *Perspectives on Murder & Aggression Violence*, 138–64. Edited by I.L. Kutash, S.B. Kutash, and L.B. Schlesinger. San Francisco: Jossey Bass, 1978.

Richardson, Ronald, and Richardson, Lois. *Birth Order and You*. Washington: Self-Counsel Press, 1990.

Roe, Anne. *The Psychology of Occupations*. New York: John Wiley and Sons, 1956.

Rose, Robert; Fogg, Louis; Helmreich, Robert; and McFadden, Terry. "Psychological Predictors of Astronaut Effectiveness." *Aviation, Space, and Environmental Medicine* 65 (Oct. 1994): 910–15.

Rosenberg, Elinor. *The Adoption Life Cycle: The Children and Their Families Through the Years*. New York: The Free Press, 1992.

Rubenstein, Ruth P. *Dress Codes: Meanings and Messages in American Culture*. Boulder, CO: Westview Press, 1995.

Sachs, Rachel; Chrisler, Joan C.; and Devlin, Anne Sloan. "Biographic and Personal Characteristics of Women in Management." *Journal of Vocational Behavior* 41 (Aug. 1992): 89–100.

Sampson, Anthony. *Company Man*. New York: Times Business Books, 1995.

Scheflen, Albert. *How Behavior Means*. New York: Anchor Press/Doubleday, 1974.

Schlesinger, L.B. "The Catathymic Crisis (1912–present): A Review and Clinical Study." *Aggression and Violent Behavior* 1 (4) (1996): 307–16.

Schlesinger, L.B. "Distinctions Between Psychopathic, Sociopathic, and Anti-Social Personality Disorder." *Psychological Reports* 47 (Aug. 1980): 15–21.

Schlossberg, Nancy K. *Counseling Adults in Transition*. New York: Springer Publication, 1984.

Schmich, Mary. "Shadow Moms Deserve a Hand for the One They Give." *Chicago Tribune*, May 10, 1998, sec. 4, p. 2.

Seligman, Kurt. *The History of Magic and the Occult*. New York: Random House Value Publishers, 1997. Serious, complete book of magic practices in countries of the Western world dating back to Mesopotamia.

Shahn, Ben. *The Shape of Content*. Cambridge: Harvard University Press, 1957.

Simon, Rita James, ed. *The Jury System in America*. CA: Sage Publications, 1975.

Sleek, Scott. "Is Impotence Only a Biological Problem?" *APA Monitor*, June 1998: 28.

Solomon, Michael A. "A Developmental, Conceptual Premise for Family Therapy." *Normal Family Process* 12, 2 (June 1973).

Sommers, J.V., and Yawkey, T.D. "Imaginary Play Companions: Contributions of Creative and Intellectual Abilities in Young Children." *Journal of Creative Behavior* 18 (1984): 77–89.

Stern, Daniel. *Diary of a Baby*. New York: Basic Books, 1990.

Stern, Daniel. *The Interpersonal World of the Human Infant*. New York: Basic Books, 1985.

Storr, Anthony. *Sexual Deviation*. Baltimore: Penguin Books, 1964.

Strier, Dorit Roer. "Coping Strategies of Immigrant Parents: Directions for Family Therapy." *Family Process* 35 (3) (Sept. 1996): 363–76.

Sutherland, Edwin H. *The Professional Thief*. Chicago: University of Chicago Press, 1937.

Suyemoto, Karen. "Self-Cutting in Female Adolescents." *Psychotherapy* 32, 1 (Spring 1995): 162–71.

Talland, George A. *Deranged Memory.* New York: Academic Press, 1965.

Taylor, Pamela J., and Kopelman, Michael D. "Amnesia for Criminal Offenses." *Psychological Medicine,* 14, (Aug. 1984): 581–88.

Tiefer, Lenore. *Sex Is Not a Natural Act and Other Essays.* Boulder, CO: Westview Press, 1995.

Tiger, Lionel. *Men in Groups.* New York: Random House, 1969.

Torrey, Fuller E. *Witchdoctors and Psychiatrists: The Common Roots of Psychotherapy and Its Future.* New Jersey: Jason Aronson Inc., 1986.

Troupp, Cathy. *Why Do We Fall In Love? The Psychology of Choosing a Partner.* New York: St. Martin's Press, 1994.

U.S. Department of Health and Human Services. *Marijuana: Facts Parents Need to Know.* National Institutes of Health, 1995, NIH Publication Number 95-4036.

Visher, Emily B., and Visher, John S. "Remarriages, Families and Stepparenting." In *Normal Family Process.* 2d ed. Edited by Froma Walsh. New York: The Guilford Press, 1993.

Vitaro, Frank; Ladouceur, Robert; and Bujold, Annie. "Predictive and Concurrent Correlates of Gambling in Early Adolescent Boys." *Journal of Early Adolescence* 16 (May 1996): 211–28.

Waehler, Charles A. "Relationship Patterns of Never-Married Men and Their Implications for Psychotherapy." *Psychotherapy* 31, 4 (Winter 1994): 632–41.

Wallace, Cameron; Mullen, Paul; Burgess, Philip; Palmer, Simon; Ruschana, David; and Brown, Chris. "Serious Criminal Offending and Mental Disorder." *British Journal of Psychiatry,* 172 (6) (June 1998): 477–484.

Wallerstein, Judith, and Kelly, Joan Berlin. *Surviving the Breakup: How Children and Parents Cope With Divorce.* New York, Basic Books, 1980.

Walters, Glenn D. *The Criminal Lifestyle: Patterns of Serious Criminal Conduct.* Newbury Park, CA: Sage Publications, 1990.

Ware, Susan. *Still Missing: Amelia Earhart and the Search for Modern Feminism.* New York: W.W. Norton and Co., 1993.

Weiss, Robert. *Marital Separation.* New York: Basic Books, 1975.

Wells, Leroy, Jr. "The Group As-A-Whole: A Systemic Socio-Analytic Perspective on Interpersonal and Group Relations." In *Advances in*

Experiential Social Processes, 165–99. Edited by C.P. Alderfer and C.L. Cooper. New York: John Wiley and Sons, 1980.

Weinberg, Martin. "Sexual Modesty, Social Meaning, and the Nudist Camp." In *Observations of Deviance*, 28–34. Edited by Jack Douglas. New York: Random House, 1970.

White, Kathleen M.; Speisman, Joseph C.; Costos, Daryl. "Young Adults and Their Parents: Individuation to Mutuality." New Directions for Child Development, Dec. 1983. Vol. 22: 61–76.

Whiteman, Dorit. "Holocaust Survivors and Escapees." *Psychotherapy* 30 #3 (Fall 1993): 443–51.

Wiley, Carol A., ed. *Women in the Martial Arts*. Berkeley: North Atlantic Books, 1992.

Wills, Anne, and Olivieri, S. "Anorexia Nervosa in Old Age." *Aging and Mental Health*, (1998): 239–45.

Wilson, James Q., and Herrnstein, Richard J. *Crimes and Human Nature*. New York: Simon and Schuster, 1985.

Wisniewski, Mark. "The Vital Element: Are Your Characters Breathing?" *The Writer* 107 (June 1994): 18–20.

Woititz, Janet Geringer. *Adult Children of Alcoholics*. Deerfield Beach, FL: Health Communications, 1983.

Zebrowitz, Leslie. *Reading Faces*. Boulder, CO: Westview Press, 1997.